DATE DUE

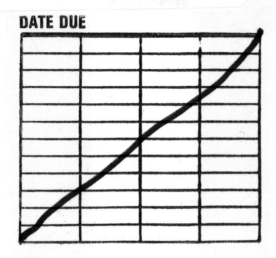

FROM POLITICS
TO POLICY

FROM POLITICS TO POLICY

A Case Study in Educational Reform

edited by
Joan M. Matthews,
Ronald G. Swanson,
and Richard M. Kerker

PRAEGER

New York
Westport, Connecticut
London

This book is intended as a case study and is not a policy statement of the State of Texas, the state agencies referenced or their assignees. The views expressed illustrate some of the diversity of the many people who were involved in the reform effort and authors' opinions may not be in accordance with the law, rules or policies of the Texas Higher Education Coordinating Board.

Library of Congress Cataloging-in-Publication Data

From politics to policy : a case study in educational reform / Joan M.
  Matthews, Ronald G. Swanson, Richard M. Kerker, editors.
     p.   cm.
  Includes bibliographical references and index.
  ISBN 0-275-93736-4 (alk. paper)
  1. Basic education—Texas—Ability testing—Case studies.
  2. College freshmen—Texas—Rating of—Case studies. 3. Texas
Academic Skills Program. 4. TASP Test.   I. Matthews, Joan McKeen.
II. Swanson, Ronald G.   III. Kerker, Richard M.
LC1035.7.T4F76   1991
378.1'664'09764—dc20   91-8074

British Library Cataloguing in Publication Data is available.

Library of Congress Catalog Card Number: 91-8074
ISBN: 0-275-93736-4

First published in 1991

Praeger Publishers, One Madison Avenue, New York, NY 10010
An imprint of Greenwood Publishing Group, Inc.

Printed in the United States of America

The paper used in this book complies with the
Permanent Paper Standard issued by the National
Information Standards Organization (Z39.48-1984).

10 9 8 7 6 5 4 3 2 1

To the students and faculty members of the Lone Star State.

Contents

Foreword

Larry Temple has long been an advocate for education. Working with the commissioner of higher education, he was the catalyst for getting the Texas Academic Skills Program underway. He commissioned the original study and, later, when the recommendations from that study had been turned into proposed legislation, Mr. Temple drew on his experience in the Johnson administration and at the state level to shepherd the bill through the legislature.

This book is about the formation and implementation of a major educational reform--one that has the potential to be the most beneficial effort to elevate the quality of undergraduate higher education in the history of the State of Texas. Like most reforms, it began with a conversation between two people.

One day in 1984, I was reading a report on the Florida rising-junior test, the College Level Academic Skills Test. I was impressed with that state's efforts to identify and correct academic deficiencies in its college students.

The testing concept was not new to Texas. We had recently begun seeing results from the Pre-Professional Skills Test used for entrance into the teacher education programs in Texas. The approach of the Texas test was similar to the one in Florida.

In Texas, students wanting to proceed in the teacher education programs were being tested during their sophomore year to determine if they had sufficient basic skills in reading, writing, and mathematics--the very foundation of the curriculum--to proceed with the upper level teacher education programs. Many of us involved in higher education were dismayed at the low scores. The unsatisfactory results were in part an indictment of the first two years of the college curriculum. But those results also signaled in no uncertain terms that Texas students were a part of the emerging national problem of college students arriving on campus underprepared to do college-level work--a focus of some recent discussions I had had with Southern Regional Education Board officials in my role as chairman of the Texas Higher Education Coordinating Board.

The Florida rising-junior test was appealing because it applied equally to all students without regard to the degree program they were pursuing. It gave the academic community in that state an opportunity to identify and correct deficiencies found in the entire higher education student body.

I discussed the Florida test with Texas higher education commissioner Ken Ashworth. We concluded that a good approach would be to create a blue-ribbon committee to review this program and make recommendations on the advisability and feasibility of such a test in Texas. The Texas Higher Education Coordinating Board quickly endorsed the idea and authorized my appointment of that blue-ribbon committee.

We intended to have every facet and interested sector of the higher education community represented on the committee. It included a student, faculty, a regent, a junior college president, senior college presidents, a private institution president, testing experts, and representatives of ethnic minorities. No committee has ever better served its state than this one.

The committee cleverly and adroitly--and unanimously--recast the question posed to it in order to give us the right answer. The question was whether Texas should have a rising-junior test--a test given to students at the end of their sophomore year. After extensive hearings throughout the state and an exhaustive study, the committee concluded that the best approach would require testing of all students upon entry into college to determine if they had the minimum basic skills to do college-level work. Why wait until students have been in college almost two years before diagnosing and remedying any academic deficiencies that burdened them when they arrived on the campus? So the committee wisely rephrased the issue to get us where we ought to be.

Happily, the report of this blue-ribbon committee coincided with work done by the Select Committee on Higher Education. The result was that the unanimous recommendation by the Committee on Testing was also unanimously endorsed and supported by the Coordinating Board and the Select Committee. To its everlasting credit, the Texas legislature enacted the legislation even though many members harbored lingering doubts about it.

When the recommendations became law in 1987, it was the job of the Coordinating Board to direct the process of implementing the program. Literally thousands of college and university faculty, staff, and students became involved in planning for the program. The success I foresee will be attributable in major part to the commitment and involvement on a voluntary basis of literally hundreds of people whose names will probably never be recorded. They made it happen.

With the testing and instructional support program that resulted--what we call the Texas Academic Skills Program, or TASP--we got a broad-gauged approach. It is one with student services and academic support services built right in.

From the beginning, we always saw the test as an inclusionary mechanism rather than an exclusionary one. It is designed to keep students in college and not keep them out. That is a factor of no little significance.

All of us on the Coordinating Board were determined to provide the necessary academic support to help entering students be successful. It is imperative to retain more of our students in school through to graduation. With this program, I know we will do so.

This book chronicles how an idea was turned into a reality. Legislators, staff, and educators built a test, a program, and the needed policies to support it while faced with uncertain funding. There were many players and much frustration. Broad policy questions intended to clarify the law and solve problems raised still more concerns. Yet somehow the seemingly endless tasks were brought to conclusion. Anthropologists refer to the concept of simultaneity when different societies tend to come up with the same idea as a solution to common problems. What will work and is working in Texas should be a model for other states to emulate.

I am convinced that all of us who had a hand in the origination, development, and implementation of this program will be proud of its legacy of enhancement of the quality of education in Texas.

Larry E. Temple

Acknowledgments

We wish to extend our gratitude to the many people who helped us bring about this book. William H. Sanford and Elena de la Garza provided us with encouragement, resources, and suggestions. Elaine M. Pearson worked unstintingly with typing of various drafts of the chapters and other materials for the book. Adelina Norris, Kay Vontz, and Daisy Horton also contributed to the typing. Special recognition is extended to Trenell S. Johnson for her patience, persistence and expertise in the final typing of the edited manuscript. Thanks go to Sally Hanaelt and Debbie Green of Senator Carl A. Parker's staff and to Greg Williams of Representative Wilhelmina R. Delco's staff for their assistance with legislative material. Jan Friese and Janice Monger gave us great help by allowing Ray Grass-hoff, our patient "first editor," to give us his suggestions.

A special thanks to the following contributors: Yolanda Chavez-Ahner, Salvador Acosta, Ramon Dominguez, Carol Kay, Martina Morales, José Rivera, David Salazar, and Sandra Tate.

Many faculty, staff, and administrators in the State of Texas were unfailingly generous in the time and valuable suggestions they provided to the Texas Higher Education Coordinating Board and the Texas Education Agency as the staffs worked together to make the Texas Academic Skills Program a reality.

To them and all the members of committees, forums, and panels that wrestled with turning politics into policy and programs go our heartfelt thanks.

Introduction: Setting the Stage

Kenneth H. Ashworth

There may be no one who knows more about the state of higher education in Texas than Ken Ashworth. Commissioner of higher education since 1975, he has seen nearly two decades of growth, retrenchment, politics, and change in the colleges and universities. He often functions as the conscience of the TASP, asking us about planning for minority student retention, innovations in computer-assisted instruction that might augment remedial interventions, or what we are doing to ensure fee waivers for needy students.

If we set utopian goals for higher education in the context of where we are today, we could rather quickly agree on one thing. All students would arrive in college able to read, write, and use mathematics at levels of competency to allow them to do college-level work. Thereby, they would grow in knowledge, skills, and competency to graduate with higher learning and assure their proper places in society.

Utopian goals are usually of two kinds, either unattainable or destructive of the social fabric. The utopian goal of competency in basic skills is both. If we admitted to college only those students fully competent in the basic skills, we would wreck our social system. To expect suddenly that our entering college students are going to have full command of the basic skills is clearly beyond what is possible.

Yet we know we need to shoot for that goal of better prepared students in our colleges. It is a goal we must pursue. But we are also thrown back on the age-old approach of change in our democracy: to make incremental improvements while we continue to do pretty much what we are currently doing.

The particular incremental change described in this book relates to the use of testing to put pressure on the educational system to make more students better prepared to do college-level work. Testing through the Texas Academic Skills Program puts pressure on many points in the system.

Ultimately, college-bound students will have to learn to work harder and take more difficult courses. They will need to realize that catching up later will cost them money and delay graduation and a job. Parents will need to know that their children are not prepared in basic skills and to recognize that their children are choosing easy courses and not working hard. Schools will be pressed to reassess public school course content and preparation and the rigor of teaching. As high failure rates reveal problems in the schools, school boards and superintendents will become involved. They will realize that ultimately the public schools will be held accountable for their graduates who still lack basic skills in college. The public will be able to see which schools are doing well or poorly, and people will demand improvements. At the very least, there are massive implications for the use of different resources, management, and curricular policies.

Consequently the TASP is not only testing deficiencies and prescribing remedies for individual students, it is also sending a message to students, teachers, parents, administrators, and the general public. The message contains the bad news about how poorly our students are prepared. But it also sends good news that there are things that can be done about what is wrong, both in terms of helping those who enter college underprepared and in terms of policy steps that can be taken to correct deficiencies in the educational system.

As Chapter 1 will reveal, the number of students who have the ability but do not possess the basics skills to succeed in college represents a generation of failure in our educational system. The Texas Higher Education Coordinating Board has been directed by the Texas legislature to act as the agent for change and give students the opportunity to master basic skills for success at the college level.

The Texas legislature's response to *A Generation of Failure: The Case for Testing and Remediation in Texas Higher Education* was to accept almost all the recommendations from the report by passing House Bill 2182. This bill requires testing for all entering college students and mandates developmental education for students who do not meet the established criteria. The law stipulates that the test should be diagnostic in nature and that recommendations from faculty at our institutions of higher education be considered in developing the test.

Thus began a most challenging period in the history of higher education in Texas. To fully address all the issues and interests that arise with such a project, we created an extensive system of committees. Literally thousands of educators were consulted to develop what is now known as the TASP.

Our objective with the program mandated by the legislature was not to create just another test. We wanted to create a holistic approach for addressing the fact that as many as 40 percent of our students do not possess basic skills in critical thinking, reading, writing, and mathematics. The test is but one of five components of the TASP. The other components-- advisement, placement, developmental education, and evalua- tion--shape a program designed so that students who do not meet the standards set for the test will be counseled positively rather than negatively.

Minorities, who are the fastest-growing segment of our population, have historically been disproportionately underprep- ared for college-level work. We were well aware of the impact the test might have on Blacks and Hispanics in Texas, so we began a thoughtful, careful process to develop a test free of bias. Test items were reviewed by committees composed of minority educators from colleges and universities around the state. These reviews will continue annually.

Although there are opposing views of the test offered under the TASP, we believe that minority students particularly need the diagnostic testing, counseling, and remedial help that the program provides. The test should be viewed, not as another obstacle, but as an opportunity to gain the skills for success that the program provides for all students. We want to use the test to sort students into the system rather than to sort students out of the system.

The success of the program needs to be measured ultimately by whether it improves retention and performance of university students. Every year, hundreds of students, frustrated by their inability to meet the challenge of college-level work, drop out of college short of graduation. By assessing students' skills early in their college career and by providing the courses, counseling, and tutoring necessary to improve those skills, the TASP hopes to help students stay in school and achieve their goals.

Our colleges and universities owe our students an education that prepares them for a job market that demands highly skilled workers. A college degree should have substance. Employers should expect a certain level of skills and knowledge from students graduating from college. To consider the alternative, which is admitting to our colleges and universities students who are not qualified, would mean downgrading the quality of higher education in Texas and being unable to provide business and industry with qualified, competent workers. Admitting underprepared students and flushing them out or downgrading graduation standards to pass them are both choices that punish students not ready for college-level work. This program, we believe, offers a far better alternative.

The TASP can be seen as a device for communicating collegiate expectations. We have sent a strong, unmistakable message of what we stand for to everyone in the state. Educational quality must be raised, minimum standards of performance are expected, and we must all rise to meet the challenge with hard work and diligence.

In developing the TASP, we chose the "road less traveled" in hopes that it will make all the difference. We have written this book for educators, policy makers, employers, students, and parents who want to learn from our Texas experience and begin to address the need for quality education all across the nation.

FROM POLITICS
TO POLICY

1
Getting Started: The Work of the Committee on Testing

Robert L. Hardesty and Joan M. Matthews

Employers, faculty members, and students have all complained about poor student preparation for college. The Committee on Testing, known informally as the Hardesty Committee, investigated, probed, and ultimately confirmed the enormity of the student preparation problem. But realizing that a serious problem exists doesn't solve it. The Committee on Testing stepped up to the issue by making some visionary recommendations that later became the basis for a legislative mandate.

ROBERT HARDESTY: THE CHAIR'S PERSPECTIVE

When the Texas Higher Education Coordinating Board decided on April 19, 1985, to establish a committee to determine if the basic skills deficit we were hearing about on our college campuses was serious enough to require state-mandated assessment and remediation, I heartily approved. But I passed it off as someone else's problem. I had problems enough at my institution, Southwest Texas State University. We were struggling with our own "rising-junior" exam.

Shortly after I was appointed to the presidency of Southwest Texas State in 1981, I received a letter of congratulations from a recent graduate. Although I appreciated the sentiments, the letter was so badly written it was embarrassing. The grammar was atrocious, the punctuation was random at best, and the sentence structure was totally incomprehensible.

At first I was shocked that one of our graduates--who I

subsequently learned had done quite well in his major--could write so poorly. But I had been taught an important lesson early in my life: Nobody's so worthless that he or she can't be used as a pitiful example. So I began showing the letter to our deans and department chairs. I learned that the writer wasn't a pitiful example after all. He wasn't even unique. He was symptomatic. And the symptoms at our university weren't limited to English. They included math as well.

The depressing fact was that we were admitting hundreds of freshmen who were woefully deficient in reading, writing, spoken communication, or math skills--and, in too many cases, graduating them with the same deficiencies four years later. They were bright enough students. They had met our entrance requirements, which were respectable. If they survived their first two years--and many did not--they usually did well in their majors. So we were not looking at students with a lack of aptitude; we were looking at students with a weakness in learned basic skills. And this was an important distinction to make, because just raising college entrance requirements, as some people were suggesting, would not solve the problem.

Two things began to concern me as I talked to educators on our campus. One, these students were falling between the academic cracks and nobody seemed able to help them. Two, we didn't know the extent of the problem.

Later, as I talked with other educators and read reports on the subject, I began to realize that we were no different than other institutions in Texas and the nation. It seemed to me that this was a terrible indictment of higher education. We didn't know the extent of the problem. We didn't know who needed help. We didn't know how to help those who needed it. We couldn't measure how effectively or ineffectively we were attacking the problem.

Worse, we seemed to have the attitude that if the students didn't learn their basic skills in grades kindergarten through 12, there was nothing *we* could or should do about it once those students reached college.

At SWT, we decided that such an unsympathetic attitude was unacceptable. We set out to break that cycle. We established a College of General Studies designed to advise lower-level students on a systematic basis, to guarantee that they received a broad, well-rounded education, and to make sure that they did *not* fall between the academic cracks. We also began designing a basic skills test that all students would be required to take and pass at the end of their sophomore year.

Out of that background, I was prepared in 1985 to follow the work of the Coordinating Board's new testing committee with keen interest. That interest was intensified considerably a few weeks later when Coordinating Board Chairman Larry Temple asked me if I would chair the committee. Because Temple is a hard man to say no to, I accepted. But I did so with some anxiety.

I knew that the road ahead was strewn with potential land mines. We were dealing with a very controversial issue. A mandated basic skills test, if that is what we decided to recommend, would not be popular. It would be an added burden to the already overburdened Texas public colleges and universities, and it would be viewed as a symbol of failure throughout the education community. High schools do not like to have to admit that they are turning out a high percentage of graduates who are deficient in the basic skills. Colleges and universities do not like to have to admit that they are doing the very same thing with the very same people, four or five years later.

A major key to the credibility of our report would be the makeup of our committee. Chairman Temple and his Coordinating Board staff did a first-rate job of putting together a balanced and distinguished group. It consisted of a regent (Larry Johnson of Texas Tech University), a superintendent of schools (James Vasquez of the Edgewood Independent School District), a faculty member (George Magner of the University of Houston in University Park), two experts on testing (Paul Kelley of the University of Texas at Austin and Marvin Veselka of the Texas Education Agency), a student (Laura Plessala of Angelo State University), and six presidents and chancellors from both the public and private sectors (Michael Nevarez of Pan American University, Ruth Shaw of El Centro College, Leonard Spearman of Texas Southern University, Sister

Elizabeth Anne Sueltenfuss of Our Lady of the Lake University, Jim Williams of Grayson County College, and myself).

We also had a first-rate staff, headed by Dr. Joan M. Matthews of the Coordinating Board, who provided the expertise we so desperately needed, scheduled our meetings, handled the burden of work between meetings, and helped us look smart. In addition, I was fortunate to be able to call upon the services of a number of very talented people at Southwest Texas State University, including Dr. Leatha Miloy, Dr. Paul Raffeld, and Carol Dochen.

We held our first meeting on August 27, 1985, and Chairman Temple gave us our charge:

a mandate . . . to review the advisability and feasibility of the establishment of a 'rising junior' type of test in our public colleges and universities in Texas and report to the Coordinating Board by September 1, 1986--a year later. You should look at all facets of this program. In addition to giving us your ultimate recommendation, we would also hope to see a thoughtful and careful analysis of both the merits and the deficiencies of such a program.

Questions he posed to the committee included the following:

1. Should such a test be designed for minimal competency in basic skills or simply to assess freshman and sophomore learning?

2. What kind of a test would be appropriate?

3. What impact would a statewide testing program have on different colleges and student groups?

4. How could institutions help students before and after they were tested?

5. What would be the costs of these tests and who should pay those costs?

Chairman Temple was clear on one point, and we held firmly to it throughout our deliberations: Such a test should never be used to weed out or reduce the number of students; it should not be used as an admission device. The primary benefits of such a test, he said, would be "to provide a measurement of both the quality of teaching and the quality of learning."

Over the next ten months, the Testing Committee held nine meetings, attended a national testing conference in Columbia, South Carolina, visited model testing programs in Florida and New Jersey, and conducted five public hearings throughout Texas to obtain testimony from more than fifty educators, students, concerned citizens, business leaders, and policy makers.

Our committee started working with the same handicaps we had begun with at Southwest Texas State: We knew there was a problem, but we didn't know its extent and we had no quick way of measuring it. We were in a Catch 22 situation. We had to know the extent of the problem before we could seriously consider recommending a statewide program of assessment; but without any formal assessment, we could only guess at the extent of the problem.

The one measurement we had was not encouraging. The Pre-Professional Skills Test (P-PST) was being used at the time to qualify aspiring education majors, usually at the end of their sophomore year. That test measured students' grasp of skills and knowledge they had been taught by the tenth grade. Historically, the P-PST judged about 40 percent of the Texas students who aspired to be teachers deficient in at least one or more of the basic skills in reading, writing, or math.

The public generally assumed that the P-PST scores were symptomatic of poor teacher education programs throughout higher education. But the critics failed to consider that students took the test *before* they entered the teacher education programs. Schools of education could hardly be blamed for the deficiencies.

The committee concluded that if the P-PST were given statewide to *all* students, the pass/fail rate would be about the same as it was for those planning to enter the teacher education program. In other words, nearly 40 percent of the sophomores at Texas public colleges and universities would fail at least one part of a 10th-grade test. That being the case, we wondered what would happen if freshmen were given an examination that measured *college-level* basic skills? Clearly, the failure rate would be much higher. Too many Texas students in higher education were not reading, communicating, or computing at the college level. We did not know who they were or where they were, but we did know that they represented a generation of failure in our educational system--a failure we could no longer afford to ignore.

The committee also learned that the basic skills problem went well beyond the state boundaries. A national study on low-achieving students indicated that the average community college freshman was reading at only the eighth grade level, and that 60 percent of the students entering community colleges needed remedial work.

But even some of the most selective and prestigious four-year institutions, such as Stanford and the University of California, were providing learning assistance or guidance to a considerable portion of their freshman classes, we learned.

In New Jersey, where the reading, writing, and math skills of some 400,000 entering freshmen had been tested since 1978, test results consistently showed that student skill deficiencies ranged from 31 percent in verbal tasks to 65 percent in algebra.

Nowhere was the failure of our schools more obvious than in the workplace. As many as 37 percent of businesses participating in a national survey reported they had been forced to teach basic reading, writing, or math skills to their employees. In fact, private corporations were educating and training their employees at an annual cost of more than $60 billion, nearly as much as the nation's colleges and universities were spending on their students. A significant portion of this business expenditure was used for remedial courses in reading, writing, and math. In fact, three out of four major corporations were training new workers in those skills.

In Texas, a bank vice president told our committee that while job applicants were well trained in finance, they often failed to pass a screening for oral and written communication skills. He told of countless letters and resumes that were discarded because of spelling, poor sentence structure or grammatical errors.

A top executive of a major aerospace corporation told us that his organization hired only top engineers from a carefully screened list of colleges and universities across the nation. Even so, this corporation was compelled to provide additional training in advanced problem solving. And, when the time came for some engineers to move into top management, poor writing and verbal communication skills hampered many of them.

Perhaps the most disturbing testimony of all came from a journalist who told of a survey of newspaper editors conducted by the Associated Press. According to the surveyed editors, journalism graduates lacked a broad education, their basic skills were insufficient, they lacked a real-world perspective, they had low reporting and writing skills, and they didn't have a newspaper-reading habit.

With this kind of information coming to us from every quarter, it soon became obvious to the testing committee that Texas was facing a basic skills problem of immense magnitude-- a problem that demanded immediate attention. "When our colleges and universities graduate thousands of students each year who cannot write a clear sentence or compute a simple mathematical problem, then we have cast a shadow on the quality of our degrees and the integrity of our diplomas," we later declared in our report.

At the outset, of course, we were considering the merits of a "rising-junior" exam. That was our charge from Coordinating Board Chairman Larry Temple. In fact, the committee's name initially was the Committee on Testing of College Sophomores.

It became clear early in our deliberations, however, that no one on the committee felt that a "rising-junior" exam was the answer. Our mandate went beyond finding a way to identify those college students who were deficient in the basic skills. We were charged with finding a way to help them through remediation. Thus it was important to identify the students who needed help as early as possible in their college careers. Finding the problem students through a 'rising junior' exam was, in effect, wasting two precious years of remediation. So our focus soon changed to a freshman examination.

As we neared our deadline in the spring of 1986 and began to shape our recommendations, the political implications of what we were doing began weighing on my mind. A mandated basic skills test would meet opposition. Civil rights leaders believed that such a test would be biased against blacks and Hispanics. Students believed they already faced too many tests. Faculty did not want to be overburdened with remediation tasks. Community college officials felt that their institutions would have to shoulder most of the burden of remediation. Education leaders and elected officials believed higher education should not be taking on a problem that should be solved in the public schools, kindergarten through 12th grade.

Clearly, we wanted to devise a plan that stood a fair chance of being adopted. Also, several potential hurdles had to be cleared--formidable ones. Our proposal would have to receive the blessing of not only the Coordinating Board, but also the legislatively mandated Select Committee on Higher Education, which was then meeting, before it even got to the legislature. And then, even if the proposal passed both the Texas House and the Texas Senate, it would still have to be approved by the Governor. That is a heavy burden of scrutiny for any public policy proposal have to withstand; it was an awesome burden of scrutiny for a proposal as controversial and as far-reaching as ours would be.

On the other hand, we did not want to water down our recommendations just to have them accepted. The solution, it seemed to me, was for the committee to present a unanimous recommendation, without a single dissenting vote. A minority report would effectively kill our proposal. And yet it was by no means certain that a unanimous recommendation was achievable. While the committee was united in its concern for the basic skills problem, I knew from private conversations that some of our members had deep concerns about a mandated test. These concerns surfaced on May 19, when we gathered to hammer out our final recommendations. As it turned out, most of the committee members shared those concerns to one degree or another, and even those who did not were moved by a spirit of accommodation that allowed us to come to a meeting of minds.

Would the test be racially unbiased? We were assured by national experts that it was possible to design an unbiased test, so the committee voted not to recommend using an existing test. We decided to recommend the development of a new test.

Would the test be used to screen out students before they were accepted by a college? Minority students would bear the heaviest burden if that happened. The committee declared that under no circumstance should a college applicant be denied admission to any Texas public college or university on the basis of his or her score on the basic skills test.

How could we be sure that remedial programs were of uniform quality and effectiveness across the state--in poor colleges as well as rich universities? We recommended that the legislature provide the necessary funding to support remediation.

When accord was reached on those stumbling blocks, the pieces of the final recommendation fell naturally into place. There wasn't a single dissenting vote on a single major issue. Not one committee member believed we could afford to ignore the problem for another generation, or another decade, or another year.

We titled our report *A Generation of Failure* and formally submitted it to the Coordinating Board on July 14, 1986. These were our recommendations:

1. Beginning in the fall of 1989, or as soon thereafter as feasible, all freshmen entering a public college or university in Texas should be tested in reading, writing, and mathematics skills at levels required to perform effectively in college. The test should be uniform across institutions and should be administered after admission. In no case should such a test bar entry to any student otherwise qualified. This assessment should be a tool of the education process, not the selection process.

2. Colleges and universities should develop strong advising programs so that appropriate course placement would occur early in the student's degree program.

3. Each public institution should be required to offer or make available non-degree-credit remedial opportunities on its own campus to those students identified by the test as needing assistance.

4. We recommended that remediation be required when a component of the basic skills test was failed. All components of the test would have to be passed on or before the completion of sixty semester credit hours of degree credit. If not, further coursework would be limited to lower division courses until all components of the test have been passed.

5. Each college and university should be required to evaluate the results and effectiveness of remediation and report annually to the Coordinating Board.

6. The Coordinating Board should be directed to have the new basic skills tests developed with the active participation at the decision-making level of faculty members from Texas colleges and universities.

7. The legislature should provide the necessary funding to develop and administer the tests and to support remediation. We declared that we would oppose a statewide basic skills test without the necessary financial support, especially for remediation.

In submitting our report, we said to the Coordinating Board:

Every year more than 110,000 freshmen enter Texas public colleges and universities. Of these, at least 30,000 cannot read, communicate, or compute at levels needed to perform effectively in higher education. Some become college drop-outs--not because they lack the ability, but because they lack the skills. Others receive degrees without ever mastering basic skills. The tragedy is that we often do not know they are deficient until it is too late to help them. We do not know who they are or where they are. This is a situation, which we can no longer afford to ignore.

JOAN MATTHEWS: THE STAFF LIAISON'S PERSPECTIVE

Committees have an often well-deserved reputation of accomplishing little. Yet at the Coordinating Board, we conduct much of our most important business through advisory committees. I have been continually intrigued with how these busy groups can be forged into working teams, especially when an important product is expected. Our committee members are usually high-level college administrators who are perennially overcommitted and overworked. But their expertise is invaluable, and those who accept the invitation to work with us have traditionally done so with graciousness and the understanding that part of the responsibility of their leadership positions is to donate their time on behalf of the state. This committee's challenge was formidable. The first task was to choose an appropriate leader, someone who would forge the group into a productive, working team. Coordinating Board Chairman Larry E. Temple asked Robert Hardesty, then the president of Southwest Texas State University, to be the committee chair. Both men had worked in the White House during Lyndon Johnson's presidency. I believe Larry Temple trusted that Bob Hardesty's political acumen would help the process of committee work.

Next, it was his job and mine to outline a methodology for accomplishing the task: how to arrange the content for an agenda of meetings to educate the members about testing and provide them with a way to research the problem and draw their conclusions.

The Committee on Testing Sophomores was given a little more than a year to accomplish its task. Although Chairman Hardesty had a testing program on his campus, not all of the other campus-based members did or were as knowledgeable. He and I decided that the first order of business was to carefully craft an educational experience for our committee members so they could learn more about the problem they had been asked to study. We gave them information basic to the problem, invited experts in certain crucial areas to address the committee, traveled to several states to study their statewide testing systems, and held hearings throughout Texas to allow input from any interested citizens. My goal as staff liaison was to load most of the basic information into the first few committee meetings. I hoped committee members would be knowledgeable testing consumers and investigators before they began traveling to other states.

I knew that every committee member was armed with personal feelings about the prospect of statewide testing, and that these feelings and opinions reflected many unanswered concerns. Statewide testing would give the legislature a new accountability tool. How would it be used? There was talk of closing some institutions. Would testing results be used to bolster arguments for closures? Could scores be used to justify reductions or increases in funding? Would testing be a disadvantage for minority students? Would they view testing as a barrier? Would they become discouraged from applying or drop out of school if they failed? Would the legislature provide the funds for the test and attendant services? Would invidious comparisons be made between schools? The prospect of such a testing program raised many specters; most were unpleasant.

Setting the Stage

To begin our task, we carefully outlined the decline of scores in the American College Test (ACT) and Scholastic Aptitude Test (SAT) programs and discussed causes. We studied changes in students' preparation for college and changes in the expectations of the professoriate when faced with underprepared students. Increased access to college and the availability of lifelong educational training has led to a growing population of older students in our colleges and universities in ways hardly imagined twenty to thirty years ago. In our state, there has also been a well-documented problem with grade inflation both at the high school and college levels.

We also set the stage by providing a context for the problem.

I presented the committee with an overview of the types of large testing programs most commonly found in higher education: entry-level assessment and placement, "rising-junior" tests, which determined if students could advance to upper-division study, and exit tests measuring the value added to the student's skills through either the major or the general education (core) component of the curriculum.

We decided to invite employers of junior and senior college students to speak to the committee because they were the consumers of our educational product. The stories they told were discouraging indeed. In sum, it appeared that our graduates were well grounded in their majors but weak in general education. Outside their fields, skill discrepancies were quite apparent. Banks had young employees who were beautifully trained in finance but couldn't communicate well orally or in writing. A newspaper editor spoke of journalism graduates who wrote poorly and had nothing of substance about which to write. A police chief spoke of training recruits (all of whom had a minimum of two years of college work) how to calculate the angles involved in a traffic accident. Practically none of the recruits could cope routinely with the simple geometry.

Last, we informed the committee of the results of the P-PST, taken at the end of the sophomore year. Forty percent of our students failed one or more sections of the test. We believed that test showed how our students might generally fare because it reflected the general education component of the first two years of college.

After having explored the problem and its dimensions nationally and within our own state, the committee turned its attention to possible testing and assessment solutions. Members heard from several experts. Dr. James Popham, who had conducted validation studies for the Texas Education Agency on the P-PST, discussed preventing minority bias on a test. For a tri-ethnic state where the minority population will become the majority in a few short years, and where there was a long and unfortunate history of segregated education, we had to be especially attentive to equitable testing content and procedures.

Other states' efforts were examined. Special attention was

given to programs in Florida, where a "rising-junior" test was in place, and New Jersey, which had an entry-level diagnostic test. Speakers from both states addressed the group.

We encouraged many of the committee members to travel to the 1985 American Association for Higher Education (AAHE) Conference on Assessment in Higher Education held in Columbia, South Carolina. Conference planners had expected 300 to 400 participants, but more than 700 people attended. Texas, like several other states, sent teams of educators or legislators to investigate large-scale or state-mandated solutions to their educational problems. We worked the conference like politicians working a room of voters. Staff members cornered people knowledgeable about testing and state programs and lined them up to meet with our group. We attended as many sessions as possible and had breakfasts, lunches, cocktails, and dinners with a long list of speakers and experts.

The Committee on Testing grew into an incredibly cohesive group of people. They quickly developed into a team of members who enjoyed working with each other despite their differences. I think much of this cohesion developed during the first trip that many of them and staff members made to South Carolina. It was a true marathon. We worked members mercilessly, but there was also time to get to know each other in more informal and enjoyable ways.

Shortly after the conference another team of committee members visited Florida. Officials at the Florida Department of Higher Education provided an excellent overview of their testing program, its purpose, and its results. Visits and interviews were arranged with a variety of officials, including the governor. Then the team divided into smaller groups and visited presidents, key administrators, faculty and students at different colleges and universities. Overall, our visit felt like a blitz, covering key institutions in the state in a few exhaustive but highly worthwhile days.

Soon another team was sent to New Jersey. They also met first with state officials to get an overview of the program, then proceeded to colleges and universities to talk with administrators, faculty, and students. The New Jersey program has been in place since 1977, so the perspective we gained was particularly useful.

In both states, our visits were valuable and productive. We learned that we did not need to "reinvent the wheel"; colleagues all over the country were willing to share their experience, advice, and problems. The politics of dealing with a state-mandated program were candidly discussed. We learned how to deal with a legislator who moves into an arena of educational policy traditionally held to be the purview of the schools, what to do to gain faculty acceptance of testing and remediation, and how other states have funded programs. Several vignettes stand out in my mind. I remember vividly an imposing and impressive woman at Florida A&M University. She met our group at the door, her hands on her hips. Before we entered she exclaimed, "Do you know this test is *ours*? *We* wrote it. This is *our* program!" Somehow, I thought to myself, this type of faculty acceptance must happen in Texas, and that thought became an important goal. When one of the Texas presidents asked a young New Jersey student how she had reacted to her need for remediation, she answered with great dignity and simplicity. "I always knew I had a problem with reading," she said. "What I didn't know was that there was something I could do about it."

Those words, too, became a hallmark for us, and our travels and study pointed to a clear direction for the committee. There was a need to diagnose students' strengths and weaknesses as early as possible after college entry and then provide programs to help with any deficiencies. The committee had heard a national expert on the effectiveness of remediation. Members became convinced that competent advising and placement had to take place for programmatic success. The vision of an entry-level testing program with appropriate services and program evaluations gradually overtook the idea of a test at the end of the sophomore year.

Cognizant of the public distrust of such a massive reform, the committee decided to hold a series of public hearings around the state. During the spring, five hearings were held in major geographic regions. We heard testimony from students, faculty and staff, administrators, systems officials, regents, employers, and parents.

After the hearings, the committee began discussing specific recommendations. As an interesting sidelight, a young doctoral student, Joyce Pollard, studied the committee's process. Her dissertation described how members of an interagency group mobilized and performed. She noted Chairman Hardesty's propensity to work toward consensus and staff roles in facilitating communication. Hardesty's goal was a set of recommendations that were totally unanimous. An excellent politician, he recognized that the conclusions of the committee could have great force on higher education in the state and he wanted no minority reports. His previous experience in the LBJ administration had finely honed his sensibilities in these matters. Joyce Pollard wrote:

Not only did the committee make recommendations, they endorsed them unanimously. Committee members, most veterans of such advisory groups, expressed surprise that the group achieved such a degree of consensus, though they agreed their work had been so thorough that "the weight of the evidence" ensured unanimity. (Pollard, 1987)

Chairman Hardesty capped the work of the committee with two presentations, first to the Coordinating Board and later to the Select Committee on Higher Education. The latter group included leadership of the legislature, so that when they accepted the committee's recommendations, we knew an attempt to pass a law mandating the program would be imminent. During the 70th session of the legislature, Chairman Hardesty helped shepherd that law into being, working with legislative staff on the wording and issues.

In fifteen months, the Committee on Testing had become a powerful voice in higher education in Texas. Members worked with great integrity, redefining their original charge to address what they believed was a more salient solution for the educational problem they learned about. With a carefully designed agenda to study and address the problem, they became a well-functioning collegial team, giving unstintingly to their task.

In her study of the group, Joyce Pollard concluded that a

certain set of strategies was used to accomplish the task successfully: (Pollard, 1987, p. 126)

1. A fundamental educational issue, which was supported by the current environment was identified.

2. A clearly defined charge with enough flexibility to allow the committee to act as it felt the evidence indicated was delivered.

3. The committee chairman, who ranked comparably with the members, was slightly more experienced with the issue and had excellent political expertise. He was able to establish the group's independence while communicating with the chairman of the State Board of Higher Education.

4. Committee members who had a vested interest in testing because of their institutions or the constituencies they served were selected.

5. A program liaison with professional skills in the issue and in interpersonal interactions was selected.

6. Professional staff support allowed committee members to concentrate on the issues instead of on logistics.

7. Information-gathering trips to out-of-state campuses as well as local meetings with consultants were conducted.

8. Public hearings were held throughout the state.

9. Press releases, press interviews, and public speaking engagements supported committee work.

10. The political implications of the issue and the entire process were mitigated rather than denied. Participation of all members was encouraged. A nonregulatory role of

the facilitating agency in regard to this interorganizational advisory committee was reinforced.

Virtually every major recommendation of the Committee on Testing was incorporated into House Bill 2182, which the Texas Legislature passed in early 1987. House Bill 2182 was the statutory basis for the TASP that exists today. The program and its history are classic examples of the sometimes rocky and winding road that took us from politics to policy.

REFERENCES

Kulick, C. C., Kulick, J. H., and Shwalb, B. J. (1983). College Programs for High-Risk and Disadvantaged Students: A Meta-Analysis of the Findings. *Review of Educational Research*, 53, 3, 397-414.

New Jersey Basic Skills Council. *Effectiveness of Remedial Programs in New Jersey Public Colleges and Universities: Fall 1982-Spring 1984.* Newark, N. J.: Department of Education.

A Generation of Failure: The Case for Testing and Remediation in Texas Higher Education (1986). Austin, Texas: Coordinating Board, Texas College and University System.

Pollard, J.S., *A Case Study of the Mobilization of an Interorganizational Collaboration in Higher Education.* Doctoral Dissertation, Texas Tech University, Lubbock, Texas, 1987.

2
Legislative Response
Carl A. Parker and Wilhelmina R. Delco

Faced with the facts and recommendations provided by the Committee on Testing, the 70th Texas Legislature developed a reasonable approach to the student underpreparation problem. The chairs of the Senate Education Committee and House Higher Education Committee used their powerful roles in convincing their peers and the public that the students' lack of basic skills portended serious long-range ethnic and economic consequences for the state. It was a testimony to their leadership that they were able to get the law passed in the face of severe budgetary limitations.

SENATOR CARL A. PARKER: THE LEGISLATIVE RATIONALE FOR THE TEXAS ACADEMIC SKILLS PROGRAM

Many Americans are aware of the unhappy state of education detailed by the National Commission on Excellence in Education in its report *A Nation at Risk* (1983)[1], but few people realize that the charges made and concerns expressed about the quality of education extended beyond the public schools to the nation's colleges and universities. The challenge for states to adopt measures for accountability and methods to foster higher levels of quality and academic excellence at all levels of education swept the country during the past decade with more than 290 state commissions charged to initiate reform.

The interest of private industry was especially stimulated when American students' achievement was compared to students in other nations. Both industrial and state leaders recognized the critical correlation between a skilled workforce and the ability of the United States to compete economically in the increasingly high-tech world economy.

Nationally, business and industry spend an estimated $210 billion for training and retraining with approximately $30 billion spent on formal educational programs. These costs represent a failure on the part of our public education system to adequately prepare a skilled workforce to meet the needs of our economy.

With the collapse of the Texas oil-based economy in the mid-1980s, state leaders organized a major economic diversification program. Higher education research was viewed as the key to economic development. At the same time the legislature began to look at the quality of the graduates from all institutions. Legislators began to hear from university faculty that public school graduates were not prepared for the academic coursework in higher education. The legislature recognized the critical need to enhance the opportunities for postsecondary education and improve the state's human resources.

The Texas Higher Education Coordinating Board appointed the Committee on Testing in 1985 to study the need for identifying and assisting students who are qualified to enter college but lack the basic skills needed to perform effectively in all their courses. In its final report, *A Generation of Failure,* the committee recommended a statewide basic skills assessment program to identify and diagnose academic deficiencies and to direct students toward appropriate remediation. They called for a test, uniform across institutions, to be administered to each student after admission. Based on test results, strong advising programs at universities would direct students to appropriate course placement, including mandatory remediation, early in students' academic careers.

Despite its extensive study and recommendations, the report supported the statewide basic skills test only if the Texas legislature appropriated the necessary financial support, specifically for the needed remediation programs. At the same time, another important joint committee was commissioned by the legislature to study reform in higher education. Larry E.

Temple, then the chair of the Coordinating Board, was asked to chair the new Select Committee on Higher Education. One of his first actions was to direct the Committee on Testing to report first to the Coordinating Board and then to the Select Committee on the problem of underpreparation of students. As did the Coordinating Board, the Select Committee on Higher Education endorsed *A Generation of Failure* and its recommendations in the final report in February 1987.

Upon the recommendations of the two committees, I, as chairman of the Senate Education Committee and member of the Select Committee on Higher Education, sponsored legislation in the 70th Texas legislature (1987) that established an assessment of each entering college student's ability to handle postsecondary coursework. The Texas Academic Skills Program (TASP) was created by House Bill 2182. Beginning in Fall 1989, the statute required all students entering college be tested for reading, writing, and mathematical skills. Students who fail any part of the exam must receive remediation from the college. My primary concern with the testing program is that it not be used to punish students by denying access to education, but that its results be used as diagnostic tools to correct academic problems and give students a chance to maximize their potential.

Funding constraints on the legislature were quite serious, so no funds were provided to develop the actual testing instrument. The law stipulated that the unit cost of the test and its development would be borne by the students taking it. In fact, the testing company that had contracted to develop and implement the TASP Test did not receive any funds for development. The company planned to recoup its cost over time. Consequently, the only state funds used to implement the testing program came with the authorization of the Coordinating Board to fill several new professional positions to assist in the development of the test and the resulting remediation efforts.

Designed to be a complete program for remediation, not just the identification of deficient academic skills, the college remediation programs were considered for funding in the 71st legislative session (1989).[2] It became a major task to determine how to fund adequately and equitably the remedial programs required under the new statute. Institutions were limited to speculation in projecting the cost of the remedial programs necessary on each campus. Some institutions had never embarked on a remedial project of this magnitude and were uncertain of the resources necessary to fund the program adequately. Although the Coordinating Board requested $36 million to fund remedial programs and fee waivers for needy students, the legislature provided less than $25 million. Public community colleges and senior general academic institutions received $23.4 million for remediation for the biennium. An additional $750,000 was provided for test fee waivers for financially needy students.

The legislature made clear its intent that institutions expend the remedial funds for a variety of different remedial programs and not place all students who fail the test in a semester-long remedial program or use a "cookie-cutter approach." Legislators realized that a passing standard had to be set for the test and some students would fail. However, not all students failing the test need the same amount of remediation. A conservative approach to funding the program and specific stipulations on the expenditures of funds were used by the legislature to force institutions to establish a prescriptive remedial program for each individual student's needs.

Examples of outstanding remedial efforts by institutions include the University of Houston-Downtown's self-paced studies and computer-assisted learning programs that allow students to complete the required noncredit coursework in less than a semester. Another is the University of Texas-Pan American, where workshops in test-taking skills, review of basic skills, tutorials, computer-assisted instruction, and reading programs are offered in addition to formal developmental courses. Remedial instruction in a formal setting, designed for those students with significant deficiencies or who learn best in a classroom setting, should be the method of last resort.

Some people argue that the TASP Test is both culturally and socially biased against minorities. The state has developed a good track record with other tests and has taken the same precautionary steps to reduce that likelihood. Questions are heavily evaluated and documented before they are placed on the test. Although any bias is unfair in an educational system, I believe that it is more rampant in the real world. It is better to detect such biases and help the student work through those differences in the academic environment than to sidestep them and leave students to experience those biases for the first time in the job market.

The TASP test will also be used to measure the basic skills for prospective teachers. Replacing the previous test, known as the Pre-Professional Skills Test, the TASP test is intended to ensure that teacher candidates are academically assessed and provided whatever remedial training they need. Because the quality of our educational system is reflected in our teachers, we must prepare them for the critical role they will play in the cultivation of our children's learning and human capital.

Although the implementation of the TASP places the burden of testing and remediation with colleges and universities, the preparation of the basic skills needed to be successful in higher education is the sole responsibility of the public education system. The legislature assigned an additional remediation role to the postsecondary system in part out of frustration with the public schools' inability to graduate students with adequate reading, writing, and computation skills.

Frustration has not driven the legislature to ignore public schools, though. Senate Bill 543, also passed during the 70th Legislative Session, requires that each high school be notified of the first-year college performance of its recent graduates. Each high school will receive the grade point average, results of the TASP Test, and grades in English and math courses. The reporting mechanism is intended to allow high schools a review of the college results and determine the effectiveness of the high school curriculum, teaching methods, and student-advising programs. Thus, student preparation for college is expected to improve over time as feedback from the TASP is utilized by the high schools.

Concurrent with the passage of the TASP Test was a package

of new reforms designed to improve the quality of instruction at the undergraduate level through the involvement of faculty. The legislature mandated that the Coordinating Board review the role and scope of each institution, that a fully transferable core curriculum be developed, and that a formula with recommendations be devised to reward tenured faculty for teaching at the baccalaureate level.

The opportunity to bridge the gap between higher education and public education has emerged. With the extensive development of remedial programs, faculty can evaluate the training and curriculum of the public school program for the first time. They can communicate their perspective on the skills necessary to succeed in a postsecondary curriculum and become involved in the learning of students at the undergraduate level. Several studies and reports have recommended that we involve all faculty in this process to build a stronger academic community for higher learning.

The extended timeline required to determine the success of programs such as TASP is an area of constant conflict between the legislature and educators. Educational institutions are guided by their own academic principles. In higher education, the accrediting bodies also subscribe standards and measures of academic quality. We know that qualitative measures take time to demonstrate results. Taxpayers want immediate results to prove that their money is being well spent on education, however, and public officials want to respond to the demands of taxpayers.

High schools will receive the first report on their graduates' performance in Fall 1990, and this information will be made public by school district. An integral role in this new initiative is that it be made available to the media. As the TASP Test becomes more routine and its results known to educators, the media can distribute this information to all Texans and allow parents and community members to judge their schools themselves. In general, it is difficult for the average citizen to know a good public school from a bad one. Soon we will be able to know which schools are preparing students for a life beyond high school graduation and which are not.

When the state finds a way to equalize funding and assure that all school districts are adequately prepared to educate their students, the legislature can begin considering options for charging the cost of remediation for inadequately prepared students at the college level back to the individual school districts. State leaders recognized that the craftsmen who failed to do their part ought to be charged by a quality control unit to fix the broken product. Thus, school districts who continually fail to prepare their recent graduates will be held responsible in theory and funding for their programs.

No new program is perfect as initially proposed and developed. For that reason, the legislature built into its law an evaluation of the assessment and remediation program. It is critical to the success of this program that all components, from the high school curriculum to the testing process to the college remedial programs, be monitored regularly to ensure that the objectives are being met. The program must be responsive to the needs of the students and guarantee the state an educated citizenry.

REPRESENTATIVE WILHELMINA R. DELCO: HOW THE TASP LAW WAS PASSED

Fundamental to any major public policy initiative is translating recommendations into law. The Select Committee on Higher Education was impaneled by the Texas Legislature, and it was to their credit that the committee was comprised of a diverse, committed, and forward-thinking group of policy makers, educational administrators, and private citizens.

The quality and breadth of the discussions in the committee, as well as the citizen input during public hearings, is in my estimation what laid the foundation for the kinds of clearly focused recommendations that were translated into legislative proposals and ultimately the new Texas law that resulted in the TASP.

Even though the Texas Legislative Council put in a tremendous number of hours to draft several bills that resulted from the Select Committee's final report, I must affirm how important clarity is to the drafting process and the timely filing and disposition of legislative proposals.

To ensure that major initiatives get the widest possible opportunity for substantive committee and floor debate, authors usually try to prefile legislation. However, there was a massive volume of testimony and public input encouraged and received by the Select Committee from around the state. Staff worked literally until the final hour to prepare and release the final report, thereby effectively eliminating the possibility of prefiling. It put us in the rather unenviable position of running with a legislative package of bills enumerated with high numbers--in the 2,000 range. Under most circumstances, this fact could have been detrimental to the legislation's passage. Approximately 3,500 bills are filed per session. When a bill is prefiled, it is assigned a low number, which results in a quick referral to committees and thus a greater chance of getting on the floor for a vote. Unless a bill numbered as high as 2,000 or above is tremendously solid, there is a much greater chance that it will become locked in committee. Given HB 2182's source--recommendations of the Select Committee on Higher Education--and its critical importance to the overall higher education reform process, it was obviously in a good position for passage from the outset.

Nevertheless, despite its positioning as a key piece of the Select Committee's recommendations, the bill was controversial and therefore subject to the pitfalls and opposition that controversial legislation receives. Of course, much of the opposition was simply a repeat of the arguments heard during the public hearing phase of the Select Committee, addressed in a most thorough fashion in the final report of the Committee on Testing, *A Generation of Failure.*

Despite its somewhat controversial image, I would have to concede that HB 2182 moved rather smoothly and uneventfully through the entire legislative process. There are specific reasons for this, which I think shed light on the absolute necessity of informed leadership in reform initiatives as well as on the role that partnerships between public officials, private citizens, agency administrators, and involved and interested professionals play in the effective and productive allocation of public funds.

In a move of historical note with respect to legislative proposals, Chairman Larry Temple convinced House Speaker Gib Lewis to coauthor HB 2181 (the Charter for Public Higher Education), which was the centerpiece of the Select Committee's recommendations. This suggested that the Speaker was coauthoring the entire package and therefore endorsing it. Since HBs 2181, 2182, and 2183 formed the core of the new higher education reforms, the speaker's coauthorship of the centerpiece obviously also provided direct benefits to HB 2182, ie, the TASP law.

In addition to the Speaker's coauthorship of HB 2181, both Senator Carl Parker, chair of the Senate Education Committee, and I, as chair of the House Higher Education Committee, were members of the Select Committee on Higher Education; and we were already on record as strongly supporting this particular initiative. Add to this the strong case for testing and remediation in Texas higher education made by the Committee on Testing, and you have the makings of a solid piece of reform legislation.

I would be remiss in not mentioning one meaningful facet of the HB 2182 process during the 70th Texas Legislature. Because of the timeline for the law, there was an agreement among involved parties that a major appropriation for the program would not be addressed until the 71st meeting of the legislature. Subsequently, the fiscal implication for the 1987-89 biennium was minimal, making support for the bill even more palatable.

More than a few forces inside the legislature precipitated the call for and passage of HB 2182. In fact, a combination of issues facing the legislature over the previous two bienniums paved the way for TASP. In 1983, when the Department of Education released its national report, *A Nation at Risk*, grave concerns were raised about the quality of American public and higher education. Here in Texas, significant reform affecting public education was passed. House Bill 72 mandated several things, but one of the most important elements required all existing and prospective teachers in the public education system to pass a basic skills test, the Texas Examination of Current Administrators and Teachers (TECAT). Unfortunately, the substandard performance of many teachers on this test called into question the quality of their preparation in our colleges and universities. It also made us think beyond teacher education and wonder about the performance of college students in general.

In addition to this, the Texas economy had taken a dramatic downturn resulting in a series of major cuts in state funding for public higher education. There was a growing demand for greater accountability from the Legislative Budget Board and House Appropriations Committee for the allocation of general revenue funds among public institutions of higher education.

As a believer in the theory that our youth are our most valuable natural resource and that the very basis and need for public funding of higher education is its advancement and service to students, I was almost relieved to see us have to face the accountability question. It forced higher education administrators, legislators, and the private sector beneficiaries of our education system to redouble efforts to do what everyone claimed they wanted to do--educate effectively and be able to demonstrate the results.

I think it became apparent to the higher education community during the 69th Texas Legislature, and subsequent special sessions, that it was "image reparation time" in the legislature. What better way for public policy makers to ensure we were getting the best student outcome for our dollars than by guaranteeing, at the very least, that high school graduates have the basic requisite skills to compete in the higher education community?

With a diagnostic test, not only can we measure the productivity of our public education system, but we can also "stop the buck" by mandating early remediation. A review of the votes in committee and on the House floor during the second and third readings of HB 2182 indicates that my colleagues agreed that this was a good first step in the direction of substantive reform.

Although the passage of HB 2182 was not impeded by any real obstacles during floor debates, it did encounter serious scrutiny by members of the Texas House and the Texas Senate. Of particular concern to members of the Hispanic delegation was the potential impact of diagnostic testing on the advancement of minorities after admission. A number of my Hispanic colleagues raised questions concerning the issue of ethnic bias and concerns about standardized tests and their use as criteria for admissions, which was nationally expressed by both Blacks and Hispanics through several civil rights organizations.

In my estimation, the Committee on Testing had done a fine job of controlling for this possibility. The committee called for a multiethnic bias advisory panel to review test preparation, an important element that strengthened my support of their recommendations. The fact that the test was also diagnostic in nature was another element contributing to my decision to support and carry the legislation. As chair of the House Higher Education Committee, I have a longstanding reputation for supporting student issues. As an African-American legislator, I faced a certain risk associated with authoring this legislation. It was perceived, especially by minorities, as a radical departure from their prevailing perceptions that standardized tests are obstacles to minority achievement.

However, I am also a parent, a former school board member, and the former chair of the Board of Educational Testing Service. I had become increasingly disillusioned with the argument that African-Americans could not pass standardized tests. Ethnic bias notwithstanding, the fact is that minority youngsters are educated from the same informational base as other youngsters. They are raised, for the most part, in American society. Except for culturally specific experiences outside of schools, they are exposed to the same stimuli and reinforcement as other youths. Admittedly, substantive bias would obviously affect test performance. On the other hand, the prospect of totally eliminating all bias is unlikely. I have argued on a number of occasions that since minority youth will ultimately be competing in a marketplace infused with much of the same bias present on some standardized tests, we would be better served if we took the position of legally minimizing the bias, then vigorously preparing our youngsters to assume the possibility of bias, and using it as a stepping stone to higher performance. I am convinced, as are many of my colleagues, that raising the level of performance of youth, as opposed to minimizing the standards by which they will be measured, should always be our position.

Finally, with respect to accountability, SB 543 authored by Senator Parker established a reporting procedure that would ensure that we maintain exact records on the performance of students and through the Texas Education Agency report this information to the appropriate school districts. This particular recommendation allows the legislature and the education agency to closely monitor the impact of public education reforms on college-bound students as a function of the TASP.

The discussion of remediation costs to be borne by the state was left to the deliberations of the next legislature. The very title of the recommendation as it appears in the Select Committee report--Testing and Remediation--indicates the inseparable necessity of the two elements for a successful academic skills program. But the Higher Education Committee was dismayed to learn early in the 71st Regular Session that a substantial decrease in the comptroller's revenue estimate for the 1989-91 biennium prompted the Legislative Budget Board to drop the $36 million remediation allocation recommended by the Coordinating Board. Subsequently, they recommended no allocation for remediation to the legislature. Had this situation held, it would have meant an indefinite delay in the implementation of TASP. I believed the importance of TASP to the overall education reform movement demanded that those of us who so vigorously fought for its passage must move immediately to ensure funding and avoid delay in the new reform program.

In addition to threatening the program as a whole, this zero budget recommendation provoked concern among the opposition to TASP about the strength of the Legislature's commitment to fulfill the mandate set forth in the Select Committee's report. Subsequently, a bill was filed stipulating that the program not be implemented unless in "each biennium at least an additional $61 million is appropriated for the design and implementation of remedial course programs." This bill did not pass. Given the declining resources of the state, coupled with the existing demands on general revenues, it was unlikely that the legislature would fund the remedial programs at such a level prior to the administration of the program and definitive evidence to the Coordinating Board of an institutional ability to address effectively the provisions set out in HB 2182 from the 70th Texas Legislature.

Forays from the program's opponents were effectively neutralized through a series of parliamentary maneuvers designed to allow the House Appropriations and Senate Finance Committees the opportunity to thoroughly review budget recommendations and to agree on a figure that represented to all supporters a good-faith effort to fund remedial costs in spite of the state's fiscal limitations.

The final appropriation for remediation was $23.4 million. While this figure was substantially lower than the $36.5 million recommended by the House Higher Education and Senate Education Committees, it represented a substantive good-faith effort toward funding a program critical to the success of higher education reform in Texas. Now the Coordinating Board and public institutions of higher education must effectively administer this program and bring to the legislature their best evaluation (with supporting data) of the full impact of this initial appropriation. Then they can make recommendations for the most efficient way to ensure the success of TASP for future generations of college youth attending Texas public colleges and universities. In my capacity as chair of the House Higher Education Committee, I am committed to revisiting this issue in terms of administrative quality and fiscal need until there is a certainty that we are administering an academic skills program that places Texas higher education where we all say we want it to be--among the best in the nation.

Even more than art, athletics, and entertainment, education has historically been the most consistent, sure path for African-Americans to move from poverty and obscurity to sustenance and privilege. So I am especially concerned that a program such as TASP fulfills its mission. Beyond this, our state and our nation must move quickly to turn this corner toward education reform and become pioneers for the advancement of the treasured principles of democracy internationally.With this goal, the quality and character of our investment in our youth speaks directly to the integrity of our commitment to excellence and leadership.

I am privileged to have been able to play a meaningful role in this massive effort to redirect the state's resources and provide for a better educated future leadership. I am grateful to the many public and private citizens who share these visions and have been willing to give freely of themselves to achieve the mandate laid out in the Texas Charter for Public Higher Education, which commits public higher education in Texas to the pursuit of excellence. Much work remains to be done, and there are new challenges to be met. I look forward to them all.

NOTES

1. *A Nation at Risk* was a report by the U.S. Department of Education, National Commission on Excellence in Education, 1983.

2. Representative Eddie Cavazos filed HB 692 during the 71st Texas Legislature in 1989 which provided for additional funding for the design and implementation of remedial course programs, but it failed.

3
Planning to Implement the Law
Richard M. Kerker, Ronald G. Swanson, and
Joan M. Matthews

It would probably be difficult enough for one state agency to oversee a massive educational reform.   In this case, two state agencies were charged with implementing the law.   Both had to coordinate with a third organization-- National Evaluation Systems, Inc.--and, to complicate matters further, different divisions within each agency wanted to be kept informed, to attend staff meetings, to contribute.   The task was a creative and fascinating one: how to turn the new law into reality.

At the time it became obvious that a law mandating a col-lege-level basic skills testing program would be passed, the commissioners of education and higher education began discussing a joint project. The Texas Education Agency (TEA) was responsible for the administration of a basic skills entrance examination for state-approved teacher education programs. It appeared that the Texas Higher Education Coordinating Board was going to be responsible for a basic skills testing program for entering college freshmen. Since the TEA was interested in replacing the existing test for teacher education candidates, it seemed a natural and beneficial marriage to have the state-mandated freshman basic skills test also serve as the entrance examination into teacher education. The dual-purpose test would not only be more cost effective for the state but also reduce the expense and testing time for teacher education candidates. The savings in time and money together with the required academic skill development component of the pro-posed legislation made the joint project an extremely attractive proposition for both agencies.

Both state agencies were involved in making this joint project a reality through the selection of the contractor, planning for the program, and policy development.

SELECTING THE CONTRACTOR

The process for selecting a contractor to develop and administer the TASP Test began before House Bill 2182 was passed by the legislature. As mentioned earlier, the TEA had already decided to replace the examination that was being used for entrance into teacher education programs. Although there were many benefits from the test instrument they were using, TEA wanted to change to a criterion-referenced test that was both developed and owned by the state. Ownership of the test would ease modifications in content or difficulty level that might be required in the future. Because of the timeline that TEA faced for a new teacher education examination, a Request For Proposals (RFP) was advertised before the legislature had passed the bill mandating the new entry-level testing program. As a result, careful language was used in the RFP asking for a test to meet the specific needs for teacher candidate testing but flexible enough to be expanded to meet the needs of the Coordinating Board's new freshman test. The assumption was made that most bidders would be aware of the pending legislation and would have great interest in the possibility of testing 120,000 to 150,000 entering freshmen per year.

Although the state wanted a custom-designed criterion-referenced test, no funds were appropriated by the legislature to cover the cost of developing it. So, the RFP clearly stated that no funds would be available to cover development or administration of the test. The company awarded the contract would have to recoup the cost of development and fund test administrations solely through examinee fees. The state also made it quite clear that the fee for the test needed to be manageable for students.

Given the rather unusual challenges presented in the RFP,

we were not sure we would receive any bids on this project. We were quite surprised and pleased at the respectable number of proposals we received from most of the major testing companies. The proposals were imaginative, innovative, and quite exciting. Our problem then became one of how to choose among so many excellent proposals.

After the first sets of proposals were received, the law mandating the testing program for freshmen was passed. Based on input from the state attorneys, the bidding process was reopened to allow existing bidders to update their proposals if they desired. Even though a very short period of time was allotted for this purpose, we were again surprised that a few new proposals were received and some elaborate and thoughtful additions were made to existing ones. Obviously, the possibility of a contract for such a large testing program was highly attractive to bidders even without upfront development funding.

Readers were invited from both state agencies and from many colleges and universities to aid in the selection of a contractor. The proposals were rated according to criteria established by the TEA. Many hours of vigorous discussion of the proposals occurred prior to a final individual vote for the top proposal.

Votes were cast anonymously so that no reader would feel pressured to follow the "party line" of his or her agency or institution. As a result of this process, National Evaluation Systems, Inc. (NES), a Massachusetts-based company specializing in custom-designed criterion-referenced tests, was recommended to both commissioners and boards as the winning contractor. The commissioners accepted this recommendation and both the Coordinating Board and the State Board of Education approved the awarding of the contract to NES.

PLANNING FOR THE IMPOSSIBLE

Once House Bill 2182 had been passed and NES had been selected to develop the test, the two state agencies began somewhat harried discussions on how we would meet the legislative requirement to have our testing program in place in only eighteen months. Opponents to the testing program (and there were many) felt that although they had lost the first skirmish in the legislature, the state could never meet such an ambitious timeline for the development of an entire program. They felt that we would not be capable of doing "the impossible" and, therefore, there was additional time to prepare for the final defeat of the program. The two state agencies were however, determined not only to make the deadline for implementation of the program but also to design, develop, and implement the best testing and remediation program in the country. The race was on!

Prior to a discussion of the specific tasks facing the State of Texas in implementing this significant education reform, it is important to describe briefly the agency staff who brought this program to life.

The Texas Higher Education Coordinating Board has a small staff relative to its responsibility for the coordination of all public postsecondary education in Texas. Although several Coordinating Board staff members were involved in part with the studies, committee meetings, and public hearings that preceded the passage of House Bill 2182, only one person served consistently as a part-time "staffer" for this project. With the passage of the legislation, this situation changed dramatically. Several staff members became increasingly occupied with the testing program. The official responsibility for this program fell in the Universities and Health Affairs Division, but staff from the areas of community colleges, financial planning, and data processing also became more and more involved in the development of the program.

A separate office of testing was created within the Universities and Health Affairs division. The office consisted of a director, a part-time graduate student completing a Ph.D. in psychometrics and statistics, and a secretary. As program development progressed, the part-time student received his doctorate and started working full-time. Eventually, two additional professional staff positions were created and an additional secretary was hired. Although the testing office had expanded, cooperation and support from other Coordinating Board areas and divisions was still critical. The TASP, more than any other program assigned to the Coordinating Board, was dependent upon intra-agency cooperation and support. Although the broadening of assignments was taxing on many already overcommitted persons, it did serve as a means to bring together people who often did not interact during their day-to-day business responsibilities. It was a high-priority project for the agency, and cooperation and assistance between divisions was essential to its success.

The TEA staff assigned to the new testing program had been in the assessment business for many years. They already administered a test for students entering teacher education programs, as well as a test required for teaching certificates. As a result, the TEA had an experienced staff of four professionals and two secretaries well-versed in the procedures necessary to design and implement a statewide testing program. Their experience proved invaluable to the effort of the new testing program. Although the lion's share of the responsibility for the new freshmen testing program rested on the shoulders of the Coordinating Board, the testing staff at TEA worked diligently on this project. Without their assistance, expertise, and experience, the Coordinating Board staff might not have been able to fulfill the legislative mandate to have the program in place by September of 1989.

The initial step in planning to implement the law was to determine what this piece of legislation really required. Lawmakers tend to have great intentions for all types of reform, especially for education. However, their good intentions are sometimes lost in the translation that becomes law. We needed to interpret the requirements of the law and, perhaps more importantly, clarify any statements that were generally stated or vague.

Although interpretation of the law and legislative intent occurred on an ongoing basis during the eighteen month development period, the critical components of the legislation were necessarily addressed quite early in the process. Since the Coordinating Board did not have a staff attorney whereas the

TEA had an entire division of attorneys, the early interpretation of the legislative requirements was the first major cooperative effort undertaken by the staffs of the two agencies. In fact, a third agency, the State Attorney General's Office, became a major player at this point and throughout the implementation process. An assistant attorney general, well-versed in testing procedures, was assigned to this project to represent the interests of the state and assist the Coordinating Board staff. He acted as the lead legal counsel in all matters related to interpretation of the law and advised us when we had interpretive latitude. Working together, we were able to ascertain what the new testing legislation required. That process enabled us to begin developing policies, rules, codes, regulations, and guidelines that provided a solid infrastructure to build a successful testing and remediation program.

In Texas, the rules and regulations for education are part of the Texas Education Code. Both the State Board of Education and the Coordinating Board operationalize their legislative mandates in the code. With the passage of the new testing legislation, it was necessary for the Coordinating Board to open yet another subchapter of the education code for postsecondary education. However, the State Board of Education already had existing rules and regulations for the testing of teacher education candidates. Therefore, their policy development and rule writing was negligible. The State Board of Education needed only to adopt the new test formally as the requirement for entrance into teacher education programs and to establish a passing standard. But as the Coordinating Board staff developed rules and regulations for the testing of entering freshmen, our colleagues at TEA were active participants, supportive and helpful.

The first major component of the new education code, Subchapter P, was a definition of terms used in the legislation. For example, who is a freshman? The legislation clearly intended this term to apply to first-time-in-college students. The institutions, however, call any student with fewer than 30 semester credit hours a freshman. This type of operation, explicitly defining the terminology used in the new program, was at times a tedious task, yet it was basic and essential. After consultation with legal staff, we would sometimes be bewildered and mildly amused at their insistence on defining terminology where we clearly understood the meaning. But it is easy to hold different assumptions about what is commonly understood, and so we worked to define all appropriate terms.

Perhaps the most interesting part of writing rules for the new program was "fixing the holes in the law." As one would expect, attempting to define the parameters of a program with the magnitude of this one almost always produces some anomalies and omissions. It was the responsibility of the testing staffs at the two state agencies to take the rather brief piece of legislation and ensure that the new program would benefit all students entering public higher education in Texas. Three major policy decisions were necessary to make this program work.

The law requires all entering students, both at community colleges and four-year universities, to be tested and given any necessary remediation. To encourage students to complete remediation early in their collegiate careers, the law explicitly prevents students from enrolling in upper-division classes beyond the sixtieth semester credit hour until all sections of the basic skills test are passed. Although this provision does not force a student out of college if the test is not passed, it does prevent the student from taking further upper-division courses or completing a certificate, associate, or baccalaureate degree. It was the clear intention of the legislators who sponsored this bill that no student would receive a degree from a Texas college or university without passing the new basic skills test. The sixty-semester-credit-hour-provision did have one major flaw. Students receiving associate degrees from community colleges do not take upper-division courses. In fact, community colleges are by law prevented from offering upper-division courses. Thus, students enrolled in community college are required to take the test and participate in remediation but they are not required to pass all sections of the test to receive their degrees. This contradiction in the law affected the majority (approximately 72 percent) of the entering freshmen in Texas. After consultation with key legislators, a provision was added to

Subchapter P stating that all students receiving TASP-applicable certificates or degrees from community colleges are required to pass all sections of the test prior to graduation.

Perhaps one of the more interesting contradictions in the law involved using performance on the test as an admission criterion in the upper-level universities. In Texas, there are nine institutions that offer only upper-division and graduate courses. These institutions award only baccalaureate and graduate degrees. They are prevented by law from offering lower-division courses, remedial courses, or precollegiate courses. The new testing legislation stated that an institution could not use performance on the basic skills test as an admission requirement, an institution must provide remediation to those students in need, and students could not take upper-division courses beyond sixty semester credit hours until they passed all sections of the test. Additionally, the new program applied to those students transferring to public colleges and universities regardless of the number of hours the students may already have received. These provisions put the upper-level institutions in an interesting situation. They were required to accept students regardless of their performance on the test; but if a student failed a section, the university could not allow him or her to take any courses nor could remediation be provided. After meeting with several representatives from upper-level institutions and consulting with legislators, the Coordinating Board rules included a provision that allowed upper-level institutions to use passage of the test as an admission requirement.

The third "fix" to the law related to the provision mandating when the testing program began. The law stated that all freshmen should participate in the program beginning in September of 1989. As mentioned earlier the term freshman has different meaning for different people. The legislators intended it to mean a first-time-entering student. The colleges and universities define a freshmen as any student with fewer than thirty semester credit hours. The Coordinating Board rules needed to state which students would be required to take the test beginning in September. After consultation with the colleges and universities, it was the belief of the staffs at the two agencies that the institutions could not be prepared in such a short time to test, advise, and provide remediation for all students who had accumulated fewer than thirty semester credit hours. Additional staff and faculty might be required to offer the advising and remediation required by this program. New instructional programs and revised registration systems needed to be developed and put into place. Quite frankly, the state was not prepared to have so many students enter the program so quickly. Clearly a rule defining the participating population of students was needed. The Coordinating Board passed such a rule exempting students from taking the test and participating in remediation if they had accumulated three or more college-level semester credit hours prior to fall 1989. This exemption was extended to students who had completed college-level work in Texas, nationally, or internationally. Further, the exemption applied to credit by examination and credit awarded for military or work experience (if acceptable to a college or university). The exemption policy required fewer students to enter the new testing and remediation program during its first year, enabling the colleges and universities to phase-in the full complement of students included under the TASP plan beginning in fall 1990. As a footnote to this policy, Texas did experience a dramatic, one-time increase in enrollment of summer school students prior to fall 1989. Apparently, our efforts to inform entering students of the rules of the program were successful.

The three problems the Coordinating Board had to remedy in board rules illustrate some of the many problems that had to be corrected. They stand as good examples for the type of efforts a state agency must enact to get from a law to an operational program. Yet there was a different, equally critical component of bringing the new testing and remediation program to life: the involvement of faculty, staff, and administrators from the colleges and universities. We believe that without input, support, and aid from the colleges and universities a program such as this one cannot come into being.

INSTITUTIONAL INVOLVEMENT

Before giving a description of the types of institutional representatives who participated in the planning for implementation of the program, it is important to note why the participation of those individuals was so critically needed.

The Coordinating Board has an enormous responsibility for the coordination of all public higher education in Texas. The higher education system in Texas includes ninety-nine individual college and university campuses serving almost 900,000 students. The challenge of coordinating such a massive system of education rests on 250 staff members serving the eighteen member Coordinating Board. Given our few numbers and the size of our tasks, we frequently must rely on the expertise of the higher education community. Typically, input from the colleges and universities is received via recommendations from Coordinating Board-sponsored advisory committees. For the development of this program, the expertise from the colleges was particularly necessary due to the range of areas the program encompassed. We needed recommendations on academic advising, financial aid, test development issues, test administration, evaluation, remediation, and policy decisions that would effect the institutions' ability to implement the program. Clearly the limited staff available to work on this project could not be expected to be experts in all of these areas.

A second and perhaps more important reason for including institutional representatives in the planning phase of this program was to give the colleges and universities a sense of ownership of the program. We believed that it was critical for the faculty and administrators, those who would be on the front lines of the program, to feel that this was their program--not one the state had arbitrarily developed and forced upon them. Looking back over the last three years, it appears that the higher education community did, in fact, claim the program. Some of the strongest early critics, after being involved in the planning of the program, have become the strongest proponents. In fact, it has become difficult for us to take credit for the success of the program because it belongs to them, not us.

The primary group of institutional representatives who have helped mold this program have been with us since the beginning of the test development process. They represent the oversight committee that provides leadership over most of the advisory committees and makes final recommendations to the commissioner of higher education and the Coordinating Board. This committee is the Texas Academic Skills Council (TASC).

The TASC is comprised of thirty members, half from community colleges and half from senior institutions. The demographic characteristics of the TASC is similar to that of the higher education community as whole. Minority representation on the TASC is higher than that found in the general academic community. The TASC members bring a range of expertise including testing and measurement, advising, remediation, and higher education administration at various levels. The position of chairperson for the council is reserved for a college president. We have had three such chairs to date, two community college presidents and currently a president from a four-year institution. Members of the Council serve a two-year or three-year term. Rotation of membership is staggered to provide continuity of the group. The members typically act as chairs or co-chairs of other advisory committees, thus providing leadership and continuity on issues brought forward to the council. The leadership and dedication of individuals who have many other responsibilities on their respective campuses have made an important positive impact on the program--one that we could not have done without.

The initial charge to the TASC called for the group to provide leadership for the other advisory committees and to act as the final recommending body to the Coordinating Board for all matters related to the new testing program. The TASC members felt that although not part of their initial charge, it was important to name the new program. At the first organizational meeting of this group a long and frequently humorous process of naming the program took place. Forty to fifty names were proposed for the program. Finally, the council agreed upon the title Texas Academic Skills Program (TASP) and appropriately renamed themselves the Texas Academic Skills

Council.

The program now had a name, a leadership advisory group, and great plans for involving hundreds of college faculty and administrators. Next began the process of identifying those individuals who would serve on the advisory committees. This became an unexpectedly difficult task. Not everyone wanted to be part of the TASP program development. Many viewed it as a legislatively inspired "evil" intended to take undue control of higher education. Others wished and hoped it would go away. On the other hand, some people feared they would not really be allowed to play a major role in program development. Somehow, they felt this was a deceptive scheme of the Coordinating Board staff to trick innocent faculty into endorsing their own demise. Fortunately there were many extremely well qualified and dedicated faculty and administrators who felt the TASP was a good idea and wanted to lend their support. Choosing committee members from this group was difficult for many reasons.

Geographically, Texas is very large with strong regional loyalties. In addition, Texans represent many diverse cultures. It was important that our advisory committee membership represented the regional and cultural diversity of the state. We also needed to represent all types of higher education institutions: community colleges, technical institutes, open-admission four-year colleges, and selective research universities. This was no small task.

The nomination process began by asking the chief academic officers from each college and university to nominate faculty members to serve on our committees. We were looking for content experts in reading, writing, and mathematics, experts in assessment, advising, remediation, and student services. In addition, the staff began deciding which institutional administrators would be appropriate to serve on a committee of chief academic officers. Once the nominations were received from the institutions, many hours were spent determining which person needed to be selected from which type of institutions from which geographic region. Special attention was given to the overrepresentation of ethnic minorities. Often we were required to go back to a particular institution asking for additional nominations because we were unable to find a person we needed or we needed additional representation from that institution. A more troublesome problem was rejecting extremely qualified nominees because their institutions were overrepresented. The selection of members for our initial committees proceeded for several months. Unfortunately, this is a process that is never completed. Replacement committee members are continuously being sought. We have retained the necessary representation on our committees as they have changed over time. It was for good reasons that the director brought a large map of the state to hang on her wall. She marked in all public colleges and universities and stuck different-colored map pins keyed to membership in the many committees. That way, we could see at a glance how the schools were represented. One of our goals was to involve representatives from every one of the ninety-nine colleges and universities in the state in the program development process. In the end, two small community colleges were holdouts. The director telephoned the presidents of each and inquired if they wanted to participate, telling them that all other institutions had. Both schools elected to send representatives to the standard-setting panels.

Aside from the council, several important advisory committees were instrumental in the planning of the TASP. Ultimately, we had twenty-eight committees: five on test development, five working on implementation issues, and eighteen ad hoc committees charged with solving very specific problems.

Five committees worked exclusively with the development of the TASP Test. These were the three content area committees (reading, writing, and mathematics), the Bias Review Committee, and the Tests and Measurements Committee.

Each of the content advisory committees consisted of thirty members, fifteen from community colleges and technical institutes and fifteen from senior institutions. They were charged with ensuring the content of the test was appropriate for the entry-level freshman, regardless of where he or she might enroll or what academic major was being pursued.

Imagine the debates that occurred between the two-year and four-year faculty on the appropriateness and difficulty level of the test materials! Although these committees were sometimes at odds with one another and the state, they provided invaluable advice on the nature of the test content.

The Bias Review Committee reviewed all test materials to ensure they would not disadvantage any students because of ethnicity, race, religion, sex, age, cultural or regional background, or handicapping condition. The thirty members of this committee represented all geographic regions of the state, types of institutions, and most importantly, the major ethnic minorities in Texas.

The Tests and Measurements Committee consisted of experts in testing who provided valuable insight from a psychometrics perspective. The membership of this committee consisted almost exclusively of testing directors from two-year and four-year institutions. They were also asked to make recommendations about test administration in the colleges. The committee considered the appropriate size of the testing rooms, writing surfaces, and the design of the score reports. The group recommended the number of proctors for each room and countless other details important to test administration. One of the most controversial and difficult changes they faced was alternative certification.

The legislation mandating TASP states that " the Board shall establish other assessment procedures to be used by institutions in exceptional cases to allow a student to enroll in upper-division courses where student test results do not meet minimum standards." This seemingly innocent clause was the source of considerable debate and discussion among the members of the Tests and Measurements Committee. Perhaps the most troublesome aspect of this statement was defining its intention and identifying the students to which it was intended to apply.

The Coordinating Board staff met with the state attorneys and spoke to key legislators in an attempt to determine the meaning of "exceptional cases" and "other assessment procedures". No clear answer was readily available. It was determined that this clause was intended to offer those students who truly possessed the basic skills measured by the TASP, but were unable to demonstrate that mastery on the test, an alternative method of assessment. It was not intended for students with handicapping conditions for whom modifications in test administration procedures were available. It was not intended for those students whose scores were depressed by test anxiety; anxiety reduction programs could be considered appropriate remedial interventions for those students. It was not intended for those students who failed the test, did not successfully complete remediation, and then wanted an out from the requirement to pass the test. It was intended only for the rare student who could not demonstrate skill mastery on a standard-ized test.

The co-chairs of the Tests and Measurements Committee had, in their collective fifty-plus years of experience, encoun-tered only two students who they believed might fall into this category. Both of these students were suffering from injury-related brain damage and simply could not demonstrate their true abilities on standardized tests. With this in mind, the committee set out to make recommendations for alternative assessment for the few students who would need this procedure due to rare and extreme circumstances.

Two principles guided the committee's recommendation. First, for students to apply for "exceptional case" status and, therefore, be eligible for alternative assessment, they must be required to demonstrate successful completion of remediation and mastery of the TASP skills. This process requires the certification from a developmental educator that the student does in fact possess the skills tested on the TASP Test. The second principle was that the alternative assessment must measure the same skills as those of the official TASP Test at the same difficulty level.

The final recommendation for alternative assessment that we accepted and was passed by the Coordinating Board outlined a procedure for institutions to follow to certify the "exceptional case" status for a student and recommend a method of alterna-tive assessment. Institutions will become the advocates for their students. They will provide documentation of skill mastery and recommend a method for assessing skill knowledge. The state will then determine if a student is eligible for alternative assessment and whether the institution's recommendation regarding assessment procedures are appropriate and acceptable. If the state agrees with an institution's recommendations, the institution will then provide the result of the alternative assessment to the state for confirmation of the fulfillment of the TASP testing requirement.

At this time, we have not received any petitions for alternative assessment. When we finally do, we will begin traveling down a pioneering trail in the assessment area. We envision alternative assessment as being special-case individualized assessment for a unique group of students. The success of these procedures should be of great interest to all those involved in student assessment.

Two other committees were instrumental in planning for the academic development aspect of the TASP: the Academic Skills Development Committee and the Academic Advising Committee. Each of these committees also had thirty members; and, as with all advisory groups, we worked hard to achieve equal geographic and ethnic representation on each committee. The Academic Advising Committee was asked to investigate the current state of academic advising in Texas colleges and universities and recommend advising models for the program. Similarly, the Academic Skills Development Committee studied the status of remedial education in Texas colleges and universities and presented models of different effective remedial interventions. Each committee achieved its charge in a slightly different manner. The advising committee presented its recommendations in a monograph sent to each college and university in the state. The skills development committee presented its recommendations at a series of regional conferences for developmental educators. Both committees serve as an example of how faculty worked on components of the TASP in different yet equally effective ways. Members and leaders on both committees were frequently asked to speak at conferences and at colleges to present their findings. Again, the work done by these committees and the assistance given to the TASP is a tribute to the quality of voluntary assistance faculty members provided to this important program.

One additional committee started out as an ad hoc group but quickly became so essential that we formalized its status and asked the co-chairs to sit on the council. We enlisted the help of eight chief academic officers, four from community colleges and four from senior institutions, to screen policy coming from the state. These administrators provided us with an insight into the internal management of higher education institutions that was critical to many of the implementation policy decisions made. The committee worked on all critical policy recommendations that allowed the institutions to implement the TASP in as efficient and fair a manner as possible. Their inclusion in the policy development of the program helped us to communicate to the colleges that we were listening to their needs and concerns. The insight and thoughtfulness provided by this group of academic officers cannot be overstated.

COMMUNICATION WITH THE INSTITUTIONS

From the beginning it became apparent that one of our most significant tasks was going to be the dissemination of information about the TASP program to the colleges and universities. We knew that much misinformation about the law and its effect on higher education existed even before the legislation was passed. We also knew that fear of change and resentment of legislative meddling in education would serve as a barrier to the flow of important information. We embarked on a multifaceted approach to getting the word about the TASP to the colleges.

One of our first major information-sharing events was a series of conferences for higher education administrators. We felt that accurate information to those in management of higher education was critical to the acceptance and success of the program. We sponsored three conferences for administrators: the first for college and university presidents, the second for vice presidents, and the third for mid-level administrators.

These conferences served as the initial briefings from the Coordinating Board staff on the policies and plans for the TASP. As would be expected, administrators showed a mixed initial reaction to these events. As people learned more about the program, their initial apprehensions gave way to positive suggestions and recommendations in nearly every case.

Following the administrators' conferences, the staffs from the two agencies began a process of communication still occurring today. We began receiving invitations to speak about the TASP from almost every college and university during their administrator meetings, faculty training seminars, and faculty association meetings. Colleges and universities from the same geographic region frequently invited us to speak to groups of faculty, staff, and administrators. We were also invited to speak at almost every professional organization meeting whose members drew from the higher education community. Although these speaking engagements took a toll on the staffs of the two agencies, they proved invaluable in getting out the word about the TASP. Many of these meeting turned into mini-press conferences with the staffs answering questions from the audience for one to two hours. This personal approach to sharing the word about the TASP not only spread programmatic information, but also helped foster a greater spirit of trust and belief in the merit of the program.

We knew that all the speeches we could possibly give could not replace the printed word. We engaged in a monumental effort of dissemination of information about the TASP to the institutions. Policy documents, clarifications, copies of the rules and regulations, and letters from our commissioner and assistant commissioner were sent to every college and university. In addition, we began producing a newsletter that contained policy statements, articles, and questions and answers about TASP. Many of the colleges and universities began publishing their own TASP information, and we contributed to these publications.

During the period of almost weekly communications with the institutions, it became obvious that an individual on each campus needed to be named as the gatherer and sharer of

TASP information. We asked each campus to identify one person to serve as a liaison for the TASP. These liaisons became the recipients of all TASP-related written material. They were responsible for its distribution on their respective campuses. The TASP liaisons became both popular and unpopular on their campuses. They were sought out for information by their colleagues but sometimes felt the sting of the "kill-the-messenger" syndrome. They became a pipeline of information to those in the field who were responsible for the implementation of the TASP. Their help was quite beneficial to the early success of the program.

COMMUNICATION WITH THE PUBLIC

Although we felt we were working hard to provide colleges and universities with information about the TASP, we realized that students, parents, and high school counselors also needed information. Together with the TEA staff we prepared information documents that were sent to all high school principals, advisors, and junior and senior students. In all, over 750,000 information brochures were sent to the high schools. In addition to the printed materials, both agencies' staffs spoke to numerous high school personnel at inservice training, workshops, and conferences.

The media became increasingly interested in the TASP. Staff members were frequently interviewed by reporters from major metropolitan area newspapers. Almost every major newspaper in the state ran stories about the new testing program. Several radio programs and community television programs were about the TASP. The media coverage of the TASP greatly increased awareness about the program statewide. During the development phase of the program, we put up a large bulletin board and displayed a cycle of several hundred TASP articles from around the state.

In spite of our best efforts, communication was and remains one of the most problematic elements of the program. We live in a large state; we have no budget specifically designated for

TASP communication efforts and are constantly frustrated by the numbers of students and school personnel who don't seem to know what they need to know about the program.

SUMMARY

Planning for implementation was a fascinating and frustrating process. First, three organizations were working together: the Coordinating Board, the TEA, and the contractor, the NES. Each of us had vested interests and different problems that had to be merged into an overarching concern for the benefit of the program and the students it served. A process of consistent and constant communication, including many conference calls and meetings, helped to keep us focused. The NES brought a wealth of expertise and an extraordinary set of high standards to our planning. The TEA had experience in developing and administering testing programs and practical experience in dealing with litigation. The Coordinating Board had never dealt with a testing program before, or the litigation sometimes associated with one, but we had a good knowledge of the politics of our constituency--the colleges and universities. The TEA is an agency with more authority to govern than the Coordinating Board; we *coordinate* and constantly must attempt to remain sensitive to the reactions of our constituents, who expect to have a significant voice in any process involving them. It put us in an interesting position. The colleges and universities wanted us to give them all the information, policies, rules, and answers they needed--preferably instantly--and fought for the right to create their own solutions, sometimes to issues clearly under our mandate. At public forums we got used to being chastised for not having provided rules and policies at the start of the development process. We typically received a great deal of policy input at those same forums.

The process never ceased to interest us. For three years, we were horrendously busy, so much so that a new staff member who joined us during an atypical lull that lasted two weeks was warned again and again that we normally didn't have the time to congregate in one office and chat for ten or fifteen minutes. Then preparation for a new semester began, and he learned what we meant. In spite of the sheer load of work, the process was intriguing because it demanded so many levels of functioning at once. We had to use our knowledge of psychometrics in planning for test development; we had to be sensitive to politics; we needed to deal with some very hostile and threatened people; we needed to know far more about public relations and a statewide communications plan than we did; we were constantly called upon as public speakers, and diplomacy was necessary at all times. Best of all was the heady task of having a major reform for which to plan; and we spent many creative hours as a staff, with national consultants and with experts from the schools talking about how to deal with topics like remediation, advising, faculty development, critical thinking, and numerous other issues that will affect students' learning and tenure in higher education. Those of us who have chosen to work in educational administration have often done so because of the opportunity to have a beneficial effect on a large group of students. Through policy and planning, the TASP afforded a particularly potent opportunity.

4
Planning for Litigation and Testing:
A Parallel Process
Kevin O'Hanlon

The day Joan M. Matthews was promoted to Director of the Texas Academic Skills Program, she gave a speech to the Coordinating Board. As she returned to her seat, an assistant commissioner beckoned her to the hall. There she was introduced to a tall, bespectacled young man who said, "Hi. I'm Kevin O'Hanlon from the State Attorney General's Office. Congratulations on your new position, and I'm here to tell you you're being sued." Litigation issues and the threat of litigation have colored the planning for the test and program, strengthening both.

The task of a public entity in creating and implementing a new standardized testing program is fraught with difficulties and not a few ironies. The courts of this nation have played an active role in the supervision of statewide testing programs in the past. It is likely that they will continue to do so in the future. It is virtually certain that a public entity wishing to implement a broad-scale testing program on the scale of the Texas Academic Skills Program (TASP) will face a series of court challenges to the testing program. Those involved in the process of test development must, from the initiation of the project, be aware of this fact of life.

The purpose of this chapter is to attempt to demystify the process. This chapter is written from the perspective of a litigator who has tried many challenges to standardized testing. My involvement with the TASP project was my first opportunity to help develop a test from the ground up. All my previous experiences had been to take the test developers' and users' decisions as given and to develop a defense out of those facts. Here was an opportunity to help shape those facts in anticipation of litigation, a rare opportunity for a litigator.

On the day the TASP project director was first appointed, I asked her how it felt to be a defendant. Obviously, she was not yet a defendant, and she was a little disconcerted to find out the likelihood of that future event.

The natural tendency, when faced with the possibility of future litigation, is to circle the wagons and assume a highly defensive mode. I submit that in the area of test development, a defensive posture is a mistake. Defensive clients most often want to limit participants in decision-making processes to those persons who will agree on a position. Defensive clients wish to keep internal dissent to a minimum. Defensive clients wish to conduct their business in private, out of the limelight. All these techniques reduce the possibility that someone will know what's going on and get mad about it. None of these techniques will work when the test developer is a public entity. The provisions of statute governing open meetings (V.A.T.S. Art. 6252-17) and open records (V.A.T.S. 6252-17a) are applicable to governmental entities. These provisions require test development activities to take place in a very public process. Nor are these provisions unique to Texas. Virtually every state in the union has statutory provisions requiring an open governmental process. This provision for public input at virtually every phase of the development process can be a very helpful tool in producing a high-quality as well as a very legally defensible test. When properly utilized, the public process is an asset, not a liability. I hope that this chapter will demonstrate the utility of this approach.

Prior to discussion of the process of test development, we must first establish a few legal principles under which test developers must operate.

It is important to note at the outset that statewide academic testing does not precisely fall within traditional protections of academic decision making.

Firmly imbedded within American jurisprudence is the notion that courts should not interfere with the process of academic decision-making. The U.S. Supreme Court has been firm in its adherence to this principle. (*Board of Curators, University of Missouri v. Horowitz*, 435 U.S. 78, 98 S.Ct 948 55 L.Ed. 2d 124 (1978). *Regents of University of Michigan v. Ewing*, 474 U.S. 214, 106 S.Ct 507, 88 L. Ed. 2d 523 (1985). The *Ewing* case involved the university medical school's use of the NBME--Part I, which is a two-day standardized written test promulgated by the National Board of Medical Examiners (NBME). In *Ewing* the plaintiff had failed the exam and was dismissed from school. Interestingly, the *Ewing* case did not involve a challenge to the NBME--Part I itself, but was only a challenge to the university's failure to give the plaintiff another opportunity to pass the examination prior to dismissal. In holding for the university, the Supreme Court wrote:

When judges are asked to review the substance of a genuinely academic decision, such as this one, they should show great respect for the faculty's professional judgment. Plainly, they may not override it unless it is such a substantial departure from accepted academic norms as to demonstrate that the person on the committee responsible did not actually exercise professional judgment. *Ewing*, Id., 474 U.S. at 225, 106 S.Ct at 513.

State courts have been equally staunch in their adherence to this principle.

In *Eiland v Wolf* 764 S.W. 2d 827 (Tex App.---Houston (1st Dist) 1989, writ den.) the court determined under a highly restrained standard of review stating that the court may not override academic judgment if *any* evidence of the exercise of professional judgment exists in the record. *Eiland*, id. at 835.

This decision is not an anomaly. Virtually all academic decisions regarding student dismissals have been reviewed by courts under similar restraints. Once a public entity enters the field of standardized testing by beginning a new standardized testing program, the same level of deference traditionally given individual academic decision making is not afforded.

The best example of this process at work is the lengthy saga of Florida's experience with the implementation of its high school graduation examination. In *Debra P. v. Turlington* a group of Florida high school students brought a class action lawsuit that challenged the State of Florida's use of the Florida State Student Assessment Test, Part II (SSAT II). The test was designed to measure functional literacy, and passing it was a necessary prerequisite for high school graduation. The test was mandated by the Educational Accountability Act of 1976, Laws of Florida 1976, Vol. 1, Ch. 76-223, pp. 489-508. The test had a significantly disparate impact on the basis of race. In 1977, for example, 78 percent of the black students failed one or both sections of the test compared to 25 percent of the white students. *Debra P. v. Turlington*, 474 F. Supp. 244, 248 (U.S. Dist. Ct. M.D. Fla., 1979). On appeal the Fifth Circuit Court of Appeals noted the trial court found the test to have content validity but determined the test did not have sufficient "curricular validity" and enjoined the state's use of the test "until it has demonstrated that the SSAT II is a fair test of that which is taught in its classrooms." *Debra P. v. Turlington*, 644 F. 2d 397, 408 (5th Cir. 1981).

In so holding the Fifth Circuit Court essentially invented a new standard of review for test development. Prior to *Debra P. v Turlington* there were three methodologies for determining test validity. Those standards were defined by the American Psychological Association, *Standards for Educational and Psychological Tests* (1974) thus:

1. *Criterion-related validity*: measures how well test items predict future performance and how test results correlate with other sought-after criteria.

2. *Content validity*: measures how well a test measures a representative sample of behaviors in the universe of situations the test is intended to represent.

3. *Construct validity*: measures how well a test reflects the concept or construct it was designed to measure.

In the *Debra P. v. Turlington* appeal, a fourth category of validity measures was created by the court as a ground to justify the delay in Florida's implementation of the SSAT II. Thus:

4. *Curricular or Instructional Validity*: measures how well a test measures content area actually taught in a given program.

After the passage of a number of years the State of Florida returned to court. Upon the demonstration by substantial evidence in the form of a study that determined curricular validity, Florida was authorized to implement the SSAT II, *Debra P. v. Turlington*, 730 F.2d 1405 (11th Cir. 1984). The study surveyed textbooks used in Florida classrooms and compared the textbooks' content to material tested by the SSAT II.

The experience of Florida with the SSAT II test illustrates the point of this chapter. Any public entity that wishes to embark upon a course of mandated educational testing must engage in significant planning from the initiation of the project to position the user for judicial review. The planning process must involve not only a thorough review of decided cases, but also a thorough, ongoing assessment of the "fairness" of the process. After all, the judicially imposed delay in Florida's use of the SSAT II was essentially a court mandate of fairness. The court felt it would not be "fair" to test students on material to which they might not have been exposed (instructional validity), even where the test items were legitimate expectations of student performance (i.e., the items had content validity).

How, then, is a test user to ensure fairness in the process and therefore reduce the likelihood for judicial intervention in a testing program? The State of Texas has adopted the content validity approach as the methodology for validating all its educational testing programs. The choice of the methodology is not mandated so much by law as by common sense. In educational testing the task is to define a series of areas upon which the test takers will be tested. It would appear that within the realm of educational testing, a content-based validation methodology best approaches validity. The content-based methodology more specifically focuses attention on the question of what students should know.

Both construct and criterion-related validity attempt to

establish skills on a pencil-and-paper test with other behaviors, sought for selection, for example, how well a pencil-and-paper test will measure a potential factory worker's ability to perform work-related tasks.

Content validation methodologies seem to fit best with the traditional academic prerogative to define curriculum.

In defining the broad content areas to be tested, a survey approach is used. To conduct the survey, a group of educators appropriate to the grade-level to be tested is assembled and members asked to give their best academic judgments as to what broad categories of subject matter a test taker should know. After survey results are reviewed, it is usual that a fairly broad consensus of subject-matter areas is generally formed. It is important to bring into this process a broad range of educational opinions. One hundred percent agreement among the educators is not necessary in the process. In fact, the process works best when there is strong debate and dissent. Dissent that appears in the process should be carefully documented and discussed. It is to be expected that educators who always have strong opinions on everything will disagree on matters of educational policy. If there is no dissent in the process, the validation study has not included a broad enough range of educational opinion. It is this very dissent that makes the process work. Once conflicting views are raised, the matter can be debated and a consensus position can be reached. The debate ensures that many views have been brought to the discussion and decreases the likelihood of a previously unconsidered issue arising once the test begins to be used. If an issue has been considered and rejected by the involved educators, evidence exists for subsequent judicial proceedings that a rational decision was made. From a litigator's standpoint, it is considerably better to defend a position that was hotly debated prior to action being taken than to be faced with defending a test against an unanticipated challenge. In other words, it is easier to defend a test against a specific challenge when the record established in the test development process demonstrates that informed educators have considered and rejected the position than to stand up and admit, "Gee, we haven't thought of that." In the former example, a judge must reverse an academic decision. In the latter, the judge gets to decide the question as one of first impression.

After the content to be tested has been selected, items are written in accordance with the previously selected content areas. Again, the items are reviewed by panels of educators. To work properly, the process should assemble a broad cross-section of educators and encourage a full range of opinion. From this full range of opinion, the best-performing items can be selected. Again, full documentation of the process should be kept. Whenever a dissenting opinion to the approach arises, it should be noted and highlighted to the reviewing panels for full discussion. In this way, a full record to support the academic consensus can be made and documented.

After items are selected by the educators, a field test is conducted; the results should be reviewed for their performance. The field test data will also be useful in determining passing standards.

This general methodology has been employed in Texas for a number of years and has served the state extremely well.

In 1985 the State of Texas implemented a test for entry into teacher education programs. The test chosen was the Pre-Professional Skills Test (P-PST), developed by the Educational Testing Service. The test has a purpose similar to the TASP Test, that is to determine whether lower-division undergraduate students had sufficient skills in reading, writing, and mathematics to qualify for upper-division undergraduate education. Indeed, the only major difference is that the state's use of the P-PST was limited to qualification for entry into teacher education programs and the TASP Test is required of all college students.

Predictably the test was challenged. The Mexican American Legal Defense and Education Fund, the League of United Latin American Citizens and the National Association for the Advancement of Colored People challenged the testing program based upon its racial impact and a series of collateral consequences arising from that impact. A preliminary injunction was held before Judge William Wayne Justice of the U.S. District

Court. The results of the preliminary injunction reported at the hearing read like a primer on everything that can be wrong with a testing program. Among the violations listed were:

1. Intentional discrimination occasioned by the state's knowledge of the expected disparate impact of the test. The court reasoned that if the state knew of a disparate impact of the test and gave it anyway, that this would be tantamount to intensing the disparate impact.

2. Disparate impact discrimination under Title VI [42 U.S.C. s2000(d)] under a Title VII [42 U.S.C. s2000(e)] employment discrimination analysis.

3. Due process violations occasioned by the lack of notice (i.e., lead time between when the test was announced and when the test was given).

4. Violations of the Equal Educational Opportunity Act. 20 U.S.C. s1703(d) See: *United States v. Texas*, 628 F. Supp. 304 (E.D. Tex. 1985).

On appeal the trial court was reversed and the injunction against the state's use of the P-PST was vacated by the Fifth Circuit Court of Appeals. In its decision in *United States v. LULAC*, 793 F.2d 636 (5th Cir. 1986), the appellate court justified its reversal of the trial court based upon the substantial validity study that was in the record. The Fifth Circuit held that the validity study constituted "substantial evidence that the test does determine whether or not education-course applicants have the knowledge of basic skills that is essential both to success in passing precertification education courses and proficiency in teaching." In short, the validation study saved the state's bacon.

Similar validation studies in connection with the state's administration of the Texas Examination of Current Administrators and Teachers (TECAT) led to the state's courts upholding a recertification examination for current teachers as legitimate exercises of the state's police power. *Texas State Teachers Association v. Star*, 711 S.W. 2d 421 (Tex. App.---Austin 1986, *writ ref'd; State v. Project Principle, Inc.*, 724 S.W. 2d 387 (Tex. 1987).

Proper validation, therefore, becomes a touchstone of a test user's defense of its testing program. As stated above, the State of Texas has used a content validation methodology using educators at the appropriate level for evaluators. It would appear to be a successful strategy based upon the litigation results thus far.

The reasons for the success of validation studies may harken back to the deference courts have traditionally paid to academic decision making. Court decisions outlining this standard were discussed at the beginning of this chapter. The key for a test user, then, is to bring academic decision making to bear in the process. Anyone who has ever been associated with academia knows that academics test virtually everything and agree on virtually nothing. Perhaps that is the power of consensus the validation provides. Since dissent within the academic process is to be expected, it is not critical if it appears within the validation process or by way of ex ante analysis provided by expert witnesses. A more critical flaw appears, not from the existence of dissenting voices within the process, but from the fact that specific issues were not addressed. The *Debra P. v. Turlington* case history can be read as a whole to stand for the proposition that a public entity will not be able to sustain a testing program unless it can demonstrate that it has deliberated upon the issue and is willing to assert a specific stance. In *Debra P.* the issue that arose apparently from out of the blue was whether or not the students had actually been taught the material they were being tested upon. In the first round, the State of Florida was unable to demonstrate that that particular issue had been seriously contemplated. In the second round of litigation, the state was able to show that students were being exposed to the tested material and the state's position was sustained.

This is the area in which developing a test and preparing for litigation are in essence two sides of one and the same task. In the development process, one must (after applying the cannons of Murphy's Law; that is, that anything that can go wrong will go wrong) seriously attempt to provide for every contingency. To the extent possible, every potential problem must be analyzed and its impact either eliminated or ameliorated to the fullest extent possible. This task is not quite as impossible as it seems. In our experience, advisory panels from diverse experiential backgrounds can and will raise a vast array of fairness type issues in the process of their deliberations. This process can be spurred by exposing an advisory panel to the myriad complaint letters that always accompany a test development effort.

After a test has been implemented, the advisory panel's role does not cease. Item bias review must be an ongoing process. Since new test items are constantly being added to the item pool, new items must be checked constantly against test statistics to determine whether they are performing properly.

Accommodations for handicapped individuals will be a continuing consideration. A well-thought-out testing program will have provided for a number of handicapped accommodations, such as braille test versions or sign language interpreters. However, every test administration brings a series of requests for additional accommodations ranging from reasonable to ridiculous. Each request must be considered and acted upon.

It is in the area of testing the handicapped that new vistas of litigation will open in the 1990s. The Americans with Disabilities Act of 1990 (ADA) was signed into law in the summer of 1990. Together with the Rehabilitation Act of 1973, 29 U.S.C. 794, and the Education for All Handicapped Children Act, 20 U.S.C. 1400 et seq. (applicable to primary and secondary school students), it has already lead to significant litigation and will do so in the future.

In some respects litigation over the rights of the handicapped operates in a different sphere from other types of allegations of test bias. Alleged test biases on the basis of sex, race, or age tend to revolve around group behavior. That is, a test is claimed to be biased because there is a significant difference in test performance among groups. For example, a group will claim a test is sexually biased if women as a group perform more poorly than men.

In the area of handicapped rights, notions of group behavior do not necessarily apply because individual handicapped litigants will claim to be more handicapped than others and therefore entitled to a greater accommodation.

The State of Texas has recently been in litigation with a teacher who claimed dyslexia after he failed a teacher certification exam. He claimed he was entitled either to an exemption from the exam or the accommodation of having someone read the exam to him and record his verbal answers. The state had, prior to the test's administration, sought advice on testing dyslexics from a group of national experts and was informed that the accommodations of more time to take the exam would be a sufficient accommodation. Additionally, the state produced evidence at trial that of all the persons who identified themselves as dyslexic who took the test, the plaintiff was the only dyslexic who failed the exam. This evidence would essentially prove that the preferred accommodations were in fact reasonable. In response to the state's position at trial, the Plaintiff responded, without evidentiary basis, that the extra time accommodation was fine for the normally dyslexic population, but he was abnormally dyslexic. This was so despite the fact that the plaintiff himself passed the test on his third try. The plaintiff lost his suit but did manage to avoid a summary judgment and drag the State through a trial and the Fifth Circuit.

The State of Texas is currently in litigation with a group of deaf teachers angry over a teacher certification exam. The test had been reviewed by deaf educators for bias and prior to the lawsuit had been modified to accommodate deaf persons. Plaintiffs in the current lawsuit acknowledge the modification but insist it was insufficient to accommodate the prelingually deaf as opposed to the nonprelingually deaf.

The challenges described above, although called discrimination lawsuits, fall into a significantly different category than the more broadly-based gender or racial suits. Typically, these suits are more about issues relating to fairness in the manner of administration as opposed to fairness in the type of material tested.

Certainly broad, categorical testing administration responses can and should be anticipated and predetermined. For example, a test administrator should anticipate dealing with blind and deaf test takers and from the outset plan accommodations for those types of disabilities. Additionally, a test administrator should provide a procedure under which a potential test taker should be allowed to request any other reasonable accommodation. Again, a panel of educators should then pass upon the individual requests. Requests should be granted when reasonable. If requests are denied, requesters should be informed of the reason, and alternative methodologies, where practical, should be suggested. Over time, if efforts are made to keep track of accommodations, the panel will develop a record of decisions that will shape the parameters of the term *reasonable accommodation.*

In summary, any agency planning for a statewide test administration must assume that the process will be the subject of future litigation. The potential for litigation does not alter the basic fact that a test, in order to do its job, must fairly and accurately measure academic skills. Surely, even without the specter of litigation, this should be the objective of any rational test giver. Legal analysis can be informative about mistakes made in the process, but in the final analysis if the test is fair, it should ultimately stand.

5
Minority Concerns:
A Response to TASP

Albert H. Kauffman

Even before the Texas Academic Skills Program was authorized by law, the Texas Education Agency and Coordinating Board staff found themselves sharing the podium on various panels with Al Kauffman from the Mexican-American Legal Defense and Educational Fund (MALDEF). Long an opponent of misuse of tests and the disparate impact of testing on minority groups, he was already involved with a coalition of minority plaintiffs in a suit against the Texas Education Agency. His concern in the case was the use of scores on an improper multiple-choice test as a sole criterion for entrance into teacher education. For him the prospect of the Texas Academic Skills Program Test raised similar issues.

I've been very lucky to be at the Mexican-American Legal Defense and Educational Fund (MALDEF) which has been organized for twenty years.[1] Modeled after the NAACP Legal Defense Fund, we started in San Antonio in 1968 and now have offices in Los Angeles, San Francisco, Washington, Chicago, and San Antonio. We work on issues such as voting, employment, immigration, and education that are crucial to the minority population in the state and, we believe, to all the population of the state and of the country. I have been doing civil rights work for about fifteen years and it's my profession and my love. I have been very lucky that we have had such an interesting docket of cases to work on. In addition to *Edgewood v. Kirby* (777 S.W. 2d 371, Tex. 1989), we have *LULAC v. Clements (U.S. v. Texas (P-PST)*, 628 F. Supp. 304 (E.D. Tex. 198, *rev'd sub nom, U.S. v. LULAC*, 793 F 2d 636 (5th Cir. 1986), a case that we filed with two important aspects. First, we are alleging that Mexican-Americans as a group have been discriminated against in the history of higher education in the State of Texas in all of the institutions. Second, areas with large Mexican-American populations, such as San Antonio, the Rio Grande Valley, and the border all the way to El Paso, have been discriminated against by the State of Texas, in that these areas have received fewer resources in higher education.

Testing is one of the most important areas of concern in civil rights litigation. I had been at MALDEF about six or eight months when someone called me on the phone and said, "You know, I want to be a teacher and I failed one part of the P-PST by two points and now I can't get into teacher education." I told her to repeat it several times because people get confused about these things. I couldn't believe it. I said, "That sounds absolutely arbitrary." I was right; it was. Nevertheless, it's the law of the State of Texas, and we challenged it in court. We ended up fighting both the State of Texas and the Educational Testing Service (ETS) in a preliminary injunction hearing that went on for about ten days. It was a real education for me, since I had to learn some testing. I'm still a novice in the area, but I had to learn in two weeks. I had some good teachers from the ETS and from the Texas Education Agency (TEA).

I have some of the same concerns about the Texas Academic Skills Program Test (TASP) that I had about the Pre-Professional Skills Test (P-PST). Consider the history of the development of the TASP from the point of view of the people who are being most directly affected by it. We must look at the test in terms of how the exams fit into the whole fabric of our society. Who are going to be the future leaders of the state? Who are going to be the future professionals? Who are going to be unemployed or the underemployed? The tests given every day have tremendous effects as people filter through the rest of the system. There are some research issues and advocacy questions that testing professionals should confront during the next few years. By working in testing before the legislature for the last three sessions, I have concluded that testing professionals have abdicated their responsibilities and have not helped develop the TASP in terms of its effect on minority populations.

Too many people have gotten caught up in the political furor of meeting higher standards instead of lending their expertise very strongly and effectively by advocating against the disparate effects of testing on minority populations.

Let's begin with the P-PST. It was made to screen prospective teacher education candidates. I had the advantage of looking back at it and listening to all the debates. I was surprised that public perceptions of the inadequacies of students came from some very select and anecdotal comments before the legislature back in 1981. A committee studied teacher education for two years and recommended an entrance test to the legislature. The legislature passed a bill in 1981 authorizing the use of a basic skills test for this purpose, and the TEA decided to use the P-PST. The agency hired Dr. James Popham to come in and bless it and validate it and he did so. The TEA then averaged scores projected by a standard-setting panel. They were people who sat around tables and looked at the test and decided on the cutoff score, even though they knew at the time the cutoff score was projected to exclude about 70 percent of minority students. Those statistics were before them, but they did it anyway. That's why we went to court and we won an injunction that stopped the test for a year, a decision reversed later by the Fifth Circuit Court of Appeals.

The Fifth Circuit never blessed the use of the P-PST; what the Fifth Circuit did was say that before a judge can tell a state it can't use the P-PST; the judge has to decide whether the test is valid or was validly used. In the process of discovery, we looked through tons of ETS records on the development of the test; but, around that time the state was deciding not to use the P-PST anymore. Instead, it began to develop a new test which became the TASP. Some of the issues of the P-PST remain. The TASP has made some changes very much along the lines we wanted, such as adding test time. It also did a little bit more on the validity process. But we are still very concerned about it, needless to say.

I've had the advantage of looking at the proposal that National Evaluation Systems, Inc. (NES) wrote to win the TASP contract. There is a lot of information about all of the

committees that would look at the test and help with development, set cutoff scores, and recommend scores, as well as how
the test is going to tie into the needs of Texans. When push
came to shove, though, the committee recommended a TASP
cutoff score of twenty, the Coordinating Board decided the
cutoff score of twenty-six should be used. I addressed one of
the meetings of the Coordinating Board and asked members if
they knew how this test was actually going to be used. I was
told it was going to be used as a diagnostic instrument. That
was the language they had learned, and they repeated it well.
Then I said, "Well, do you know that this is going to end
people's college education if they can't pass it?" They said,
"You're too negative." Perhaps I am. But if people don't pass
the test, their college careers are ended.   If the test has
anything like the effects the P-PST has had after multiple
testings and despite well-meaning people developing remedial
programs, we'll still end up losing about half our minority
students. If you look at the number of teachers graduating
because of the P-PST and all teacher certification tests, their
numbers are down, and the number of minority teachers is
going down even more.

   We're concerned about the possibility of misuse in several
parts of the testing system. First of all, what is in the test
obviously is of crucial interest to all of us. But so is how the
test is used ultimately in terms of deciding people's futures.
The legislature has said we need to be tough, we need to be
rough; we need to set standards and make people meet them,
but I believe there hasn't been nearly enough discussion about
the populations the tests do affect adversely and the amount of
the effect on them. Who are going to be the leaders and who
are going to be the manual laborers during the next fifty to
seventy-five years? Are there going to be enough white middle-
class people to run all companies and industries? I don't think
there will be, and I continue to believe that testing screens out
too many minorities. It's a critical societal issue.

   Next, let's consider the use of multiple criteria. The TASP
is, in my mind, being used as a sole criterion. Now, I once had
the disadvantage of doing a very stupid thing for a lawyer,

cross-examining a witness who was smarter than I was and who knew more about the topic than I did. But I did it anyway when I cross-examined the vice president of ETS and said, "Now, look at these guidelines. Aren't these the National Teacher Exam guidelines?" "Oh yes, they are." I asked, "Didn't you sign them?" "Oh yes, we did." "Aren't they all true?" "Oh yes." "Weren't you involved in them?" "Oh yes." "Doesn't it say right here that these tests should not be used as a sole criteria; but should be used as one of multiple criteria?" "Oh yes, it definitely says that." "Do you believe that?" "Oh yes." And then he started smiling, and I figured I was being set up, which is not very good for a lawyer. So I went on anyway and asked the stupid question: "When I got into Law School if you had higher LSAT scores, you could have lower grades. If you had lower grades and lower LSAT scores, but you had written legal documents that people had used and quoted, maybe you could get in anyway, and that is multiple criteria." And he responded, "Yes." And I said, "Well now, the P-PST doesn't work like that. If you fail one of three parts, you're out." He responded, "Yes." And I asked, "Is that multiple criteria?" He said, "Yes." Then I asked the stupid question, "What's the difference?" He said, "Well, what you're talking about is multiple compensatory criteria--one thing can compensate for the other. In our minds, the P-PST is multiple criteria because it's one of a lot of things you have to do." I said, "Well then, if you had to take your tetanus test and take the P-PST, would you have multiple criteria?" He said, "Yes."

So that's where multiple criteria is, and unfortunately that's the way the term multiple criteria is used in Texas. It's a crucial point because tests are not perfect instruments; they are still, to a great extent, works of art and not of science, and therefore so much weight should not be put upon them and scores shouldn't be used as a sole criterion. Test results might be one of many aspects of a person's performance to study. The ETS and NES and the American College Testing Program (ACT) will confirm that scores shouldn't be used as a sole criterion but as just another indicator so people can make intelligent decisions. But the fact is that test scores are used as sole criterion with devastating effects. The TASP contains a very high-stakes test. If it is not passed, a college career is over. So we are very concerned and we'll keep fighting until somehow we can get people to look beyond the test scores to the student.

We have turned our concerns into some recommendations. There was a bill in the 71st Texas Legislature sponsored last year by Representative Cavazos, Senator Barrientos, and Senator Edwards that sought to make the TASP a multiple criterion, saying that scores couldn't count more than half of a total index score, allowing the student to meet the TASP criteria. Students still had to take the test, so it could still be used as a diagnostic instrument. It would still be possible to use results to judge how well the junior colleges and colleges are doing; students could still receive all the remedial help they need. But the bill would have allowed the student to pass the requirement some other way--by making better grades in college, having made better grades in high school, or having done something else of note in college, for example. In other words, it would have forced colleges to look at the total student. The bill did not pass. The only people we had fighting the battle were the Coordinating Board, and they were fighting against us on the issue.

We even asked for more money for remediation. Instead of the $36 million the Coordinating Board asked for, Representative Cavazos asked for $60 million, of which $36 million was to be given to all the universities and an additional $25 million to those junior colleges and colleges showing the most improvement over a few years. Instead of the $61 million we got $22 million.

Validity is also an important issue. We feel that when a test has the impact of the TASP, we must also see people who do better on the TASP also do better in college. We'd like to know that people who do better on the TASP do better in the real world. No matter how well meaning, it's simply not enough to leave it to the panels. We just don't believe that this instrument or the content validity method of having the panels look at the questions and deciding they're valid is sufficient.

Somehow the test has to be related to the real world, especially on a high-stakes test, especially when the standards are projected to exclude a third of our minority students.

Military testing provides an interesting case. In the late 1960s, Secretary of Defense McNamara was concerned about an adequate number of people coming into the army. In spite of the war on poverty going on in the streets, many people just couldn't get into the army. McNamara proposed letting 100,000 people in, even if they scored below the cutoff score on the intricate battery of tests the army uses, the Armed Forces Qualifying Test (AFQT). So they let into the services a group called Category Four (the fourth of five groups), people who scored between the tenth and thirtieth percentile. They let in 100,000 of them. As it turned out, the services liked the idea, so they let in many more than 100,000. The process continued for several years. Many studies were conducted on what became known as "The Hundred Thousand." There is very little difference between the performance of these Category Four people in the army and the performance of the people who were in Categories One and Two and Three given the indicators that the armed services think were important: that is, completing training, promotions, eligibility for reenlistment, and job proficiency. Now I think those sound like topics that might also relate to the TASP; at least I hope they do. We need a study like that on the TASP. The test is being used right now, and such a study has not been done. We think it should be done. The results might be similar to the army's where several hundred thousand people would have been excluded from the armed services by a paper-and-pencil test. Many years later, a lot of those people are E3s and E4s and are now working their way up through the ranks. At the time everybody felt the sky was falling; those in the services worried that the corps would be destroyed. Twenty years later, it turns out that the test just didn't make any difference.

Then another thing happened. There was an interesting mistake made when the military used a test called the Armed Services Vocational Aptitude Battery (ASVAB) back in the late 1970s. They "misnormed" it. That is a very ambiguous term.

It meant that while they thought that only five percent of the people getting in were Category Four people, actually thirty percent were Category Four people. Because of misnorming, the military ended up with an extra 25-30 percent of their total entry into the armed services from this low group. Those people were studied. This time, though, nobody even knew about the study; it was one of those natural, blind experiments that people would always like to do but never had the power to do. This time they did because of the misnorming error. Four or five years later there was almost no difference in performance of the Category Four people versus the performance of the people who were "competent" in the One, Two, and Three levels. Certainly, most of the Category Four people performed a little bit lower; but the average entrance percentiles of the Category Four people were around twenty or twenty-two, while the average entrance percentiles of the other people were around sixty. But when all the indicators were considered, such as sergeants measuring performance, staying in the service, rising in ranks, disciplinary records, and so on, there were only two or three points difference, rather than the forty points difference on the test. So I think it does call into question some of the validity of just using a test as a sole criterion.

Bias must also be considered. It is probably the most sensitive issue in testing today. It is certainly the one that causes the strongest negative reaction from the testing experts and from the decision makers, the legislators. Whatever you want to say about it, it's clear that minority students are still generally about one standard deviation behind Anglo students on tests as a whole. Some questions work differently than others. Some questions show much greater differences between minority and Anglo scores than others. Nobody really knows why. But there are some things going on, and they seem to relate somehow to language differences: first language, language acquisition, cultural differences; all those things somehow fit in. But it does have a disparate effect, and we recommended that everything possible be done to delete those items with the greatest differences. As I understand it, the NES did some of that item elimination as it developed the test.

I wrote a ten-page form on all the information I thought would be helpful in looking at the test and sent it to everybody connected with TASP test development. I sent it to people at the Coordinating Board, the TEA, and all the major committees that were developing the TASP, but did not receive any feedback.

Remediation is crucial. I've read extensively about the New Jersey testing program and the Florida testing program, which, as I understand it, were used as models for the TASP. First of all, the New Jersey plan does not use the test as the ultimate killer the way Texas does. The New Jersey test is really much more of a remedial program. If a student fails the test, he or she has to take some courses. First, there is some proof that remediation helps people learn things. I'm not disagreeing with that, and I'm also not disagreeing that students need some help. If students take remedial courses, they can learn something from them that will help them. But a separate question is whether remedial courses help people pass tests. That is a very important distinction that escapes the legislators. For example, there is not a lot of data saying that if a student failed the TASP or P-PST by two or three points and then took a set of courses, he or she then had a 60 or 70 or 80 percent chance of passing the test. Those data do not exist. As a matter of fact, for the people who are more than two or three points below the cutoff lines, their future success getting above the cutoffs is not very good. And the probability trees show for those people who fail to pass the test the chances the second time are much lower. The numbers of people retaking and passing the test keep getting smaller. I worked with lots of people who have taken the P-PST five or six times, have taken every remedial course, and still couldn't pass the test. It leads me to believe that there is not a lot of data showing that if you take these tests, you are going to pass them. Given the TASP Test results, with an overall failure rate of 41.9 percent for Mexican-Americans, 44.5 percent for Blacks, and about 22.4 percent for Anglos (figures based on the September 22, 1990 test administration), I do not feel really secure that those numbers are going to improve much.

New Jersey found, after about ten years, that incoming freshmen were still failing the tests at the same level they did before. If the tests are normalized over a period of time, the percentage passing on entering college is not much different than it was ten years before. The Scholastic Aptitude Test (SAT) results over the last twenty years have been studied, and there simply has not been all that much change. Facing that prospect certainly does concern us at MALDEF.

Next, is the test diagnostic? Diagnostic results should lead students to remediation. One of the best selling points of these tests is that they are not supposed to be exclusionary. Rather, a three-hour test will tell an incoming student what strengths and weaknesses are seen. On this there is a split among the testing companies. But if there are only four or five questions on each skill, you cannot give somebody a lot of good diagnostic information. So, is this test really diagnostic? I do not think it's fully diagnostic; and even if it is, we have no proof yet that it is going to improve the scores.

Most important of all are the societal implications of testing. Let me illustrate what happens to Mexican-Americans, although the same thing happens to Blacks. Mexican-Americans now constitute over 40 percent of the first graders in the State of Texas, over 55 or 60 percent of kindergarten and below. They include 31 percent of all students in public schools; 25 percent of the high school graduates; 18 percent of the people in junior college; 12 percent of the people in four-year colleges; 8 percent of the graduates of college; 4 percent of the Masters and 1 percent of the PhDs--just in Texas. At each step along the line there are tests. Tests are not the only thing going on, there's no doubt about that. But if these numbers continue to fall at the same time that the percentage of students in the public schools is increasing and the percentage of unemployed among minorities is increasing, we'll have a distorted system without enough minorities in positions of power and leadership and it's going to get worse. You are at the gates, and the gates are being closed.

In Florida, after a year on the College-Level Academic Skills Test (CLAST), there was a move to increase the test scores.

Some people who had supported the test looked at a study and found that if they raised the tests scores, only three hundred Blacks in the State of Florida would be able to progress into their junior year. Florida didn't raise the scores. Somewhere along the line they decided that there must be some balance. We can't let the testing people determine who is going to make it and who is not.

The testing community has benefitted recently by a comprehensive report on testing issued by a broad-based commission from the fields of education and employment, military as well as civil rights organizations, testing companies and testing defense attorneys. The report is entitled, *From Gatekeeper to Gateway: Transforming Testing in America,* a report of the National Commission on Testing and Public Policy, published by the National Commission on Testing and Public Policy. The commission included the past president of the College Board, the governor of Arkansas, directors of the NAACP Legal Defense Fund, MALDEF and the Intercultural Development Research Association (IDRA), testing and training officials of Pacific Bell and AETNA Insurance Company, testing experts, and Dr. Robert Linn and Dr. Thomas Sticht with technical help from the chief of personnel of the City of Los Angeles and the director of testing for the Defense Department. The commission was chaired by the vice president of the Apple Computer Company and former Education Dean of the University of California at Berkeley.

The conclusions of the commission are especially relevant to the TASP because, in my opinion, the state and the Coordinating Board have violated most of the principles and standards recommended by the commissioners. The commission made three major findings and eight recommendations:

A. America must revamp the way it develops and utilizes human talent, and to do that, educational and employment testing must be restructured.

B. Current testing, predominantly multiple choice in format, is overrelied upon, lacks adequate public accountability, sometimes leads to unfairness in the allocation of opportunities, and too often undermines vital social policies.

1. Tests may mislead as indicators of performance.
2. Testing can result in unfairness.
3. There is too much educational testing.
4. Testing practices can undermine social policies.
5. Tests are the subject of insufficient public accountability.

C. To help promote greater development of the talents of all our people, alternative forms of assessment must be developed and more critically judged and used, so that testing and assessment open gates of opportunity rather than close them off.

1. Testing policies and practices must be reoriented to promote the development of all human talent.

2. Testing programs should be redirected from overreliance on multiple-choice tests toward alternative forms of assessment.

3. Test scores should be used only when they differentiate on the basis of characteristics relevant to the opportunities being allocated.

4. The more test scores disproportionately deny opportunities to minorities, the greater the need to show that the tests measure characteristics relevant to the opportunities being allocated.

5. Test scores are imperfect measures and should not be used alone to make important decisions about individuals, groups, or institutions; in the allocations of opportunities, individuals' past performance and relevant experience must be considered.

6. More efficient and effective assessment strategies are needed to hold institutions accountable.

7. The enterprise of testing must be subjected to greater public accountability.

8. Research and development programs must be expanded to create assessments that promote the development of the talents of all our peoples.

Unfortunately, the TASP violates these principles.

1. Specifically, the TASP structure has not been reoriented to promote the development of human talent but in fact is being used as a screening instrument to cut out those persons who have not met the "standards" of the test.

2. The test is multiple-choice and does not allow alternative forms of assessment.[2]

3. There is no proof that the test scores are differentiating on the basis of characteristics relevant to the opportunities being allocated; specifically, the testing commission recommended that "evidence should be accumulated to show how well test scores reflect real life educational or job performance."

4. Even though the test has very significant differential impact upon Black and Mexican-American students, the test is already being used to refer students to remedial courses, or to prevent them from taking upper-level courses.

5. The test scores on the TASP are being used alone to make important decisions about individuals whose past performance and relevant experience are not being considered in the TASP Test.

6. The TASP Test is not only a diagnostic instrument; its major thrust is as a screening instrument in practice. As recommended by the commission, sampling could be done to measure the quality of remedial programs in universities and community colleges. Similarly the test could be used only as a diagnostic instrument and not used in any way to prevent students from taking college-level courses or moving from remedial to college-track programs. The structure of the TASP and its use are the same as the structure and use of the P-PST.

7. The process is not being subjected to greater public scrutiny; indeed, not as much information about the process of validity and bias of the test is being disseminated as was disseminated about the P-PST.

8. There is simply no proof that the Coordinating Board or any of the universities is working to develop less discriminatory, more diagnostic-oriented, and fairer tests. The recent modest efforts of the Coordinating Board to develop alternative procedures are punitive in nature, putting on the student the burden of proving through a detailed, cumbersome, and embarrassing administrative process that the student might succeed even though he or she has "failed" the tests.

I submit that each of these factual statements and conclusions is supported by research in the area of testing and public policy. I would be happy to supply a bibliography on request. In general, I recommend to the reader a consideration of the bibliography listed in the report from *Gatekeeper to Gateway: Transforming Testing in America*, as well as the papers presented in two other reports of the National Commission of Testing and Public Policy: *Test Policy and the Politics of Opportunity Allocation: The Work Place and the Law*, and *Test Policy and Test Performance: Education, Language, and Culture*, both edited by Bernard R. Gifford, Kluwer Academic Publishers, 1989. The materials on military testing are described in a paper by Thomas Sticht. Another source of materials used in the preparation of this study was the report *Fairness in Employment Testing, Validity Generalization, Minority Issues and the General Aptitude Test* by the National Research Counsel, Washington, D.C., National Academy Press, (1989).

Unfortunately, the TASP is being used as a sole criterion to place students and restrict their educational progress. We cannot forget that the students who are being screened out, especially the minority students, are the survivors of the dropouts, the extremely poor, and the discriminatees who have miraculously survived the system and gone to college. Losing any of these, let alone half, is a tragedy.

People have already asked us if we are going to sue on this test. Well, I don't know. I haven't had clients come to me yet and ask me to sue. But I will say that obviously we are looking very closely; we have to. It's hard for me to sit down with the head of LULAC and GI Forum and have them tell me that they're losing half of their kids, that there are no more Mexican-American teachers and no more Mexican-Americans going into law school, and have me reply, "Yeah, but it's all scientifically done." I have a rough time with that; so I'll just keep working on it.

NOTES

1. This chapter is adapted from a speech given by Mr. Kauffman in September 1989 to the Texas Association of College Testing Officials.

2. The essay portion of the TASP Test constitutes an alternative form of assessment to multiple-choice. (Editors)

6
Test Development

Paula M. Nassif and
Richard M. Kerker

Developing a test is a complex, time-consuming, and expensive undertaking. Selection of a testing company is one of the most important decisions a state can make. National Evaluation Systems, Inc. (NES), specializes in custom-designed, criterion-referenced tests. Throughout the 18-month test development period, we came to appreciate greatly the careful, systematic, and detailed approach that National Evaluation Systems, Inc. (NES) brought to the program. Ultimately, the development process involved thousands of Texas educators and millions of dollars for a test that would be administered to up to 200,000 Texas students each year.

INTRODUCTION

The development process of a large-scale instructional and testing program has at its heart the construction of the testing instrument. However, all test development activities must be completed mindful of the larger context for which the test is being developed and for which it will be used. As a result, during the development process, it is important to bear in mind the background that prompted the development of both the program and the test, and it is essential to examine the ongoing test construction activities frequently to ensure that the test continues to match the intended purpose and goals of the program.

This chapter includes background information that was used to guide the test development process and a description of the test development process itself, specifically identifying key steps and outlining the processes used to achieve each step. The collaboration of the Texas Higher Education Coordinating Board (THECB), the Texas Education Agency (TEA), and the contractor, National Evaluation Systems, Inc. (NES), is discussed during each key step of the test development process. Activities surrounding the involvement of Texas educators, bias prevention, and validity are also discussed. Information about continued test development and continued involvement of Texas educators is also included. Finally, a description of the operational TASP Test is provided.

BACKGROUND

House Bill 2182 includes specific mandates governing the development of the TASP Test. A discussion of these legislative mandates is essential to understanding many of the test development activities.

The legislation states that "in developing the test, the Board shall consider the recommendations of faculty from various institutions of higher education." With the clear directive to involve faculty, the design of the test development activity needed to be sensitive to two factors. First, Texas is a large, diverse state with a complex and extensive system of higher education, and the number and selection of faculty to be involved in the program had to reflect these dimensions. The process involved selecting a substantial number of faculty based on several factors including type of institution, geographic location, gender, and ethnic/racial characteristics. Second, faculty recommendations about the test and items were collected in a variety of ways. At several key decision points during the development of the test, both face-to-face meetings and surveys were used to collect these ideas.

The legislation states that all students entering public institutions of higher education must be tested in reading, writing, and mathematics skills, so key elements that affected the test design concerned the definition of reading, writing, and math skills as they are used in programs at the college level.

As part of the test development process, entry-level college skills in each of these three content areas needed to be defined. The definitions had to be clear and provide a reasonable description of college academic skills. These skills definitions needed to be available during the test development process. In fact, they were ultimately disseminated statewide.

The definition of the academic skills had to encompass a broad range of skills needed by entry-level students in the courses they typically take in the freshman year. Therefore, the skills measured by the test were developed with relationship to the level of reading, writing, and mathematics encountered across the range of courses that an entry-level college student might elect or be required to take.

Faculty have a hands-on perspective on the content of college-level courses. They know the types of skills in reading, writing, and math that students should have in order to learn effectively in those courses. By asking faculty to provide this information during the test development process, the groups involved in writing and editing the test questions were better able to identify and focus on the skills and skill levels that are relevant to undergraduate programs.

The legislation is clear about several characteristics of the test. It states, "The same [test] shall be used at all institutions of higher education." Further, it states that the test "shall be of a diagnostic nature."

The test instrument needed to have comparable content and be of comparable difficulty from one test administration to the next. The procedures for defining the content of the test in relation to stated skills and for developing test questions according to an agreed-upon test blueprint facilitated the creation of tests that were comparable in content from one administration to the next. The comparable level of difficulty of the test was provided through a statistical equating procedure.

In creating the blueprint of the test from the skills, efforts were made to provide a balanced group of items across the skills measured by the test so that results could be reported by the total score for each section of the test as well as by each skill or group of skills measured by the items. In developing the test, a balance was reached between the level of detail of the diagnostic information and the amount of testing deemed reasonable by the organizations involved in developing the test. The result was a test that nearly everybody could complete in four hours or less. Each student's answers provide reasonable information concerning his or her strengths and weaknesses in the skill areas being tested and everyone receives this information as part of the examinee score report. Appendix 4 shows the basic outline of the examinee score report. This information is used to assist in the assessment and advisement component of the TASP in determining appropriate remediation.

ROLE OF THE STATE AGENCIES

The THECB and the TEA were involved in test development from initial planning through the review of final test materials and testing policies. The constant involvement of both groups ensured that the emerging test materials were consonant with the principles and aims of the TASP.

The THECB was primarily responsible for ensuring that the test materials were appropriately addressing their audience of concern: entering freshman-level students in Texas public colleges and universities. The target group of the TEA was students, whether in public or private institutions, who were preparing to enter teacher education programs. The dynamic involvement of both groups with NES, and the consideration of input from educators in Texas, ensured a coordinated instructional and testing program.

Typically, all three agencies were involved in discussions on the design and implementation of each step in the TASP test development and administration planning. For some specific tasks, one or the other of the agencies might have initiated the effort. For example, the nomination and selection of Texas educators to serve on various committees was done by both agencies. For technical activities, a preliminary discussion initiated by the contractor would take place with the two agencies. Discussion continued, sometimes with draft plans, to lay out and consider procedures, steps, and implications. All three groups would come together to implement the finally selected approach.

Most of the operational implementation of activities was completed by the contractor hired for that purpose. However, the two agencies appeared at and monitored all public functions such as committee meetings and the pilot test. The staff at the two agencies also closely monitored the contractor's work on a constant, ongoing basis.

The outcomes of this highly interactive process were that each of the Texas agencies ultimately designed and implemented programs that addressed the needs of their two audiences. Further, they ensured that the program addressed issues in the State of Texas and that the program was customized to their specific needs--a goal from the start of the program. Ultimately, the program customized both the test development activities and products and, in particular, administration procedures and policies.

The three agencies met frequently to plan upcoming activities and also to review past events. Meetings would last from one to two days, involving several members of the three agencies. There was virtually daily telephone contact among the three agencies for the purpose of information sharing, task definition, and sharing results of completed tasks.

INVOLVEMENT OF TEXAS EDUCATORS

An important feature of the test development process was the continuous involvement of Texas educators in the designing, reviewing, trying, shaping, validating, and refining of the testing program. The principle involvement of Texas educators was with ongoing review and input sessions termed review cycles. Throughout the development of the TASP Test, four review cycles were held. In January and February 1988, the first review cycle was held to look at the draft list of skills for the testing program. The second review cycle, in May and June 1988, was held to review the skills survey results and make recommendations for the list of skills that would be eligible for testing. A second purpose of the second review cycle was to review the test and item specifications that NES had drafted for the testing program. In September 1988, the third review cycle had as its focus the draft test items corresponding to the skills eligible for testing. The purpose of the fourth review cycle, in November and December 1988, was to review the test items together with item tryout results and to refine the content of the items for use in actual administrations of the TASP Test.

There were three principal groups of Texas educators who participated in the review cycles. First, approximately 300 Texas college faculty, chosen by the THECB and the TEA to reflect the racial, gender, ethnic, regional, and educational (or institutional) diversity of Texas, formed Regional Review Forums. The Regional Review Forums met at six sites around the state. Input from the Regional Review Forums at each of the four review cycles was gathered and summarized for consideration by the TASP Bias Review Panel and Content Advisory Committees (described below) and by the THECB and TEA.

A second component group of the review cycles was the TASP Bias Review Panel. The THECB and TEA selected approximately thirty Texas educators representing the various minority groups in Texas. The focus of the Bias Review Committee was to review test materials for potential bias and produce recommendations to be considered by the Content Advisory Committees and the THECB and TEA.

The THECB and TEA established one Content Advisory Committee for each of the three test areas (reading, writing, and mathematics) of the TASP. Each committee was comprised of thirty college educators, for a total of ninety, who reviewed the test materials (including a review for bias). The Content Advisory Committees considered and incorporated comments from the Regional Review Forums and the Bias Review Panel into final recommendations to the THECB and TEA.

After the test materials had been through four review cycles, the test items were submitted to a Content Validation Panel, composed of approximately sixty college faculty across the three test areas. The Content Validation Panel provided an independent reconfirmation of the validity of the test items that had been developed and refined through the draft-review-refine process. The Content Validation Panel reviewed the items for accuracy, match to the skills, and freedom from bias.

Several hundred college faculty, representing a variety of academic disciplines, types of schools, regions, and demographic backgrounds constituted the Standard Setting Panel. This panel reviewed a sample of test items and provided information to be used by the THECB and State Board of Education in setting the passing scores for each test area.

TEST DEVELOPMENT PROCESS

In addition to the test development process, the agencies paid consistent and continuing attention to bias prevention and the validity of the test. NES began in 1987 by reviewing the skill requirements for graduation from public high schools in the State of Texas, college freshman-level course descriptions, syllabi, textbooks, and study materials, and it identified prerequisite skills for effective performance in an entry-level undergraduate program of study. From this review, NES constructed a preliminary skills list. These skills and sub-skills were presented for review to Texas postsecondary faculty during the first review cycle meetings in January and February 1988. At those meetings, Texas educators comprising the TASP Regional Review Forums, the TASP Bias Review Panel, and the TASP Content Advisory Committees reviewed the skills list from several different perspectives.

The Regional Review Forums were asked to consider whether the list adequately covered the important basic skills all entry-level students should possess. Additionally, they were asked to consider whether the list was at the appropriate level of difficulty and could be understood by students and educators preparing students for the test.

The Bias Review Panel studied whether the skills list contained any element that could disadvantage an individual because of his or her gender, race, ethnicity, nationality, religion, age, handicapping condition, or cultural, economic, or geographical background.

The Content Advisory Committees advised whether the skills list was complete, organized in a manner that would provide diagnostic information, accurately stated, measurable, teachable, and free from bias. Additionally, the Content Advisory Committees were asked if the skills and subskills represented significant knowledge that entry-level students should possess at the appropriate level of difficulty.

Using all the input from the first review cycle, revisions were made to the skills list. National Evaluation Systems then conducted a skills survey in the spring of 1988 using the revised list of twenty-eight academic skills. The purpose of the survey was to collect information about the skills from general college and university faculty, teacher education faculty, public school teachers, entering freshman-level students, and teacher education students.

Approximately 3,400 general college and university faculty were asked to review each of the twenty-eight reading, mathematics, and writing skills and answer the survey question: "How important is it for entering freshman-level students to have this skill to perform effectively in undergraduate certificate or degree programs in Texas?" Approximately 800 teacher education faculty were asked: "How important is it for students entering teacher education programs to have this skill to perform effectively in undergraduate teacher education programs in Texas?" Approximately 500 public school teachers were asked: "How important is it for you to have this skill to perform your job effectively as a teacher in Texas?"

Respondents in each group were given a five-point scale, ranging from one equals no importance to five equals very great importance, to answer each question. The mean importance ratings (the arithmetic averages of the responses on the five-point response scale) were calculated by skill for each group.

Committee members reviewed the skills survey results at their meetings in May and June 1988 to make recommendations for the list of skills that would be eligible for testing. On the basis of the skills survey results and the review of the Texas faculty members attending the Regional Review Forums, Bias Review Panel meetings, and Content Advisory Committee meetings, all twenty-eight skills were recommended as eligible for testing and the two state education boards adopted the full list of skills as eligible for testing.

During the spring of 1988, NES developed test and item specifications for the three test areas. These specifications served to establish a link between the skills and subskills and the test items that were to be developed. They provided guidance to item writers on how the items were to be written and what the items were to address. During the second review cycle of meetings in May and June, 1988, committee members reviewed the specifications and sample items written to illustrate the use of the specifications.

The Regional Review Forums also reviewed test specifications and sample items from the perspective of whether the specifications were appropriate, comprehensive, and free from bias. They were also asked whether the sample items matched the skills, were written at the appropriate level of difficulty, were significant, and were free of bias.

The Bias Review Panel was asked to review the specifications and sample items to determine if the content and language could disadvantage an individual because of gender, race, ethnicity, religion, nationality, or cultural, economic, or geographic background. The Bias Review Panel was also asked whether the specifications and items contained material that could be deemed offensive or reflected a stereotypical view of any group. Finally, the panel was asked whether the specifications and sample items represented content that is typical of the Texas population.

The Content Advisory Committees reviewed the test specifications and sample items for appropriateness, skills match, comprehensiveness, significance, accuracy, and freedom from bias.

Working with the skills approved by the state and revised item specifications, draft test items were developed by NES.

During the item writing process, items were subjected to several NES internal reviews. The items were reviewed on an ongoing basis by an equity review board, content area specialists, and technical editors. Initial drafts of items were pilot tested on groups of freshman-level students and revised where necessary.

Over 600 draft test items, including twenty-five writing sample assignments were developed by NES for the initial item bank during the summer of 1988. During the third review cycle the draft test items were reviewed by the Regional Review Forums, the Bias Review Panel, and the Content Advisory Committees to determine if the items were appropriate, accurate, free from bias, and matched the skills.

In October 1988 approximately 5,600 freshman-level and entry-level teacher education college students from across the state participated in a tryout of TASP test items. The purpose of the item tryout was to collect empirical data on how the test items performed.

Participants received one of sixteen item tryout booklets containing either a subset of reading and mathematics items or a subset of writing multiple-choice items and one of the writing sample assignments.

The item-level data generated included p-values, item-to-skill and item-to-test point biserial correlations, and differential item performance between groups. Data generated from the scoring of the examinee essays included means and score distributions.

The data collected from the item tryout were used by the advisory committees in the fourth review cycle meetings to review the test items and to refine the content of the items, where necessary, for use in actual administrations of the TASP Test. The criteria for this review cycle was similar to those used during the review of the draft test items.

As a final confirmation of the appropriateness of the content of the item bank, Content Validation Panels were convened in six cities across the State of Texas. The Content Validation Panels were each composed of approximately twenty Texas educators who were specialists in the areas of reading, mathematics, or writing and who had not previously been involved in the TASP test development. At these meetings panel members reviewed the test items and writing sample assignments and provided a dichotomous judgment on the validity of each item. For an item to be considered valid, the reviewer had to find that the item matched the skill it was intended to measure, that it was accurate, and that it was free of bias. At least 61 percent of the reviewers had to approve an item for it to remain in the item bank.

STANDARD SETTING

The final step in the test development process that involved Texas educators was the standard-setting procedure. In January 1989, Standard-Setting Panels were convened in six cities across the State of Texas. The Standard-Setting Panels were composed of 291 Texas educators representative of the broad range of academic disciplines and institutions in the state. At these meetings, faculty were asked to imagine a hypothetical group of entering freshman-level students who have the minimum level of skill to perform effectively in undergraduate certificate or degree programs in Texas, to review each item; and to answer the question: "What percentage of this group of students would answer the item correctly?" Faculty were given a ten-point scale, ranging from one equals zero to ten percent to ten equals 91 to one hundred percent to answer this question.

Faculty also reviewed two writing sample assignments that were part of the October item tryout. They were provided with four student writing samples per assignment; each sample was assigned a holistic score of 1 (undeveloped), 2, 3, or 4 (fully developed). Faculty were asked to imagine a hypothetical group of entering freshman-level students who have the minimum level of skill to perform effectively in undergraduate certificate or degree programs in Texas and answer the question: "Based on the sample papers provided, which of the four points on the rating scale represents the level of writing that would be achieved by this group?" To answer this question, faculty were given a four-point scale ranging from 1 to 4.

After the meetings, item-level ratings were calculated, by test section, using a formula for computing medians from categorical data. The sum of the item-level ratings for the items selected for the first operational form of the TASP Test was calculated to produce a suggested preliminary cut score for each section.

The THECB and the State Board of Education met in January and February 1989 respectively, to review the standard-setting results and establish a preliminary cut score for each test section. Final cut scores were established by the THECB and the State Board of Education after the first administration of the TASP Test in the spring of 1989.

VALIDATION OF THE TASP TEST

The legislation that mandated the development of the TASP Test contains a statement of the central validation concern for the Test. It states simply that the "testing instrument be designed to provide a comparison of the skill level of the individual student with the skill level necessary to perform effectively in an undergraduate degree program." Efforts to accumulate evidence in support of the test were guided by this purpose.

In the planning stages of the test development effort, the decision was made to incorporate validation procedures at each step in the test development process, to use multiple sources of validity evidence, and, in some cases, to use multiple data collection methodologies to cross-check validation evidence and to provide an additional measure of confidence in the validation results.

Several sources were used to accumulate validity evidence throughout the development of the TASP Test. The first source was the process of expert review. Approximately 450 Texas educators, representing all institutions and a cross-section of content areas, were directly involved in expert reviews of the TASP Test. A second source of validity evidence was documentary. The State of Texas has a well-defined high school curriculum and established assessment requirements for high school graduation. These requirements establish a range of precollegiate skills students are expected to have. In conjunction with college-level course descriptions, syllabi, textbooks, and study materials, these sources of documentary information established a range of skills appropriate for the TASP Test. Finally, empirical evidence of validity was collected through several types of activities. To validate the skills to be tested, surveys of faculty were conducted. To validate test items, an item tryout was conducted and validity data were collected from content experts and other educators.

The tremendous amount of time devoted to the development of the test by Texas educators, the extensive supervision of the development materials and procedures by the two state agencies, and the painstaking job done by NES have assured the content validity of the TASP Test.

SUMMARY OF BIAS PREVENTION EFFORTS

Given the significance of the TASP on the higher education of the citizens of Texas, and the tremendous ethnic and cultural diversity of the state, it is important to reiterate the procedures implemented to assure that the TASP Test is fair for all students entering college in Texas.

Throughout the preceding discussion of the test development process, mention of the efforts to prevent bias occurred frequently. The prevention of bias was a major focus of test development beginning with the program's inception. Bias prevention was planned and implemented, not as a one-step review (which is often the case in testing programs), but as a dynamic process involving the participation of many people at several stages of development of the test.

The test developers at NES were guided in their efforts to ensure the fairness of the TASP Test by the *American Psychological Association Standards for Educational and Psychological Testing* (1985). These standards enumerate specific precautions and activities that are to be followed to insure fair testing. In addition to these standards, NES staff were well versed in bias prevention issues addressed in numerous test development guides and books (e.g., *Handbook of Methods for Detecting Test Bias,* Berk, 1982). An internal equity review panel responsible for the review of all test development materials was established by NES before they were submitted to the State of Texas for review and approval. The extensive internal equity review process by NES could have been deemed sufficient by most organizations involved in test development. For the TASP, however, it was only one aspect of the efforts to prevent bias.

A second approach to bias prevention in the TASP program was the involvement of hundreds of Texas postsecondary faculty. These faculty, comprising several advisory committees, were provided materials sensitizing them to bias in testing and offering practical advice about detecting and preventing potential bias in test materials. Five groups of Texas educators were assembled to review test materials at one or more stages during the test development process. One of their major roles was to review all test materials with the explicit intent to ensure that no potential bias existed. These faculty took this challenge very seriously. Many an afternoon meeting was spent discussing whether a single test item might prove disadvantageous to a particular group of students because of the language used. In the end, all the items that compose the TASP bank of test items were deemed free from bias by literally hundreds of Texas faculty.

For a more detailed discussion of the work of the Bias Review Panel, please see the following chapter.

THE TASP TEST

The discussion thus far has focused on the test development process. What follows is a brief description of the product of that process, the TASP Test.

The TASP Test consists of three sections: reading, mathematics, and writing. Each section is designed to measure a student's academic skills in relation to a standard of competence established by the State of Texas.

The reading section includes reading selections similar to

those found in course materials (e.g., textbooks, lab manuals) students are likely to encounter during their first year of college. Each reading selection is approximately 300 to 700 words in length. Students are asked to answer several multiple-choice questions about each selection.

The mathematics section contains multiple-choice questions covering three general areas: fundamental mathematics, algebra, and geometry. The test questions focus on a student's ability to perform mathematical operations and/or solve problems. Appropriate formulas are provided to students for use in performing some of the computations. Students may not use calculators during the test.

The writing section consists of two parts: a group of multiple-choice questions and a writing sample. The multiple-choice part of the test assesses student skills in various elements of effective writing. The writing sample requires students to demonstrate their ability to communicate effectively by writing on a given topic. Students are asked to provide a writing sample of approximately 300 to 600 words. Topics allow examinees to draw from personal experiences and general knowledge. Students are not allowed to use dictionaries.

To satisfy the requirements of the TASP, a student must achieve a passing score for each test section. Students may elect to take one, two, or all three sections at any given administration. They receive all three sections and are given a five-hour block of time to complete the test. Students may work on the test sections in any order they choose and the individual sections are not timed separately.

TEST UPDATING

The test development procedures described earlier form the foundation for the development of new test items. Since test forms change with each administration, new item development is an ongoing process.

The process for developing test items at NES involves a team of people with varying expertise and perspectives working to ensure that the tests are reflective of skills entering students should have to perform effectively in college. After the items have been written, they are checked for clarity, accuracy, readability, freedom from bias, and appropriateness of the level of difficulty. The draft test items are then reviewed by the Bias Review Panel and the Content Advisory Committees using the same criteria from the review of the initial TASP item bank.

Once the new test items have been reviewed and any necessary revisions have been made, they are ready to appear as nonscoreable items on actual TASP Test administrations. Presenting the new items to students taking the official TASP Test permits the state to collect item-level data under actual testing conditions. These data are then reviewed to determine the difficulty level and appropriateness of each item.

SUMMARY

The development of the TASP Test was a major accomplishment for the two state agencies and NES. Given the 18-month development timeline, many people, both inside and outside the educational community, thought it could not be done. That such a quality product was produced under this type of pressure is a tribute to the literally hundreds of higher education faculty and administrators who contributed to the effort. Texas has a quality, state-of-the-art basic skills test that supports a quality educational program. The TASP reflects Texas' commitment to improve higher education for all its citizens.

7
The Prevention of Bias

*Milton R. Bryant, José Roberto Juárez, and
Ronald G. Swanson*

*Texas has a minority population that will soon become the majority. In
addition, testing programs have typically been subject to attack by minority group
advocates because of bias considerations. In fairness to all students who would
have to take the Texas Academic Skills Program Test, we were determined to
make the test as free from bias as humanly possible. The Texas Academic
Skills Program bias prevention effort was monumental and involved sensitizing
to bias issues virtually everyone involved in test development.*

BACKGROUND

The Case for Bias Prevention

The development of a bias-free test was declared a top
priority from the beginning of the Texas Academic Skills
Program (TASP). Educators and administrators recognized that
the ethnic and age demographics of Texas are changing and
that Texas is rapidly becoming a "minority-majority" state. This
will be true in both the school-age population and the population as a whole in the early twenty-first century.

It has been well established that minorities (blacks and
Hispanics) do not do as well as whites on standardized tests.
This fact, coupled with demographic projections for the state,
produced an assumption that the state and the test developer,
National Evaluation Systems, Inc. (NES), might face a court

challenge if differential test performance was due to factors other than differential educational preparation. The history of differential educational preparation for minorities made it even more important to provide a bias-free test. Doing so not only would help guard against potential litigation but also was the right thing to do. Therefore, the prevention of bias was a specific goal of developers of the TASP Test.

Texas Demographics: Population Growth

From 1970 to 1985, the population of Texas grew 46.2 percent while the population of the United States grew only 17.4 percent.[1] The Texas population is projected to grow another 14.6 percent from 1985 to the year 2000, while the national population is expected to increase by 11.8 percent. Most of this growth has been in urban areas, where more than 80 percent of the population now lives.[2] Regionally, the Dallas and Houston areas account for nearly half the total population in the state. It is anticipated that the growth (primarily Hispanics) will increase dramatically by the year 2025.

By the year 2000, more than 45 percent of the Texas population is projected to be made up of Asians, blacks, and Hispanics. By the year 2035, these groups will comprise more than 55 percent of the state's population. Of course, blacks and Hispanics will represent the overwhelming majority of these minorities.

Whereas the black and white populations are aging, the Hispanic population is growing younger. By 2000, blacks and whites will comprise approximately 45 percent of the 45 to 64 year age group. By 2025, these same ethnic groups will comprise more than 52 percent of the same age group.[3] Of course, Asians and Hispanics will also age, but their effect on the total population will be offset by the higher birth rate in the Hispanic population along with the increased immigration of Hispanics into Texas. When the baby-boom generation (born from 1945 to 1965) reaches retirement age in about 2025, the number of Asians and Hispanics in the 0-14 age group will far outweigh the number of blacks and whites in the same group.

The birth rate in the Hispanic population is also significant. According to 1980 census data, the average family size was 4.16 for Hispanics, 3.66 for blacks, and 3.07 for whites.[4] Coupled with the fact that Mexico supplies Texas with more immigrants than any other country, it is clear that minorities, particularly Hispanics, will make up a significant proportion of the population in Texas after the year 2000. These figures will certainly impact higher education in Texas in the very near future.

Texas Population: Place Bound

In 1984, more than 94 percent of the college-enrolled students in Texas were residents of the state.[5] That proportion is almost 10 percent above the national average for students attending college in their home state.[6] The fact that Texas students tend to stay close to home supports the argument for focusing on the minority population. Education costs and socioeconomic conditions in Texas play a major role in a student's decision about where to go to school. Students are often "place bound" by these conditions.

The need for a bias-free test is even more clear when this lack of mobility, which is often found in economically deprived areas of the state where many minorities live, is recognized.

Texas Population: Disparities in Educational Attainment

Between 1985 and 2025, it is projected that the proportion of blacks and Hispanics in the labor force will increase from 30.3 to 43.9 percent while the proportion of whites will decrease from 68.3 to 54.8 percent.[7] Although minorities are a significant proportion of the labor force, their educational attainment levels do not complement this fact. Fewer blacks and Hispanics complete high school than whites. In the 1986-1987 school year blacks and Hispanics constituted 46.2 percent of high school enrollments but only 37.2 percent of high school graduates.[8]

Whites, on the other hand, represented 51.8 percent of the enrollments and 61 percent of the graduates. This statistic is startling when the need to have a better educated minority population is so overwhelming. As a result of the underrepresentation of minorities among high school graduates, minorities are overrepresented in the unskilled occupations such as operators, fabricators, and laborers. In addition, blacks are highly represented in service occupations.[9]

Minorities also tend to be significantly underrepresented in the ratio of college enrollment to relative proportion of the population. In Texas, this ratio is .54.[10] In 1984, whites made up 76.6 percent of the enrollments in four-year institutions.[11] Whites also received 83 percent of the baccalaureate degrees. Although blacks and Hispanics represented 20.9 percent of four-year institution enrollments, they received only 14.8 percent of the baccalaureate degrees. The ratio of graduates to enrollees must be increased for minorities. There is sufficient evidence to indicate that the effort to enroll and retain more minorities in college should be enhanced.

Texas Students: Grade Inflation

Grade inflation has been documented in Texas secondary schools. In 1988, almost 35 percent of a group of Texas high school seniors reported they were A or B students in comparison to 28 percent nationally. But Texas students tend to average approximately ten points below the national average in both the SAT Verbal and SAT Mathematics scores.[12] Texas students, like other U.S. students, are perceived or perceive themselves to be better students than they really are.

As Texas becomes a "minority-majority" state, more emphasis must be given to upgrading the educational level of all students, particularly minorities. The quality of and the commitment to education at all levels must be a societal concern and goal. Society will continue to look to institutions of higher learning for providing assistance in solving this problem. Therefore, the State of Texas has made the commitment toward resolution of this problem with the establishment and implementation of the TASP.

BIAS DEFINED

Bias: What's It All About?

Because of the sensitivities involved in the issue of bias, bias prevention was given special attention. The first task was to define bias. Is a test biased simply because a larger percentage of certain groups fail it? The temptation was to answer yes, but different performance by different groups on tests involving simple math problems kept surfacing. Is a test requiring specific knowledge of addition, subtraction, multiplication, division, fractions, ratios, and geometry biased because a larger percentage of minority members do not pass it? The obvious answer is no. Either one knows those skills or one does not, and results have nothing to do with race, ethnicity, or gender. Word problems, because of the narrative in which the questions are embedded, could, however, be phrased in such a way that they favor one group over another. As a result, special attention was paid to these.

We also realized that poor performance on the test could be the effect of societal discrimination in distributing funds for education. How could students from low property value districts receive the same education as those from higher property value districts? How could students whose parents come from the low socioeconomic strata compete with those whose parents were more fortunate?

Bias in reading and writing tests was a more difficult matter. Students from the lower socioeconomic strata are often not exposed to some of the Western-oriented cultural aspects included in standardized tests. Assumptions about what these students could be expected to know and be familiar with had to be reviewed carefully. How many minorities, for example, can answer questions assuming a knowledge of skiing resorts or aquatic sports? Our assumption, however, was that the existence of unfamiliar cultural topics did not mean that reading and writing skills could not be tested. There had to be some way of determining if a person had the writing, reading, and math skills necessary for college-level work.

Bias: A Definition

While there are many ways to define bias, our TASP Bias Review Panel chose a definition that refers to a "person's potential disadvantage in responding to test materials because of his or her gender, race, ethnicity, nationality, religion, age, handicapping condition or cultural, economic, or geographic background." When a test is biased, inaccurate information is received and inaccurate decisions may be made about the person who took the test. Subgroups of people may be disadvantaged because they may be unable to demonstrate their skills or knowledge fair as a result of bias in the testing instrument. In other words, a tested individual or group will not have adequate opportunity to demonstrate or give evidence for skills they possess if the test they take is biased against them. Bias is not associated with a test that identifies those who do not possess the skills measured. Bias occurs when factors other than the skills in question influence test results.

BIAS PREVENTION

Bias: Everyone's Concern

Prior to the TASP, teacher candidates in the State of Texas had to pass a basic skills test known as the Pre-Professional Skills Test (P-PST) before they could enter upper-division education coursework. The results of the P-PST were dismal for minorities. Between March 1984 and November 1986 only 28 percent of blacks and 42.6 percent of Hispanics passed the test, while 78.8 percent of whites passed it.[13] If there were biased items in the P-PST, we certainly did not want similar items in the (TASP) Test.

Sensitizing everyone involved in the development of the test to bias issues and bias prevention became a high priority. Principles in *Bias Concerns in Test Development*, a guide published by NES, were adopted. All participants were sensitized to avoid language that would reinforce or perpetuate bias. They were to avoid stereotyping that would, for example, assume that certain groups deserved a particular fate, lacked positive qualities, were linked to poverty or crime, or lacked intelligence. The roles and achievements of females, minorities, and persons with disabilities were to be fairly represented within the test. These qualities were to be presented in primary and secondary characters in a variety of settings. The characters had to exhibit nonstereotypical behavior.

The *Bias Concerns* guide included examples of biased questions. "Analyze the causes for the preeminence of Western Civilization since the Middle Ages" obviously displays cultural and ethnic bias. So does "Analyze the effects of poor diet on black women" because it singles out one sex and one ethnic group. The guide contained nonbiased ways to express potentially biased terms or phrases. Numerous examples of potentially biased test items were included with explanations.

Every person associated with the development of the TASP test was given a copy of the guide. *Bias Concerns in Test Development* was reviewed by representatives of the Bias Review Panel and other Texas educators familiar with minority concerns in the state. Based on these reviews, the manual was expanded and a new edition was made available to all persons associated with the development of the TASP Test. Prevention of bias was a central factor in its design and implementation.

We simply had to make every effort to produce a bias free test, and that message was frequently repeated at Bias Review Panel meetings, as well as at every other committee meeting. National Evaluation Systems, Inc. set the pace in this effort by sensitizing everyone involved with test development to bias prevention. Members of every statewide committee, as well as the Regional Review Panels and the Coordinating Board staff, were sensitized to the issue of test bias.

Bias Review Process

The original Texas Academic Skills Council (TASC) was made up of higher education experts from throughout the state. Several statewide advisory committees were formed to counsel and advise the state on various aspects of the program. The chairs of those committees made up the TASC. When it was noted that the Bias Review Panel had the only minority chair, other co-chairs were appointed. Co-chairs for the Bias Review Panel were both minority members, while most other committees ultimately had an Anglo and a minority member as co-chairs. The co-chair concept worked well because it gave flexibility when illness or other business kept one of the co-chairs from attending a meeting. It also permitted continuity when a co-chair's term ended.

Content advisory committees for reading, writing, and mathematics were appointed, as were committees for test and measurements, academic skills development, advisement and placement, English as a second language, evaluation, and faculty development committees. Every public institution of higher education in the state was invited to suggest potential members for these committees. Persons were chosen to balance gender, region, and type and size of institution. There was a deliberate proportional overrepresentation of minorities on all of the committees. Of the 623 people who served on committees, 12.5 percent were black, 20.4 percent were Hispanic, and 63.7 percent were Anglo.[14] Twenty-five of the thirty Bias Review Panel members identified themselves as minority members, including two who represented the handicapped community. A Hispanic was appointed as chair, with a black as co-chair.

The first meeting, on February 1, 1988, was a tense one. Minority members representing community colleges, universities and upper-level institutions from every region were, to say the least, skeptical of the need for the state-imposed TASP. They asked why minorities should be involved in legitimizing a process that had often hurt their own interests. They also wondered if minority concerns could really be addressed.

Many of the minority concerns were addressed by Coordinating Board, TEA, and NES representatives. The extensive and continuous regional and statewide review process, which included thousands of Texas educators, allayed some of the fears. In the opinion of the co-chairs, however, most of the panel members did not immediately buy into the process, and a few never did. This review process was a strenuous, but necessary task.

The Bias Review Panel, as well as other groups, had the same kinds of questions at its first meeting on February 1, 1988. Will the Texas legislature really provide money for remedial programs? Was the $24 fee too high? Will institutions do away with the ACT and SAT tests? Can a single test based on competency also provide diagnostic information? Must students studying for a certificate pass the TASP? How will the media interpret data, especially from colleges that educate mostly minorities? How will second-language speakers be handled? Since writing is greatly influenced by culture, can a bias-free writing test be developed? The panel members vented their frustrations on the co-chairs and the Coordinating Board, TEA, and NES representatives. They seemed to believe the TASP was one more hurdle for minorities, and they wondered where the idea had come from.

That was the perfect question. Many of the minorities on the Bias Review Panel were surprised to find out that a black state legislator, Representative Wilhelmina Delco, was one of the chief sponsors of the legislation. Although that piece of information did not calm everyone, it made swallowing the bitter pill easier. Representative Delco had spoken to the TASC on August 21, 1987, and assured the members that she had not sponsored discriminatory legislation. She had worked with lawyers from the Mexican-American Legal Defense and Education Fund (MALDEF) and National Association for the Advancement of Colored People (NAACP). The intent of the legislature was to address educational deficiencies through remediation so that students could have a better chance of success in college. She unequivocally answered yes when asked if she intended that students working on certificates pass the

TASP. When told that many students being trained for industry would not pass, Representative Delco said industry should do its own training for below-college-level skills. Higher education had been funded on the basis of warm bodies for too long, she said, adding that it was now time to expect results.

After hearing Representative Delco's philosophy, the Bias Review Panel recommended that nationality be added to the bias review criteria, which already included gender, race, ethnicity, religion, age, handicapping condition, or cultural, economic, or geographic background. The panel then divided into math, writing, and reading subcommittees.

Bias Review Panel Concerns

The Bias Review Panel had two major concerns. One was the procedure adopted for each of the meetings. The Bias Review Panel would meet after the eight regional forums, but prior to the meetings of the reading, writing, and math content advisory committees. The recommendations from the Bias Review Panel would be sent to the content committees by NES, TEA, and CB staff. The Bias Review Panel felt that the process should be reversed with the content committees meeting first and sending their recommendations to the Bias Review Panel for evaluation. This procedure remained a bone of contention throughout the process and was never resolved to some of the members' satisfaction.

Related to the above, the Bias Review Panel's second major concern was that it never received concrete feedback on changes or deletions it recommended. At a November 29-30, 1988 meeting the state gave the only gratifying answer to the panel. The members were assured that their deliberations were presented to each of the content committees. Content committees had to justify the rejection of any Bias Review Panel recommendations. The chair and co-chair of the Bias Review Panel also noted that it would be folly for NES to use any item that had been declared biased by the Bias Review Panel.

The plan for allowing review of materials first by the

Regional Review Forums, then by the Bias Review Panel, and then by the Content Advisory Committees was followed throughout. A skills list was presented first. After input from all three groups, the list was sent to thousands of Texas educators for their comments. Test questions were carefully developed after survey results had been given to the three groups. Finally, field test results were provided to the committees in late November 1988.

The confidential nature of all documents, even committee members' personal notes, was galling--but necessary. Test security is a cardinal principle of companies that develop standardized tests. This necessary precaution, however, only made it more important that the Bias Review Panel be informed of the disposition of its recommendations.

Preventing Biased Test Items

Because material used during the meetings was collected and kept confidential, it is impossible to provide examples of materials that were found to be biased. We can, however, recall the gist of some examples.

Interestingly, the Bias Review Panel recommended the complete deletion of very few items. One was a reading selection which portrayed women as docile individuals with little understanding of economics. Another led the reader to believe that Mexican-Americans would never achieve political power because of their own inadequacies. A third selection portrayed black Americans in only subservient types of employment while another depicted Chinese Americans as primarily itinerant railroad workers. Still another depicted Mexican-Americans predominantly in the role of migrant workers.

The Bias Review Panel's concern with these materials was based upon the possible reaction of minority students who took the test. For example, black Americans have played subservient roles, Chinese-Americans have worked as itinerant railroad employees, and Mexican-Americans have been migrant workers. The panel felt the emotional reactions of minority students to those items might interfere with their test performance. The panel wanted to minimize that possibility.

Recommending the elimination of passages was easier than working to develop viable replacements for items recommended for deletion. The Bias Review Panel recommended, for example, a study of minority business publications and magazines as sources for such material. In fact, objectionable materials were ultimately eliminated and replaced with materials that presented a more positive picture of minorities.

The necessary security precautions sometimes meant the panel worked without its own written record of the previous meeting. This led to some controversy. For example, the Mathematics Content Advisory Committee reported that the Bias Review Panel considered Math Skill 14 (solving problems involving quadratic equations) too difficult and that it recommended its deletion. The Bias Panel did not take such a position but, rather, did what it was instructed to do. It had been told that these skills that had received a rating below 3.5 (out of a possible 5) in the faculty survey instrument would be considered deleted unless a strong argument could be made for their inclusion. Skill 14 was the only skill which all faculty groups rated below 3.5. Since there was unanimity among 2,000+ postsecondary faculty and public school teachers surveyed, the Bias Review Panel simply endorsed their perception. The Mathematics Content Advisory Committee co-chair, however, argued persuasively to retain the skill and, ultimately, that skill was retained.

A more common approach for the panel was to recommend changes to make test items acceptable. All the essay-writing prompts, for example, were checked to make sure there were no cultural references that would favor one group of students over another. If a specific Greek playwright was mentioned in the prompt, the name was deleted. Words considered esoteric for students in the poorer school districts were replaced with more common terms. A word problem that asked the student to help develop a budget for a specified family income was modified because students from some segments of the population would not be able to identify with the income figure or the concept of budgeting. Another problem, which dealt with hourly wages paid to laborers, had to be adjusted to better reflect what a laborer might expect to make in Texas.

Similarly, problems that required figuring a portion of an income tax return or the area of a kitchen were changed because students not familiar with the concepts of income tax and kitchen (as a separate room in a house) could be at a disadvantage. At first it was feared that certain students would not be able to identify with the word sprocket used in a math problem. A labeled diagram of a sprocket was included to end the controversy.

Overall, no one on the Bias Review Panel objected to having minority students learn about budgets, income taxes, kitchens, or sprockets. But they also believed students should not have to learn about them on a high-stakes test.

The Bias Review Panel made sure that three principles were always kept in mind. The co-chairs repeatedly insisted that high-quality developmental education, with low student-teacher ratios, be adequately funded. They also insisted that remedial credit hours not count toward the nine or fifteen semester credit hours a student could earn before taking the test. The panelists also felt that students should not be prohibited from taking junior-level courses because of the results of a single test. Other criteria should be considered. That message was reinforced by many minority educators who made presentations to the TASP Council on May 26-27, 1988.

Graduated Versus Full Implementation

After the description of necessary skills was approved and items were field tested, there was concern about the impact the TASP Test might have on minorities. Although the Bias Review Panel was able to meet the goal of reviewing and acting on the test materials per se, the materials review process did not allow enough time to address the overall effect of the test on minorities. The co-chairs of the panel discussed with many of its members a graduated approach to TASP implementation as one possibly helpful measure.

A graduated approach to program implementation was considered essential for four reasons. First, minorities believed that replacing the P-PST with the TASP Test for teacher certification programs would continue underrepresentation of minorities in teaching. The problem could become even worse, they feared, because all students would have to pass the TASP Test. Second, nonminority as well as minority faculty were disgruntled about the possibility of changing roles for teachers. Given the results of the field tests, schools could end up with very few students in their college-level classes and faculty might have to be retrained to teach remedial courses. Most faculty were not hired to teach remedial English, reading, or math, and they had no desire to be so trained. Third, the Texas legislature had not yet appropriated any funds for remediation. "No funds, no TASP" was the strong sentiment of the Bias Review Panel. Fourth, the state appeared to be attempting to solve in one year the results of more than a century and a half of what most members of the Bias Review Panel believed was outright discrimination against minorities.

The Bias Review Panel chair offered Laredo Junior College's (LJC) experience in gradually phasing in higher entry-level standards as a model. Long before the TASP, officials at LJC realized that its students were often unprepared when they transferred to its main feeder school, Laredo State University (LSU). Only 50 percent of the transfer students could pass LSU's English test. Only 33 percent of the students who took the P-PST passed all three portions of the test. Something was amiss.

After a full year of study, research, animated discussions, and planning, the LJC Board approved a policy that required in 1985 a seventh-grade reading level for entry into the school's college-transfer courses. The reading requirement increased to eighth-grade level in 1986, ninth-grade level in 1987, ten-and-a-half-school-year level in 1988, and, by sheer coincidence, twelfth-grade level in 1989--which was to be the year of the TASP. Such an approach prevented the transfer of instructors from their disciplines to remedial work.

The high school students soon got the message that LJC was serious about its mandatory placement policy and that they could not take college transfer courses without mastery of some basic academic skills. Students in occupational programs were not discouraged because they could enroll concurrently in their chosen disciplines and remedial courses if they were within one grade of the skill prerequisite.

The TASP Council formally considered the graduated approach on December 16, 1988. The Coordinating Board staff's recommendation was to set a preliminary cut-score prior to the first administration of the test in March 1989. They suggested a review of the score after the results of the test were known. The cut-score could be lowered, but not raised, for those who took the March test.

The Bias Review Panel chair noted that everyone was in favor of higher quality, but proposed to the council establishing a cutoff score to ensure that only a certain percentage of minorities would fail the test for the first year. The score could be raised each year thereafter, he said. Such an approach, he argued, would allow the secondary school system to prepare students for the test. It would not require faculty to teach remedial courses, a proposal they would hate. After a long and impassioned discussion, a vote was taken. Although the minutes of the session did not record the vote of each member, the Bias Review Panel chair jotted down the result: eight against the graduated approach and seven for it, with two abstentions. There were minority members on both sides.

A compromise recommendation to the commissioner of higher education was adopted unanimously: "Improving the standards of higher education is the purpose of the TASP and the cut scores should reflect it," but "in so doing, sensitivity to the unique needs of special populations must be considered." The TASP Council decided not to be vague in its intentions but rather to send a strong message to the elementary and secondary schools that they must improve their product.

Whether remediation will work or not statewide remains to be seen. Perhaps the Coordinating Board took the right approach by adopting a fixed cut-score from the beginning. As mentioned above, the Bias Review Panel was concerned not just with the test but also with the more global issue of different levels of academic preparation for minorities. It felt compelled, therefore, to report at the December 1988, TASP Council meeting that "most panel members felt that the real bias issue had not been addressed. Minorities will continue to score below others as long as they receive inadequate, underfinanced educations at the elementary and secondary school level." This message must be broadcast throughout the Coordinating Board and the TEA.

The Result

As is evident from the material in this chapter, the prevention of bias is a very important if not emotionally laden endeavor. Nevertheless, we found that it is possible to sensitize people to be aware of and prevent the inclusion of biased materials on a test. Although the procedures may not have made everyone happy, in the end there was almost unanimous approval of the test as being as bias-free as is humanly possible. But that doesn't happen by accident. As this chapter has pointed out, hard work, effort, and dedication by a lot of people was necessary. It must also be mentioned that the minority group members asked to participate in this task did so willingly and with great energy in spite of their being "overtasked" for membership on statewide committees. It was a great temptation to call repeatedly on already overcommitted minority group members in order to derive the proper demographic make-up of a committee--and, alas, it was a temptation that could not be resisted at times.

This project has been very useful in the continuing bias prevention effort. The Bias Review Panel continues to exist and function, as do the three content advisory committees and a number of other committees as well. As long as the test exists, the services of these committees will be needed to continuously monitor new test items. The most important aspect of the entire bias prevention program was the justified assumption that bias prevention is truly everybody's business.

NOTES

1. *Demography and Higher Education in the Changing Southwest Texas*, Western Interstate Commission for Higher Education (WICHE), March 1988.

2. F. Ray Marshall and Leon F. Bouvier, *Population Changes and the Future of Texas*, A Publication of the Population Reference Bureau, Inc., Washington, D.C., 1986.

3. Ibid.

4. Ibid.

5. V. Johns and D. W. Viehland, "Migration Patterns of First-Time Freshmen in the United States," *Research in Higher Education*, vol. 30, no. 5, 1989.

6. Southern Region Education Board, *SREB Fact Book on Higher Education*, Atlanta, Georgia, 1988.

7. Murdock, S. H., Hamm, R. B., Beckman, K. P., and Hwang, S. S., *The Future Population of Texas: Alternative Scenarios of Growth and Their Implication for Public and Private Services*, Texas Agricultural Experiment Station in Cooperation with the Texas Department of Commerce, College Station, Texas, 1988.

8. *Demography and Higher Education. . .*, WICHE, March 1988.

9. Marshall and Bouvier, *Population Changes*.

10. Ibid.

11. Ibid.

12. *PSAT/NMSQT Summary Report and Summary Report Worksheet*, Admissions Testing Program of the College Board, 1988.

13. *"Pre-Professional Skills Test Longitudinal Data, March 1984 through November 1986,"* accompanying Albert H. Kauffman, staff attorney, Mexican-American Legal Defense and Education Fund, to Dear Friends, March 24, 1987.

14. *"Council Committees,"* attached to April 8, 1988 TASP Council minutes.

8
Addressing Special Needs: The Handicapped and Testing

Ronald G. Swanson and Pamela Tackett

The hallmark of any good testing program is how fairness and accessibility for handicapped persons are addressed. There is a delicate balance between providing testing accommodations for handicapped students and maintaining fairness and equitability for all other persons taking the test. Yet another consideration is how to determine what, if any, accommodations to grant without lowering the standards of the test. As interesting and complex as dealing with persons with special needs can be, it is also a serious and demanding facet of any testing program.

A major concern in any large testing program is to provide adequate test accessibility for students with special needs. These students warrant significant attention and consideration during development and administration of the test. In this chapter, persons with special needs will be defined, legal requirements will be reviewed, implementation policies will be described, and some of the unique problems faced in making provisions for these students will be examined.

DEFINING TERMS

For clarity and to ensure that no student's special problems were overlooked, persons with "special needs" were identified in four main categories: visually impaired, hearing impaired, mobility impaired, and learning disabled. Of course, the categories are not mutually exclusive. An individual may have multiple handicapping conditions.

Those examinees who require alternative test dates due to religious reasons were another category that was dealt with independently. The Texas Academic Skills Program (TASP) Test is administered on Saturdays, but the personal beliefs of some religious groups forbid them to take the test on that day of the week. To accommodate this group, alternative test dates and sites were identified and application procedures clearly specified in the registration bulletin.

Providing accommodations for persons with special needs to assure fair access to the test, while neither advantaging nor disadvantaging these persons relative to other test takers, is critically important in maintaining the integrity of the testing program. Great care must be taken to ensure that the such accommodations provided to students with special needs do not give them an unfair advantage over others who take the test without special accommodations. Only accommodations truly needed by the person with special needs should be granted. On the other hand, sufficient accommodation must be rendered to allow a handicapped person a fair chance to demonstrate knowledge of the skills being measured on the TASP Test.

Magnifying devices and large print or braille editions of the test are standard accommodations for the visually impaired. Videotaped sign language versions of the test were developed specifically for the hearing impaired. Students with mobility impairments may use mechanical devices that permit them to indicate their answer choices. They may also be provided with a scribe.

SPECIAL NEEDS AND THE LAW

In developing a high-stakes testing program, the state must comply with the specific statutory requirements as well as address pertinent laws, court cases, precedents, and professional guidelines. The two state agencies involved in developing the TASP Test, which were the Texas Education Agency (TEA) and the Texas Higher Education Coordinating Board (THECB), sought advice about treatment of individuals with special needs from TEA's chief legal counsel and counsel from the state Attorney General's Office. The TASP Test administration guidelines were inclined toward inclusiveness, rather than exclusiveness, because access to the test was a vital element in giving an equal opportunity to everyone to pursue higher education in a state-supported institution.

As the administration policies were developed, it became apparent that there were no provisions for exemption from the TASP Test for students in state-supported institutions of higher education who pursued a baccalaureate degree, an associate's degree, or a certificate from programs that had nine or more semester credit hours of general education course requirements. However, students deemed to be either blind or deaf, as specified in *Texas Education Code* Section 51.306(1)(a) [House Bill 1196, 71st Texas Legislature], and who entered state-supported institutions prior to September 1, 1991, and who met the definitions specified in this law, were to be exempted from the TASP Test. Beginning in September 1991, hearing-impaired and visually impaired persons must meet the same requirements as other individuals. The state will give these examinees the opportunity to take the test with appropriate accommodations. Exemptions are not allowed for students enrolled in Texas teacher certification programs in state-approved public or private institutions.

The state reviewed appropriate sources for information about handicaps to determine how these might affect the administration of the TASP Test. The American Psychological Association's *Standards for Educational and Psychological Testing*; the *Rehabilitation Act of 1973*, Section 504; the *Code of Fair Testing Practices in Education*; the Equal Employment Opportunity Commission guidelines for developing tests; and practices from other testing programs for handicapped persons were researched and used in developing the procedures fr accommodating persons who desire to take the TASP Test.

Staff members from the Coordinating Board and TEA researched the laws relevant to persons with special needs and found that Section 504 of the *Rehabilitation Act of 1973* passed by the U.S. Congress provides that

No otherwise qualified handicapped individual in the United States. . . shall, solely by reason of his handicap, be excluded from participation in, be denied the benefits of, or be subjected to discrimination under any program or activity receiving Federal financial assistance. (29 U.S.C. Section 794)

It was necessary to review the potential needs that could possibly arise because this section of the Rehabilitation Act applied to both of the involved state agencies. The state wanted to assure examinees that an appropriate system for handling their special needs existed for the vast majority of students in the Texas higher education student population. Ultimately, the state defined categories of arrangements for special administrations of the TASP Test. Those categories will be discussed later in this chapter.

The *Education of All Handicapped Children Act of 1975* (Public Law 94-142) requires public schools to provide a number of specified services to handicapped students. This legislation, however, applies only to preschool, elementary, and secondary school children between the ages of three and twenty-one years old.

Section 504 of the *Rehabilitation Act of 1973* was amended to identify the specific protections to be provided for learning-disabled students in higher education. Whereas Public Law 94-142 outlined extensive and detailed policies, procedures, and services public schools (kindergarten through twelfth grade) are required to provide, Section 504 provided only very general guidelines for postsecondary education. In addition, court cases have established clear precedent that while institutions of higher education must make college accessible to all who are qualified, regardless of handicap, they in no way must lower their standards or exempt or waive important degree require-ments. Section 504 permits institutions of higher education to uphold academic standards and does not make it a requirement to substitute or waive courses even though it does require them to provide reasonable accommodations when necessary. Conse-quently, legal requirements for modifying test administrations for students with learning disabilities do not exist.

However, the state judged that these individuals, in most cases, have progressed through the public education system and should be given the same opportunity for success in the college environment. Thus, the testing time was extended to eight hours for examinees with documented learning disabilities.

Two specific rulings that supported these actions of the state were considered in developing the administration policies of the TASP Test. In November 1989, the U.S. District Court for the Western District of Texas ruled in favor of the state in the case of *David Chapline v. Central Education Agency* (Texas Education Agency). Chapline argued that he had been wrongfully terminated from his teaching position in a public school district because of his failure to complete successfully a requirement for continued employment in the schools, the Texas Examination of Current Administrators and Teachers (TECAT). Chapline alleged that his handicap, dyslexia (a type of learning disability), caused him to fail the TECAT, resulting in the loss of his job. Even though he had been granted additional time to take the test, the plaintiff argued that the conduct of the state was discriminatory under Section 504 of the *Rehabilitation Act*. He sought damages as well as an injunction enjoining the state from future discriminatory conduct under Section 504, that is, not to require him to pass the examination to retain his job. Noting Section 504 of the *Rehabilitation Act of 1973* (see above), the court stated:

under Section 706(8)(B), an individual with handicaps is any person who (1) has a physical or mental impairment which substantially limits one or more of such person's major life activities, (2) has a record of such impairment, or (3) is regarded as having such an impairment. 29U.S.C. Section 706(8)(B). The regulations promulgated by the Department of Justice under Section 504 define physical or mental impairment as including any mental or psychological disorder, such as mental retardation, organic brain syndrome, emotional or mental illness, and specific learning disabilities. The term physical or mental impairment includes, but is not limited to, such diseases and conditions as orthopedic, visual, speech, and hearing impairments,. . .See *Department of Justice Guidelines on Non-Discrimination on the Basis of Handicap and ederally Assisted Program*, 28 C.F.R.41.31(b)(1)(ii). These regulations also define major life activities as functions such as caring for oneself, performing manual tasks, walking, seeing, hearing, speaking, breathing, learning, and working. Id. at 41.31(b)(2).

The basic purpose of Section 504 is to ensure that handicapped individuals are not denied jobs or other benefits because of the prejudiced attitudes or ignorance of others. Section 504 has been construed as prohibiting disadvantageous treatment, rather than mandating differential treatment. *Brennan v. Stewart*, 834 F.2d 1248, 1259-60 (5th Cir. 1988) (quoting *School Board of Nassau County v. Arline*, 107 S. Ct. 1123 (1987) and *Wimberly v. Labor & Industrial Relations Commission*, 107 S. Ct. 821 (1987).

The court in the Chapline case ruled that the state violated neither the defendant's Section 504 rights nor his due process rights. It was clear from this ruling that the state had no legal obligation to accommodate persons with learning disabilities by providing special administration procedures. The court said that differential treatment could not be granted. Thus, the state could not waive requirements to pass examinations. However, the state did feel that to allow extra time for individuals taking the TASP Test who have appropriate documentation of their learning disabilities was a reasonable accommodation, did not unfairly advantage a learning-disabled individual, and did not constitute a waiver from the testing requirement.

A second ruling with legal standing that supports the actions of the state agencies in implementing guidelines for dealing with handicapped persons was issued by the U.S. Office of Civil Rights (USOCR) in December 1989. This case was filed against the TEA by an examinee who had not passed the Pre-Professional Skills Test (P-PST), which was the basic skills test required for admission to teacher education programs in Texas at the time. The complainant in the case said that she should not be required to meet the testing standards because of handicapping conditions defined as developmental aphasia and juvenile diabetes. In its findings, the USOCR concluded that the TEA did not discriminate against the complainant by requiring her to take a basic skills test. The USOCR stated:

the evidence indicates that the skill, level of achievement, and other factors the test purports to measure are essential to the program of instruction being pursued and are reasonable and necessary to the proper use. . .Background information is available to indicate the validity of the tests as predictors of success in the field of education. Additionally, evidence presented demonstrated that the testing service was responsible for scheduling special arrangement for the complainant during the testing. Modifications have been made to reasonably accommodate examinees during testing. Therefore, the TEA is in compliance with [applicable laws]. (Ruling of USOCR, Regional Office, Dallas, Texas, 1989)

MEETING THE REQUIREMENTS--AND BEYOND

Clarifying the requirements of the law was the first step; then came implementing these requirements, which often are only minimum standards. In actual practice, it is often necessary and even desirable to go beyond the minimum to ensure that test accessibility and fairness are inherent to the testing program.

A classification system was developed to allow the state agencies and the testing company to categorize special needs students by the nature and extent of the arrangements they required. Four categories were specified:

Type A: These arrangements require no alteration of regular testing conditions or arrangements before the day of the test and are available at all test sites. They include special seating, proximity to a door or a restroom, seating near the front of the room, frequent breaks, and magnifying glasses.

Type B: These arrangements require moderate alterations in testing conditions or procedures that must be planned before the day of the test. These special accommodations can be available at all test sites. These arrangments may include large print tests, written copies of the directions, allowing answers to be circled in the test booklet rather than responded to on the answer sheet, and sign language interpreters for the instructions given to the test by the proctors.

Type C: These arrangements are available at selected test sites only. They require substantial changes in testing conditions and/or testing materials. They include a Braille version of the test and/or special assistance to the examinee, which may require a

> separate testing room; videotaped versions of the test in sign language at selected predetermined sites; use of mechanical aids provided by the examinees for recording essay responses; and extra time beyond the 5-hour testing period.

Type D: These are special, unforeseen cases that require prior documentation of the need and type of arrangement and approval by the state agencies. Each case is reviewed separately.

In all but Type A, prior documentation must be provided before the end of the regular registration period to allow time for review of the documents and arrangement of the appropriate accommodations. All these requirements are included in the registration bulletin. The *TASP Test Registration Bulletin* lists specific application procedures for students who need special accommodations because of visual, hearing, or physical impairments. They must submit a letter describing the handicapping condition and the necessary special arrangements, submit a registration form with proper payment prior to the normal registration deadline, and submit a diagnostic statement from a qualified professional with a license or credentials appropriate to diagnose the disability (e.g., a physician for the mobility impaired or an ophthalmologist for the visually impaired). The diagnostic statement must be written on the qualified professional's letterhead.

Persons with learning disabilities or attention-deficit disorder must submit a letter requesting special test administration and specifying the desired special accommodations, a completed registration form with proper payment, and any one of the following documents:

1. A full educational history with complete documentation, including testing results to support recommendations for special services.

2. A neuropsychological test battery interpreted by a quali-

fied professional whose license or credentials are appropriate to diagnose the disability.

3. An evaluation by a qualified professional verifying physical abnormalities as evidenced by a computerized axial tomography (CAT) scan, magnetic resonance imaging (MRI), electroencephalogram (EEG), or brain topography mapping test.

In some cases, an examinee is contacted directly to discuss suitable arrangements. All examinees receive confirmation regarding any special procedures that have been approved and arranged before the date of the test administration for which the examinee has registered.

The above steps are described in the registration bulletin to assure examinees that all requests are treated in the same manner and that subjective judgments on the part of the state and the testing company are removed from the decision-making process regarding special accommodations.

During test development, persons with special needs were represented on the Bias Review Committee to ensure consideration of bias issues regarding handicaps. In addition, the test was reviewed by persons from both the blind and deaf communities, and consultants were used in developing both the braille and videotaped materials. Staff members also briefed members of statewide organizations representing the interests of handicapped persons about program requirements and available accommodations. Special test sessions of hearing and sight-impaired persons were conducted to identify their special or unique problems in responding to the items in the test.

Persons with learning disabilities posed a difficult set of policy problems. Even though federal laws and court rulings have not required special accommodations for them, debate among educators has continued. There is little agreement about defining learning disabilities and necessary accommodations. Even experts in the diagnosis of learning disabilities have not reached consensus about its definition or if accommodations are appropriate. For these reasons, additional time to complete the TASP Test has been the primary accommodation allowed for students with learning disabilities.

FACING UNIQUE PROBLEMS

As mentioned, House Bill (HB) 1196 exempted blind and deaf students from the TASP Test until September 1991. The primary reason for the exemption was not simply to exempt from the test students with hearing or visual impairments but rather, to allow the Coordinating Board time to identify remediation specifically designed to meet their needs. If any student fails one or more of the three test sections, he or she must by law enter a program to remediate the deficiency. The authors of HB 1196 were concerned with the availability of appropriate remedial activities for blind and deaf students who might fail portions of the test. Texas teachers were available to teach remedial reading, mathematics, and writing skills, but there was a question about their expertise to remediate blind or deaf students who needed help. The exemption gave time to develop appropriate remediation strategies, while possible solutions were investigated by a special committee appointed solely for this purpose.

The legislation specifically required the THECB to "prepare and adopt a program of remedial courses that have been determined by qualified professionals to be fully accessible to and unbiased toward deaf and blind students, to be used on and after September 1, 1991, to meet the requirements of Section 51.306, *Education Code*." The Committee for Students with Special Needs was formed with experts on hearing impairments, visual impairments, mobility impairments, and learning disabilities appointed from two-year and four-year institutions of higher education. Also included were representatives from the Texas Rehabilitation Commission, the Texas Commission for the Blind, and various centers at colleges and universities that deal with students with special needs.

The committee was charged to produce a monograph, to be sent to state colleges and universities, that addressed a review of state and federal laws that affect handicapped students in higher education; a review of the services and accommodations available to handicapped students; recommendations for appropriate curricular accommodations, remediation programs, and model instructional programs for handicapped students; and recommendations for remediation of deaf and blind students as required by HB 1196.

An inconsistency in Texas laws requiring testing soon surfaced. Many Texas high school students with physical or mental impairments or learning disabilities have been exempt from taking the high school minimum skills test required for graduation. The tests are given at each odd-numbered school grade (grades three, five, seven and nine), with the exit-level test required for graduation administered at the eleventh grade. Based upon a review procedure used to identify and develop special instructional arrangements, students with special needs may be exempt from having to take the tests. Consequently, students who have never participated in minimum skills assessment during their public school education face a required exam that measures their basic skills in reading, mathematics, and writing when they arrive at college. This inconsistency has resulted in a great deal of misunderstanding and resentment on the part of affected students and parents, since there is no provision for exemptions under the TASP.

A provision for alternative methods of assessment was included in the law to give students who cannot demonstrate their skills on the TASP Test another opportunity to reflect mastery of those skills. However, it must be clear that alternative assessment is in no way associated with accommodations granted to persons with special needs. Accommodations are simply ways of permitting persons with certain handicapping conditions an opportunity to have fair access to the TASP Test. Accommodations for these students still involves the taking of the test. Alternative assessment, described in a policy adopted by the THECB involves procedures other than administration of the TASP Test for measuring the same skills at the same level of difficulty. It may be that persons with special needs might indeed qualify for alternative assessment, but the requirements and purposes for this assessment are different and are not addressed in this chapter.

Translating the TASP Test into braille for visually impaired students presented problems. Certain words, expressions, phrases, and graphics were difficult to translate into braille. Many of the test items that included such material were modified without significantly altering the skill measured by the item. In a few cases, however, items had to be substituted because modifications were not feasible. Examples include graphics that are a part of some mathematics items. When circular pie charts or diagonal lines on graphs were reproduced in braille, the computer-generated printouts resulted in diagrams that could be misleading to the examinee. A ratcheting effect in the braille caused circles to look and feel as though they were oval shaped, and lines became stair-stepped or "rough" feeling. Both effects tended to draw attention away from the primary purpose of those particular items. The blind examinees who received these items in a special pilot test recommended that those diagrams be hand drawn, or that other items be substituted.

Another challenge had to do with the wide variety of requested accommodations for taking the test. Some requests for accommodation asked for no more than allowing a student to use a magnifying device or a large-print edition of the test. Other requests were much more thought provoking and involved. For example, what sort of accommodations should be provided for paraplegic students with limited or no movement capability or limited ability to communicate answers? How should an albino student who must remain in near darkness be accommodated? Or what about the disabled student who wants to type a writing sample with a device, attached to his or her head, for striking typewriter keys? These and many other accommodation requests had to be dealt with in as fair and equitable a manner as possible without significantly advantaging or disadvantaging any student.

Written rules are fine, but not everyone will fit into the provisions specified in a written set of rules. There are human concerns that transcend formal policy at times. A good example of this is the paraplegic student with no movement capability. While answers to multiple-choice items are possible with these students, the production of a written sample proved to be impossible. Hence for these students the writing portion of the test consisted solely of multiple-choice items and the written essay was waived.

Accommodations for learning disabilities caused different problems. The most common accommodation granted thus far for learning disabilities has been extra time, and it has been a great challenge to determine which students should be granted that accommodation. Determining the appropriate accommodation has been difficult for several reasons:

1. It is difficult to find any two "experts" who agree about what learning disabilities are, much less how to accommodate for them.

2. Diagnosticians provided a wide variety of test batteries to the state that purport to document the learning disability in an individual. In some cases, the test battery results were deemed inappropriate by the state and accommodations were denied.

3. Parents and teachers apply for accommodations for students they consider to have learning disabilities, but the documentation does not indicate a true disability. Some of these students have tested IQs in the seventies. The parents and teachers truly believe that the student is learning disabled and persist in efforts for special accommodations because similar efforts have been successful throughout the student's public school years. These parents become upset when TASP accommodations for their children are denied. Each case poses a special problem for the state; and although extra time can be given as an accommodation for learning-disabled students, it is not given automatically or without proper documentation.

THE CONTINUING CHALLENGE

As long as there are mandated testing programs, the challenge of dealing with persons with special needs will continue.
A balance between test requirements and appropriate accommodations to assure fairness for all examinees will be sought.
Those who must develop and implement large-scale testing
programs must remember that many factors enter into the
testing equation: economic factors, political factors, legal
precedents, and other practicalities. However, the true bottom
line in the testing of persons with special needs is to ensure that
granted accommodations are necessary and fair.

9
Testing for Two Purposes: Teacher Education and Basic Skills Certification

Marvin Veselka, Nolan Wood, and Pamela Tackett

Coincidentally, the Texas Education Agency was seeking a basic skills test for admission to teacher education candidacy at the same time that the Texas Academic Skills Program law was passed. The Texas Education Agency and the Coordinating Board joined forces to develop a test to serve both their purposes. What resulted was a truly beneficial team effort with those responsible for kindergarten to twelfth grade education in the state in close cooperation with those responsible for higher education.

Testing students for admission to teacher education programs has been a national trend for a number of years. In the State of Texas, the implementation of a basic skills testing program for this purpose was debated in the legislature, tried and upheld by the courts, and finally accepted by institutions of higher education. In less than a decade, Texas' policies moved from open-admission teacher education programs to programs requiring students to pass a single test in reading, mathematics, and writing. This was the first step toward upgrading the higher education system in Texas. Students must meet this requirement and other academic and/or experiential standards applied by public colleges and universities to gain access to teacher education courses and a career as a public school teacher. Now the State of Texas has taken a dramatic step by requiring acceptable performance on a basic skills test for all students attending any public college or university, regardless of major field of study, entering college-level degree or certificate programs.

BACKGROUND OF BASIC SKILLS TESTING IN HIGHER EDUCATION

In 1979, the governor of Texas established an advisory committee on public school education. One part of the committee's final report addressed competency testing of future teachers. The report called for tests that would assure the public that its teachers had the academic and professional knowledge necessary for adequate performance in the classroom. At the same time, the Commission on Standards for the Teaching Profession was created by the legislature to focus on quality teacher preparation through institutions of higher education. This commission immediately sought evidence for the need and public support for testing of teacher candidates.

As a result of their work, the Commission on Standards for the Teaching Profession recommended two types of testing: testing in basic skills to gain entry to the professional courses for teacher preparation and certification testing in subject areas and pedagogy after completing a teacher education program. Accepted by the State Board of Education, these recommendations were passed on to the Texas Legislature, which mandated both types of testing through Senate Bill 50 in 1981.

Subsequently, the Texas Education Agency (TEA), which regulates elementary and secondary public schools and teachers, undertook a study of ways to implement the testing legislation. During this same period, the Educational Testing Service (ETS) was developing a standardized test for determining the basic skills of persons considering entry into higher education professional programs. This test, the Pre-Professional Skills Test (P-PST), was field tested by ETS on a national sample of students in higher education institutions, including eight university campuses in Texas. The TEA was asked to review data from this field test; it further studied the P-PST for validity as an admission test for teacher education programs. Following this study, the P-PST was adopted by the State Board of Education. It was first administered to students in Texas in March 1984.

Texas encountered its first legal challenge to the P-PST. An ongoing lawsuit was enjoined by the Mexican-American Legal Defense and Education Fund (MALDEF) in the U.S. District Court. Pending a full trial on the merits of the P-PST, the organization was granted an injunction that prohibited the use of test results as a criterion for admission to teacher education programs. Satisfactory performance on the test remained a requirement, however, for teacher certification during the injunction. The injunction was reversed and vacated in 1986 by the U.S. Court of Appeals for the Fifth Circuit. The appellate court upheld the state's right to require competency in basic skills for future teachers and ruled that the state had taken appropriate steps to establish that the P-PST was a valid measure of those skills.

With the legal challenge to the testing program resulting in a ruling in favor of the State of Texas, the State Board of Education began to review actions it could take to help students meet the testing requirement. The board determined that an inherent weakness in the state program was the lack of sufficient information to allow students to prepare for the test or, when needed, to remediate successfully. In making this statement about the P-PST, the board followed a pattern established in the early 1980s in Texas' public school student assessment program. The test should provide feedback useful to the students and to the institutions charged with teaching the skills being measured.

The State Board of Education concluded that the P-PST lacked some of the features desired in a state-mandated testing program. The board directed the TEA to develop and quickly initiate a plan for implementing a testing program to achieve the goals set forth by the board for assessment instruments. The board's directive coincided with planning that had just begun for another statewide testing program. Approved by the legislature in 1987, and effective in the fall of 1989, House Bill 2182 required basic skills testing of all students entering state-supported higher education institutions in Texas. This law eliminated the need for a separate testing program for admission to teacher education courses in virtually all institutions except privately supported universities with approved teacher education programs. Consequently, the TEA and the Texas Higher Education Coordinating Board (THECB), which was authorized to implement House Bill 2182, joined forces to develop one testing program for all students entering public institutions of higher education in Texas.

RESHAPING BASIC SKILLS TESTING FOR HIGHER EDUCATION

The development of a large-scale testing program that will eventually test 150,000 to 200,000 students each year is a unique challenge for most education agencies and testing companies. Even though there have been many programs developed to test larger populations, few, if any, other programs have been developed with the complexities of Texas' new basic skills testing program for higher education--the Texas Academic Skills Program (TASP) Test. Two state agencies--the TEA, responsible for administering the public school system of the state, and the THECB, which works with colleges and universities--have jointly planned the implementation of this program. Because the missions of these agencies differ considerably, special attention had to be given to meeting many different needs. Accommodating the needs of the colleges and universities while enforcing a state mandate for assessment was a challenge. The TEA, with its experience in administering the P-PST for virtually the same purposes as the TASP Test, had already encountered many of the issues that had to be faced in developing a new test. On the other hand, the THECB had facilitated dialogue with colleges and universities that added immeasurably to the quality of the new program.

The legislation requiring testing of all students also mandated remediation for those not performing at an acceptable level. Therefore, the TASP was designed to guide appropriate instruction for each individual student. The legislation and program for teacher education admissions testing had not addressed remediation. Hence, the TASP addressed an important feature not available in the previous testing program.

As noted earlier, the state's philosophy about measurement of a specific curriculum or particular objectives was at the center of the development of the Texas Academic Skills Program. The legislation mandating the program stipulated that a diagnostic test be administered to public college and university students. Consequently, a criterion-referenced testing program was designed with college and university faculty members identifying the skills needed for entering college freshmen. Test items that measure the identified skills have been painstakingly written, and the test format assures feedback about acceptable performance relative to these skills. Because this significant feature was noticeably absent from the P-PST, it is believed to be the single aspect of the TASP Test that will benefit students and the entire education community. A test designed to allow students to recognize their problems early on and to improve their skills in the areas in which they are deficient should increase access to higher education for all students.

Fairness to students was the basis for decisions in all aspects of this program. The concepts of fairness and bias prevention were considered in decisions including the definition of the test content, material to be used in the test items, administration of the test, scoring practices, and reporting results to students. Every attempt was made to consider the problems students encounter in testing situations and to treat these with sensitivity while maintaining the integrity of the program.

Historically, state-mandated testing programs have had a greater adverse impact on those minority students who have suffered a lack of educational opportunities. In Texas, passing rates for minority students are considerably lower than for other students. In developing the skills to be measured on the TASP Test, the removal of racial, ethnic, or gender biases was considered one of the most important activities. Material in the test items was examined to assure all groups that their social and ethnic values were included or appropriately addressed. Consequently, the TASP Test encompasses materials not usually seen on tests and excludes material that might previously have been detrimental to some groups.

CHANGING THE RELATIONSHIP BETWEEN SECONDARY SCHOOL EDUCATION AND HIGHER EDUCATION

The TASP will benefit Texas public secondary education and higher education in a manner earlier considered to be only peripheral to the implementation of the program, but which now has the potential for far-reaching impact. For the first time, the higher education community has defined the basic skills or competencies all students should have as they begin their postsecondary education.[1] Consequently, the high schools will be able to counsel students about the preparation needed for college and direct them to the courses with the specific curriculum necessary for successful performance on the test and in college. Texas has many open-admissions postsecondary institutions where students are enrolled regardless of their high school preparation. These institutions left high schools without targets or preparation guidelines for students. Now those students who are underprepared when they enter college will be in remediation programs to target their specific needs.

The joint development work on the TASP between two state agencies charged with assuring quality education in Texas has been a first step in establishing a new cooperative relationship for improving education for the state. To see testing as the total response to an educational problem is an inappropriate use of tests. But because basic skills testing in the college setting was first instituted to assure the state of highly qualified teachers, the logical next step of requiring this type of testing for all college students will bring about a much closer relationship between secondary and postsecondary educators.

Reform has always begun with the identification of a particular problem. Unfortunately, this has resulted in finger pointing at that segment of education believed to be at fault. Not all this finger pointing has been bad. Because of it, problems have been examined in the proper perspective and new ways to facilitate changes have been explored. Public and postsecondary sectors of the education community should be sharing those instructional approaches proven to be effective.

Accountability indicators were built into the legislation for basic skills testing for entering higher education students. There will be an opportunity for each institution to evaluate itself in relation to its institutional mission and the preparation of its students to be successful in that institution. These institutions will report the effectiveness of their remedial programs for those students who did not perform successfully on their initial attempts at the TASP Test. In addition, with appropriate privacy safeguards, student test scores will be reported to the high schools. Reports on the success of the high schools will be sent to both the THECB and the State Board of Education. The two state agencies involved in this testing program will need to continue working together to assure that this evaluation of institutions is conducted appropriately and accurately.

There are potential dangers in reporting assessment data to the public. These dangers were experienced in the public school sector in Texas when people judged the education community before they understood the context in which instruction was delivered. However, such dangers are out-weighed by the need to inform the public about the adequacy of the educational system in Texas for preparing individuals for a useful and productive life. Plans are underway to develop a reporting system to benefit all groups.

Although the State Board of Education was the first body charged with developing a basic skills testing program in higher education, the role of this board in the Texas Academic Skills Program will change. In effect, the law requiring the TASP Test will preempt the law and policies relating to students entering teacher preparation programs (except for students enrolled in private universities in Texas). All incoming college freshmen will be tested for basic skills competency via the TASP Test, and if they plan to enter the teaching profession, they will no longer face other tests before they enter teacher education courses.

The State Board of Education and the Texas Education Agency will continue to review the impact of this program. The team effort exhibited by the two state agencies resulted in the development and implementation of a program which met common goals. There will be a continuing need to examine the public school curriculum and the adequacy of the public schools to prepare students to succeed in a college or university. The State Board of Education, which has faced many difficult issues related to testing, will continue to have many new problems requiring ongoing communication between the board, the public schools, and the higher education community.

NOTE

In addition to the twenty-eight skills identified as appropriate for testing on the TASP Test, eighty-two faculty members from secondary and postsecondary institutions worked on the Instructional Competency Project, which defined comprehensive reading, writing, and mathematical competencies necessary to succeed in college. A report of their project was widely distributed to all colleges, universities, and secondary schools in Texas. For additional information about this project, refer to *Improvement for Undergraduate Education in Texas: College-level Competencies*, Texas Higher Education Coordinating Board, June 1989.

10
Implementation in Community Colleges
Dan Angel, Roberto Reyes, and
Charles B. Florio

The community colleges were especially proactive in planning for implementation of the Texas Academic Skills Program law on their campuses. Most colleges already had testing and placement programs and appropriate remedial courses in place. Thus, they had an excellent appreciation of the complexities involved prior to the law going into effect. Nevertheless, unique problems arose during program implementation that affected large urban community colleges differently than small, rural colleges.

DAN ANGEL: THE COMMUNITY COLLEGE CONTEXT

When the Texas Academic Skills Program (TASP) was approved by the state legislature in 1987, the Texas public community and junior colleges knew the new testing instrument was going to affect them much more than the other elements of higher education. Since the legislation required tests of first-time students within a specified period, one only had to note that 57,000 (24 percent) fell into the first-time student category in 1987 at Texas public senior institutions. The other 161,000 (74 percent) enrolled in higher education for the first time at a community college.

Also, junior colleges enrolled the majority of entering minority students. In fall 1987, three of every five blacks and two of every three Hispanics enrolled in higher education attended community colleges. Furthermore, a 1986-1987 survey of Texas public community colleges had already indicated that an estimated 40 percent of entering students needed remediation in reading, 43 percent in writing, and 54 percent in math even before TASP was begun.

The Community College Context

To say that the forty-nine community college districts in Texas did not receive TASP with open arms would be something of an understatement. There were strong feelings of resentment on several fronts.

First, the community colleges felt they had been responsive to the remedial needs of the students. More than half the districts had begun remedial testing on their own dime, and some of these programs had been very successful. Several of the presidents felt these model testing programs could have and should have been adopted rather than spending the time, resources, and duplicative efforts to establish a new statewide test.

Second, some of the leadership questioned why this new wrinkle in the "no pass, no play" legislation of a few years earlier, wherein failing high school students were prohibited from participating in sponsored extracurricular activities, had to be expanded to academic opportunity. Many worried that this new "testing barrier" would be insurmountable for minority, low-income, and less well-prepared students. They feared the test would at the least discourage students, if not make them confirmed failures outright. Then, too, perhaps financial aid would be denied for remedial courses, making the matter worse. At the very least, students trying to get a community college education would have to stay in school a semester or a year longer. Students who already had significant barriers would just have the high bar raised a notch.

Third, the State of Texas had acted more like Uncle Scrooge than Huey, Dewey, and Louie when providing cash for remedial programs. Although Texas community college funding is provided on a cost-of-program funding scale, there are no extra dollars for the additional support services for students who need remediation. Using reasonable estimates, we calculated that remediation needs could double. But when the support levels were already inadequate, the commissioner of higher education had recommended only enough money to increase remedial support by one-half. Community college officials could foresee massive unmet needs for remediation after verifying their students needed it and this was a major concern.

Coming Out of the Chute

In January 1988, the commissioner of higher education invited Texas educational leaders to Austin to discuss plans for test development and implementation by fall 1989. The half-day, January 1988 conference was really the first exposure to the TASP for the majority of those who attended. The briefing provided short comments from state educational leaders, some handout materials, and a rather thorough explanation of the New Jersey testing experience, which had begun a decade earlier.

Although the process had to begin at some time, it would be safe to say that the briefing raised more questions than it answered. Many in the audience thought they were seeing a film sequel to *The Gods Must Be Crazy*. It seemed impossible to develop and implement a test of this magnitude within eighteen months. There was very little information available. Several doubted that the effort would be successful.

The "Bird Dog" Committee

There is an old Texas saying for something that won't work: "That dog won't hunt." Thus it came as little surprise when the Association of Texas Public Community and Junior Colleges (TPC/JCA) named a "bird dog" committee "to attend to, monitor, and report on pertinent actions regarding the development of the TASP and its impact on Texas community colleges."

Before I get into further details, let me share what my deep involvement with TASP has been for the last two years. I have been involved in six significant ways: I (1) served as chairman of the Texas Public Community and Junior College Association Oversight Committee--the "bird dog" group, (2) presented the TPCJCA testimony before the Texas Higher Education Coordinating Board, (3) co-hosted a statewide conference on TASP, (4) hosted a two-hour television show regarding TASP implementation, (5) chaired a faculty development committee on the expected shortages of reading teachers, and (6) was a member of the advisory committee that recommended the distribution of money.

Over the next few months, issues began to multiply rather than divide.

Issue Discovery

Although starting slowly, and then gathering speed, the Oversight Committee members soon felt like the old lady who lived in a shoe with so many issues, she didn't know what to do!

First came issues based on rumor and frustration: (1) the test would be transfer dominated; (2) it would push vocational and technical students to private schools; (3) business and industrial contractual arrangements would be derailed; (4) massive amounts of institutional money would be diverted to remediation; (5) "strangulation" reporting requirements would be forthcoming; and, (6) the test would be used to denote institutional success, eventually leading to direct state funding.

Next came issues of legitimate concern: How many testing centers would there be? Would the test be truly diagnostic? How much turnaround time would be involved in receiving test scores? What would be the level of difficulty of test questions? What would be a passing score? Would financial aid be available for people taking remedial courses? Would community colleges be allowed to administer the tests?

Third, there was great concern with bias. The two major Texas minority groups took different avenues of action regarding this issue.

The Texas Association of Black Personnel in Higher Education went on record in the spring of 1988 at its fifteenth annual conference in Fort Worth, Texas, as supporters of the TASP. Their support was not unqualified. They sought model remediation programs of a pilot nature, adequate financial aid, test sites at all community colleges, and changes in test content. Finally, they asked that test questions be as generic as possible.

The Mexican-American Legal Defense and Education Fund (MALDEF), took hearty exception to the test from its inception. They challenged the test on five major counts: the lack of multiple criteria, concern about adequate money for remediation, concern about the scientific accuracy of test scores, the impact on minority students, and the lack of lead time for developing remedial education courses.

To deal with these issues, the Bias Review Panel was one of the more than twenty committees formed to develop the test. Also, the State Attorney General's Office provided legal advice as the test was developed.

Constructive Criticism

Although all major meetings of the statewide TPC/JCA included a discussion on TASP development, some of the membership seemed to feel it was difficult to criticize TASP to the "bird dog" committee. One letter, written in May of 1988, said very straightforwardly, "I've encountered three major objections to suggested changes: (1) We have known about this for a long time and should have objected earlier if we had concerns; (2) if we express concerns now, it will appear that we are opposed to assessment and remediation, thus creating political problems for ourselves; and (3) the TASP is needed just as legislated."

These feelings seemed to be widespread and deeply felt. We decided that a meeting with the commissioner of higher education was necessary to present the concerns of Texas community colleges.

In June 1988, a two-hour meeting with the commissioner of

higher education allowed us to voice complaints frankly. The commissioner was equally candid about his game plan. Although the meeting in itself accomplished little, it set the stage for some meaningful dialogue with the commissioner's staff that was to mitigate many of the major issues.

Major Issues

Two major issues seemed to resolve themselves very quickly: the number of testing sites and the bulging backlog of those students in need of being tested and remediated.

In spite of rumors that there would be only a select few testing centers that would administer the test, the number of locations seemed to multiply like gremlins exposed to water. It was soon evident that any institution that seriously wanted to be a testing center could be. Most colleges opted to become centers.

The solution to pent-up demand for remediation versus inadequacies of financial resources appeared easily. The Coordinating Board and the Texas Education Agency decided to employ an old legislative strategy and "grandfather" (exempt) anyone who had taken at least one three-hour credit college-level course prior to fall 1989. The demand was simply too big to start any other way.

Community College Clout

Texas community colleges were directly responsible for some major changes in the TASP. They worked hard for these changes and they won!

The victories were in cost, the choice of a nine or fifteen semester credit hour rule, the creation of two tests, exemptions, and refocusing on diagnostic and remedial needs.

Cost. Since the State of Texas had employed National Evaluation Systems, Inc. (NES) to develop the test and the legislature had passed the development costs on to students, there was a lack of control from the very beginning regarding how much students would be charged.

When a figure of $29 surfaced, community college leaders went into a seizure. In a state where several of the community colleges still charged only $4 per credit hour, students would be faced with an up-front cost of $29 to take the test and a repeated cost for retaking any sections they failed. This seemed like a major barrier to access in the minds of community college leaders. No other group spoke of the cost as frequently or successfully, and they are directly responsible for reducing the charge to $24.

Two Test Forms. Another issue that sent community college leaders into a frenzy was the turnaround time for getting results from the official TASP Test. Originally, new program specifications indicated six to eight weeks would be necessary. That figure didn't seem to bother senior universities who expected students to compete for a spot several months in advance, but for the community colleges it was a massive problem.

Junior colleges have open admissions, and thousands of students show up at registration without any prior indication they planned to attend college. Those students would not have taken the test if it were given only five times a year, and results would not be available for placement. For the entire first semester, students would be taking courses as if the statewide testing program did not exist, forcing them and the colleges to ignore anything the test would reveal regarding remedial skills. It also meant that remedial classes for skills necessary for success in the first semester would not be offered until the second semester.

The community colleges also wanted to be able to test their students on the spot and at any time of their choosing. The Coordinating Board and the Texas Education Agency refused to let the official test be given by anyone except program officials in order to maintain ultimate security for the test.

As battle lines were drawn, the idea of having two tests surfaced: the official certification form and a campus version, the Pre-TASP Test (PTT). Local community colleges could now give the PTT, get immediate results, and use the data for placement at the time of student need. The PTT also costs $2.50, and colleges could administer it free or for a minimum cost of up to $3.00.

The Nine or Fifteen Semester Credit Hour Choice. An accommodation was made to allow students adequate time for remediation. Also, two test versions allowed a student to take either the TASP Test before completing nine hours of college work or before completing up to fifteen hours of college work *if* he or she had taken the PTT (or a corresponding diagnostic test given at the institutional level upon entry).

Exempt Students. One of the most ticklish issues raised about the TASP legislation was that it applied to both credit and certificate students. That requirement did not wear well with community college leaders who felt there were several groups of students who should not be obligated to take the TASP Test. These included vocational and technical students, certificate students, clock-hour students, and casual or occasional students. After much debate, discussion, and gnashing of teeth, a significant exemption policy was enacted. Any student was exempt from taking the TASP Test if he or she was enrolled in a certificate program that contained fewer than nine semester credit hours of general education courses.

Refocusing. The fact that the test was the first part of the TASP seemed to focus everyone's attention on passing the test to become a "rising junior." That is, in order to take upper-division courses after sixty hours, which constitutes the junior level of college, a student must pass all sections of the test. Less attention seemed to be paid to the fact that a student also had to pass the test to obtain a community college degree and that the thrust of the program was the appropriate placement and the required remediation. The last significant community college victory refocused attention on the remedial nature of the program.

1989 Results

The TASP Test was given to 56,781 students during 1989. That number represented about one-third of those who were expected to take the test. There were significant differences in performance among whites, blacks, and Hispanics, as well as between four-year and two-year college students taking the test.

Nearly 82 percent of students enrolled in senior universities passed all sections of the test. Ethnic group breakdown for the senior universities showed 87 percent of whites, 62 percent of blacks, and 70 percent of Hispanics passed all sections of the test.

For students enrolled in community colleges, 56 percent passed the entire test. Further analysis showed 63 percent of whites, 23 percent of blacks, and 43 percent of Hispanics passed all sections.

It is important to note that only 17 percent of first-time freshmen enrolled in Texas public community colleges took the test in 1989, but the results demonstrate that the important burden of remediation will definitely fall at the community college level. That burden will be much greater for black and Hispanic students.

Major Implementation Problems

In spite of the specific legislative directive, public pressure, and focused community college concerns, a number of issues caused difficulty with program implementation. These included the large number of people involved, a general lack of information, changing rules and regulations, institutional policy decisions, and, of course, money.

Number of People. The TASP was brought to Texas with a literal cast of thousands. There were more than twenty statewide and regional committees, numerous institutional representatives, hundreds of content advisors for question development, and hundreds of others who were in charge of campus implementation guidelines and procedures.

The Cecil B. DeMille approach had advantages and disadvantages. The biggest advantage was that people involved in the process had an opportunity to actively participate in its development and felt somewhat responsible for the result. The biggest disadvantage was that so many people were involved that the right hand many times did not know what the left was doing. Many of the committees believed that what they had decided was final, not realizing that other committees might come to a different conclusion and that the Coordinating Board would make the final decision.

Lack of Information. Throughout the development process, very little written information was available in the field. The newsletter that was attempted came infrequently, often with dated and previously known information. The TASP telephone hotline was not established until March 1989. In addition to the general lack of field information, very little was done to inform the general public and students that the test was coming.

Changing Rules and Regulations. Some of the lack of information cited above was caused by the fact that the rules and regulations were constantly in a state of flux. In some cases rules came late, and in other cases they were changed shortly after they came forth. Most of this difficultly could have been avoided with a longer development period for the test.

Institutional Implementation Decisions. Late in the game several sheets of important policy decisions for institutions were developed by the TASP Committee of Chief Academic Officers and delivered to institutional representatives. The lists were long, comprehensive, and complex. Such lists had been needed much earlier.

Money. Without a doubt the most serious problem in implementing TASP was money. Due to a faltering state economy, Texas community colleges had been hard hit by lack of state funding in the 1987-1988 biennium.

The new TASP monies were inadequate by any scale of measurement. First, the commissioner of higher education, realizing the Texas Legislature was going to be tightfisted, requested only enough dollars for about half the new need. This amount was reduced in the legislative process from the original request of $36 million to approximately $23 million over the 1989-1990 biennium. One example of the inadequate funding is demonstrated at Austin Community College (ACC) in the capital city of Texas. In 1989-1990 ACC spent $450,000 on TASP and received $245,000 in state funding. In 1990-1991, ACC will spend $460,000 in direct TASP costs and will receive $345,000 from the state. Neither of these gaps considers indirect costs, which are sizeable.

Although these were major problems, the public community colleges in Texas have tried to handle them with the poise and consideration expected and deserved by Texas higher education students.

Conclusions

Texas community colleges did not welcome the TASP with open arms, but they did have a significant impact on the program during its early formation. It is clear that the bulk of the TASP burden will rest on their shoulders. As the importance of the "grandfather" clause wanes and as more students surpass the nine or fifteen semester credit hours trigger, thousands of Texas students will come to know the TASP program firsthand.

The testing program in Texas is here to stay. It is up to all of us to be sure that it is a test that "sorts people in."

ROBERTO REYES: EL PASO COMMUNITY COLLEGE

The Community and the College

El Paso Community College (EPCC) in El Paso, Texas, is a

comprehensive community college with a strong commitment and record of service to its unique, multicultural environment. The community served by the college is characterized by geographical proximity to Mexico, by high minority populations, low-income levels, and low education levels. El Paso is located at the far western tip of the state, bounded by the U.S.-Mexican border and the state of New Mexico.

Of El Paso residents twenty-five years of age and over, approximately 28 percent have completed less than eight years of schooling. Statewide, 22 percent of the population is in the same category. This figure rises dramatically for Hispanics. Half of Hispanic women and 40 percent of Hispanic men in El Paso have completed less than eight years of education. According to the projected 1990 U.S. Census data, 70 percent of the 600,000 inhabitants of the district's service area are Hispanic, and 29 percent of their families live below the poverty level. Persons under eighteen account for more than 35 percent of El Paso's population. Consequently, a large number of students at EPCC are young, Hispanic and from low-income families that have little experience dealing with a postsecondary educational environment.

The college is located in the largest metropolitan region on the United States-Mexico border. With its sister city--Ciudad Juarez--El Paso is in a geographic area that has approximately one and one-half million inhabitants. For decades, it has been a principal place of passage from Mexico to the United States. El Paso Community College's location has provided a unique opportunity to provide access for thousands of first-generation Mexican-Americans into the socioeconomic mainstream of U.S. society.

The El Paso County Community College District was established as a county-junior college district in June 1969 when citizens voted to create the district and elected a seven member board of trustees. State funds were appropriated to the district in 1971, and 901 students were enrolled that fall. Local financial support and long-range financial stability became a reality in 1975-1976 when taxes were levied for the first time to support facilities development and operations.

Now a multicampus community college offering a wide range of general, vocational, technical, and career programs, the college currently offers the associate of arts and the associate of science degrees in academic transfer programs, the associate of applied science degree in fifty-seven occupational fields, and the certificates of completion in twenty-seven technical areas. In addition, EPCC has a comprehensive, noncredit continuing education program which offers general interest classes for the community, General Education Development (GED), a wide range of vocational classes, and several community-based English-as-a-Second-Language courses.

The college currently ranks third among all institutions of higher education in the continental United States in numbers of Hispanic students enrolled. During the fall 1989 semester, 74.6 percent of the 16,557 students enrolled in credit courses were Hispanic, 20 percent were non-Hispanic whites, 3.7 percent were black, and 1.7 percent were native Americans, Asian or nonresident aliens. In addition, 59.7 percent of students enrolled in fall 1989 were women. Both the number and percentage of minorities enrolled at the college continue to grow steadily. During the spring semester 1990, a total of 17,098 students were enrolled in credit courses. Of that number, 74.8 percent were Hispanic, 19.7 percent were non-Hispanic white, 3.8 percent were black, and 1.7 percent were native American, Asian or nonresident aliens.

General Institutional Response

Throughout the process, EPCC's response to TASP has been proactive within the institution and across the state. Soon after passage of HB 2182 in 1987, EPCC sought and received an appointment to the state's Texas Academic Skills Council. The council is comprised of two and four-year college and university educators charged with providing procedural and policy advice to the commissioner of higher education on TASP issues. The college has also encouraged and supported the participation of EPCC faculty and administrators in statewide and regional

TASP Test development and implementation activities. Representatives from EPCC served on committees, participated in regional and state conferences, and developed and reviewed test questions and procedures. The college has also been represented on the committees for reading, writing, bias review, academic skills development, advisement and placement, faculty development, and English as a second language, as well as the Special Committee of Academic Officers. Twelve college faculty participated in the El Paso area Regional Review Forums and in the Standard-Setting Committee that recommended the TASP Test cut-scores.

Concurrently with institutional involvement on a statewide level, the college began comprehensive and detailed planning for its internal response to TASP prior to the mandated fall 1989 implementation date. As a first step in 1987, the college established an internal Steering Committee, which in turn appointed subcommittees for advising, test administration, remediation/instruction, recordkeeping or tracking, faculty development, public relations, and curriculum development. These committees were charged with developing plans and procedures to implement the TASP at EPCC by the fall of 1989. The TASP Steering Committee at EPCC consisted of chairpersons from each subcommittee and the chairs of the English, Math and Science, Communications, and Developmental Studies Divisions and coordinated and supervised the work of the subcommittees. They ensured all relevant groups were brought into the process and that developed procedures coincided with state mandates and requirements.

The college specifically responded to TASP in the areas of college admissions, student reporting and tracking, advising, and remediation. In these areas TASP has had great impact. The planned changes were tested in a pilot program during the 1989-1990 academic year. Some improvements are being made.

Admissions Response

The requirements mandated by the TASP, and specifically

the need for identification of TASP-vulnerable students by the Admissions Office, has had several positive effects on the college's admissions procedures. In the process of evaluating student records and admissions placement, for example, the college clarified the relationship between nontraditional course credits, such as credit by exam, prior experience, and challenge exams, and TASP-mandated nine and fifteen credit hour requirements. It was necessary to determine if those credits exempted students from TASP requirements and if those credits counted toward the nine and fifteen credit hour test requirements. The admissions process has also been improved with more timely written explanations of the intake, testing, and orientation procedures required at the college.

The college's mail registration process used by 40 to 50 percent of all students was given considerable attention. Course booklets and mail registration information packets advised registering students for the first time that they must attend a new-student orientation and see a counselor before registering. New students who did not follow these procedures were advised by mail of the new TASP requirements, such as the need to take the TASP Test before completing nine semester credit hours of coursework.

In addition, the Admissions Office is now working more closely with other college departments in providing information and services to new and returning students. One important component of this process has been the establishment of a partnership between student intake and admission personnel during registration periods. An intake and admissions team has been formed at each campus within the College's multicampus district. It uniformly provides students with the same consistent information.

Problems that emerged in the admission system are being resolved. For example, the college presently assigns a computer-generated identification number to each student, but the TASP Test identifies students by their social security numbers. To match students with their test scores, Admissions Office personnel have had to convert each student's social security number to its appropriate college identification number. The

Admissions Office is implementing changes that will allow it to identify students initially by their social security numbers. The Admissions Office also has had problems identifying the TASP status of transferring students when transcripts are delayed or incomplete information is received. Admissions personnel hope to resolve this problem by working more closely with other institutions and with statewide committees.

Reporting and Tracking

For TASP reporting and tracking, a new process has been established by the college making extensive use of computer resources and close cooperation between all relevant departments. We decided to develop a computer system for monitoring, with special emphasis in advising and placement because we anticipated a large number of students would need remediation. We implemented an extensive system of checks and balances to ensure that new students participate in a six-step process of student intake, admission, assessment (in-house testing), new-student orientation, advising, and registration. Texas Academic Skills Program information must be incorporated at each step of the process:

Intake. Students first complete their admission forms and are advised of their TASP status. An intake person completes each testing referral slip so that information on test scores will be identical to the student's admission application. Thus, the admission application first identifies a student for all tracking purposes.

Admission. After data from an admission form is put into the computer, the student's initial TASP status is posted as a series of flags on the student's computer record.

Testing. The Office of Testing Services requires each student to present the testing referral slip before he or she takes any test. The slip proves that the student has gone through the intake process. Then the student must supply demographic information. After verification, the ASSET Test is administered for local assessment. The test is scan-scored and results are immediately loaded into the main student data bank. The main computer system then re-determines the testing status of the student and modifies the set of test status flags in the student's record. The computer also identifies recommended remedial courses for each student whose score falls within the lower ranges.

New-Student Orientation. The advising staff flags the counseling portion of the main student records system to indicate when new-student orientation was completed.

Advising. Remedial courses recommended for any student can be called up on the advising computer screen. Test status is also flagged. Advisors develop an educational plan (the TASP Advising Record) for each student. The plan indicates recommended remedial courses, tutoring, or computer assisted instruction. For non-course-based remediation, the advisor must indicate the remediation subject, when remediation should be attempted, and the number of hours required for the student to comply with TASP regulations. This information must match the information put on an "alternate remediation" contract signed by the student. Again, a system flag is created to indicate that the student has been advised.

Registration. At registration, the computer checks all TASP status flags, placement test records, and the courses in which the student is enrolling. A student who has not been tested or advised, or who has failed to enroll in any of the recommended remediation options, is denied registration. He or she must redo the missed step. A student who does not register for appropriate remediation is advised immediately. The system will not allow a needed remedial course to be dropped. A student flagged as out of compliance with TASP (one who did not take TASP as required or someone who dropped out of required remediation) can register only in remedial courses. The advising and registration steps are also used for returning TASP-vulnerable students.

Advising Response

The task of implementing many of the objectives of the TASP has been the responsibility of the college's counseling staff. Counselors must be well-informed about Coordinating Board policy, as well as about EPCC's interpretation and implementation of that policy. In the first year of TASP implementation, an intensive training program gave counselors and intake student assistants information they needed about TASP requirements and new EPCC processes.

Remediation Response

The developmental education Program at EPCC has taken a leading role in preparing the college for the TASP challenges. We have been fortunate to have a Title III grant to support many of our efforts toward improving remedial education and it also helped improve the monitoring and tracking system.

One of the most important steps accomplished with Title III resources relates to course revision and curriculum development. Prior to making revisions in the curriculum, our developmental educators conducted a basic skills survey. Instructors who taught remedial or entry-level classes were asked to respond to a questionnaire that listed all the basic skills necessary to enter and to be successful in their courses. Using this data, as well as a list of TASP skills and instructor input from all the affected divisions, the Course Development Committee made the necessary course revisions and piloted the courses. The revised curriculum is undergoing evaluation.

Concern with course revision was also focused on the method of delivery. The developmental education staff studied instructor characteristics determined to be most helpful to high-risk students. This information was used in faculty training at EPCC and will continue to be updated and coordinated with faculty development activities. In addition, institutions similar to EPCC were identified through a separate national survey. Those institutions will become information sources for proven successful innovative learning strategies. A compilation of this data, coupled with the existing experience of our own faculty, will be used to improve teaching methodologies.

Since we anticipated that the implementation of TASP would identify more students in need of basic skills than we could enroll in remedial courses, we also decided to strengthen alternative remediation resources. We focused on tutoring and computer-assisted instruction. To ensure consistency, quality, and success for remedial students, a comprehensive tutorial management program was fully studied, planned, and implemented. The tutorial program has specific criteria for the selection of tutors, and it requires ongoing tutor training with a comprehensive tutor's handbook. Using the experience and knowledge of developmental education faculty, as well as consultants, all tutoring sessions are content sound and highly correlated to the TASP objectives. Student levels and specific needs are addressed in remediation groups. All efforts in the alternative remediation have been documented via a comprehensive database program developed specifically for this purpose. Demographic data, as well as content area of remediation, time on task, and progress are accurately logged into the database and are readily accessible.

The developmental education division has also upgraded its computer-assisted instruction system and has explored additional computer alternatives. Vendors were invited to demonstrate computer-assisted instruction (CAI) systems, which were evaluated by faculty. We have put out a bid for a software curriculum correlated to TASP objectives and remediation needs. In addition, plans are underway to expand the physical space and facilities available for remediation. The expansion will provide additional tutoring space and appropriate housing for the proposed state-of-the-art CAI system.

The developmental education program has also worked

closely with the English, Math and Science, and Communications Divisions to ensure that changes made in remediation programs adequately prepare students for success in entry-level college courses. As part of these cooperative efforts, division chairs and faculty in English, math, and reading have worked with the developmental education group to revise and reexamine course objectives.

Conclusions

In planning and implementing TASP requirements, we have seen beneficial results as well as serious challenges. Now, many college departments are working more closely to provide solutions for the many TASP-related concerns. The offices of admissions, testing, and counseling have enjoyed closer cooperation. Additionally, the developmental education area has been brought into a closer working relationship with key academic departments, such as English, communications, and math, through their joint work on course development and identification of key skills.

Preparation for the TASP and its actual implementation has made us identify actual and potential weaknesses in our admissions and advising processes. We have taken steps to improve those processes. Moreover, the necessity under TASP for careful and accurate monitoring of student progress has added impetus and urgency to our own goal of improving monitoring and tracking of student progress. Stimulated by the TASP, the college has increased concentration on the improvement of remedial courses and alternative remediation strategies.

It is also clear, however, that TASP is straining institutions like ours. The college, which has experienced steady and rapid growth since its inception, is a relatively young institution in a community that is severely economically depressed and has a low tax base. Because of the community's economic conditions, the college's board and the community have been reluctant to approve significant local tax increases. The need for additional resources has been further exacerbated by our recent unsuccess-

ful bid for a bond issue to pay for an expansion and improvement of facilities. Yet TASP requires even more new services
and points toward the need to expand facilities.

For example, a successful placement and monitoring system
in a large community college makes sophisticated computer
equipment almost a necessity. The monitoring and placement
systems devised by EPCC in response to TASP requirements
are dependent on the use of computers to provide the necessary
checks and balances. Even though we began planning before
the initiation of TASP and have the resources of a Title III
grant to provide partial support for increased personnel and
equipment needs, our resources have been stretched tightly.

As of fall 1989, many students were exempt from TASP
because of their prior college academic credit. But this
situation will change in the future. As more high school
students and older adults who have never attended college
request admission to EPCC, and as current students graduate,
the number of students who are eligible for TASP will increase
dramatically.

The need for increased and improved monitoring and
advising is, however, only part of the challenge posed by TASP.
Equally important is the very real need for more effective
remediation. This is particularly critical for an institution like
EPCC which serves large numbers of Hispanic students. With
the initiation of TASP, many educators were very concerned
that the TASP requirements would pose additional barriers for
minorities pursuing higher education. although there are no
definitive results proving this, preliminary analyses of test
results statewide suggest that minority populations are failing to
pass the TASP Test in disproportionately larger numbers than
majority populations.

Although the enrollment at EPCC remains strong and grows,
the college is concerned that unless effective remediation and
critical support services are available for students, particularly
marginal high school graduates or adults returning to education
with weak skills, they will be discouraged from initiating college
studies. If they do enroll, they could find themselves in
continuous remediation and may become statistics in higher

education's minority dropout problem. If TASP is to fulfill its goals, which means ensuring that students attending Texas institutions of higher education have the necessary academic skills to pursue college work and that Texas college graduates have competitive social and economic opportunities, it is vitally important that students be afforded all opportunities to correct skills deficiencies. This requires not only an effective remediation curriculum and personnel well-prepared and trained in working with students with skill deficiencies, but also an array of remediation strategies utilizing the latest technologies and research. If our institution and the State of Texas fail to provide the necessary resources to ensure that the TASP fulfills its promise, we will be doing a disservice not only to our students and our citizens, but also to the economic well-being of the state.

CHARLES B. FLORIO: KILGORE COLLEGE

Kilgore College is a 55-year-old, comprehensive public community college in the piney woods of northeast Texas and in the heart of the great East Texas oil field. Approximately 150 full-time faculty service the 4,600 students enrolled in semester-length credit courses. Kilgore is a city of 13,000 population 120 miles east of Dallas, 60 miles west of Shreveport, Louisiana, and 10 miles southwest of Longview, Texas.

Degrees and Certificates

Kilgore College offers four associate degrees and forty certificate programs. Students earn the associate degree upon completion of either a two-year university parallel program or a comparable occupational program. University parallel programs, which include considerable coursework in general education and give broad exposure to lower-division baccalaureate work, enable students to enter four-year institutions as juniors. Occupational programs also include coursework in general education along with a concentration of coursework in a specific technical or vocational field. These programs prepare students with the knowledge and level of skills necessary to enter the job market at various levels and to compete effectively. Certificates of completion provide students with appropriate entry-level job skills.

The university parallel program offers the associate of arts, associate of fine arts, and associate of science degrees. The associate of applied science degree is offered through the occupational education program.

General Education Requirement

General education is the basic core of courses that emphasizes the liberal arts and sciences. These courses are designed not only to help students understand and appreciate their heritage but also to enable them to prepare for responsible citizenship and successful living in a rapidly changing and highly technological world. One component of this general education core contributes to developing competence in reading, writing, oral communications, and fundamental mathematical skills. Consequently, associate degrees awarded by Kilgore College include a minimum of fifteen semester credit hours of general education courses drawn from the following broad areas of general education disciplines: (1) the humanities or fine arts, (2) the natural sciences or mathematics, and (3) the social or behavioral sciences. Most of the forty certificates of completion require general education coursework, but none includes the nine or more semester credit hours that would cause students to face TASP requirements.

Testing and Placement Program

Prior to the TASP, All first-time entering freshmen and transfer students with fewer than fifteen college-level semester credit hours were required to submit scores of the American

College Test (ACT) or the Scholastic Aptitude Test (SAT) along with their admissions applications and transcripts. Students who did not submit scores were required to take the ACT on a residual basis prior to registration. However, students who enrolled in seven or fewer credit hours in a semester and who did not enroll in English or mathematics courses were exempt from taking the ACT or SAT. This exception was determined at the urging of the college officials responsible for off-campus and evening instruction. Thus, the college had a dual testing and placement policy--one for full-time students and one for part-time students.

Students whose scores were extremely low on the ACT, SAT, or residual ACT tests were placed in specified developmental education courses that did not carry degree credit. After preliminary placement in developmental education classes, students were asked to take the Nelson-Denny Reading Test, the Descriptive Test of Mathematical Skills of the College Board, and the Kilgore College English Diagnostic Test. As a result of this additional testing, approximately 10 percent of students placed in developmental education courses were required to change their course schedules. Consequently, many students, including those who registered early during the summer orientation sessions, were closed out of desired courses. This caused some problems for many students. Some of these students had to exchange book purchases; revise work schedules, car pools, and baby-sitting arrangements; adjust fee payments; and forego preferred instructors. Nevertheless, college studies indicated and developmental education faculty believed that low ACT or SAT scores alone were not specific enough to serve as placement criteria. Precise testing and placement of students must override other considerations.

Students who needed to improve their reading and writing skills were not restricted from taking college-level courses that required college-level reading and writing skills. Instead, academic counselors and faculty members used their professional judgment in helping students select appropriate college-level courses. However, all students were required to take mathematics courses in sequence.

A New Beginning for Developmental Education

House Bill (HB) 2182 (the TASP law) changed developmental education at Kilgore College more than any previous event. Although Kilgore College had been providing developmental education since 1978, the college became engrossed in it in fall 1989.

At the beginning of the development of TASP, Stewart H. McLaurin was president of Kilgore College and the Texas Public Community Junior College Association. Honored as an outstanding community college leader by the University of Texas at Austin and the Texas legislature, Dr. McLaurin died January 11, 1989, at age fifty. But he had been an early advocate of the goals of the TASP, having testified before the Select Committee on Higher Education and having participated in the development of HB 2182.

Dr. McLaurin's first step to implement TASP at Kilgore College was to appoint me as the TASP liaison officer for the college. Next, I was asked to chair the nine-member Ad Hoc Committee on the TASP, a committee that is still in place. Other members include the dean of occupational education, the registrar and director of admissions, the director of counseling and new student relations, the dean of the Kilgore College Longview Center, the director of the computer center, the director of the Communications Division, the director of the Engineering and Sciences Division, and the director of the Social Sciences Division. The latter three directors are responsible for developmental courses in reading, writing, mathematics, and human development. The charge to the committee was "to make recommendations regarding policies and procedures that might be adopted to implement TASP" at Kilgore College. Some of these recommendations are presented to the academic council while others are implemented directly through the organizational structure of the college. We have made many recommendations concerning the college's compliance with HB 2182 requirements for testing, academic advisement, course placement, remediation, evaluation, and reporting.

Faculty Participation in the Development of the TASP Test

Prior to the appointment of the Ad Hoc Committee on TASP, the names of fifteen Kilgore College faculty members were forwarded to the Texas Higher Education Coordinating Board and the Texas Education Agency. These faculty were nominated to serve on TASP committees set up to establish the content of the TASP Test, to provide feedback about the content of the test through regional review panels, and to review the test for potential bias.

During the fall of 1988, thirteen of these faculty participated in a survey on campus to collect data on the skills that community college faculty consider important for effective performance by first-time entering freshmen in undergraduate certificate or degree programs.

Six of these fifteen faculty members served on a Content Advisory Committee to help validate the TASP Test. They were to see that the test does, in fact, measure the basic skills necessary for success in college-level courses.

In addition, seven of these fifteen faculty also served on the Standard-Setting Panel on January 3, 1989, in Dallas. Although the participants were on holiday vacations at the time, they gladly agreed to serve. They helped review the TASP Test and advised the Texas Higher Education Coordinating Board about the standards for each section of the test.

Educating the College Community

Although fifteen Kilgore College faculty members had been nominated for significant involvement in the development of the TASP Test, we invited Joan M. Matthews, the Coordinating Board's director for the TASP, to provide TASP orientation for all professional employees at Kilgore College. She gave the opening-day professional development address and workshop on August 22, 1988. The administration believed it was important for everyone to learn as much as possible about the program. Knowledge about the TASP would help implement and adopt it. We would internalize the TASP and use it as a guiding principle of educational philosophy and practice. Dr. Matthews discussed the need for and the goals of the TASP and emphasized benefits of the TASP to teaching.

After Dr. Matthews' visit, members of all the instructional divisions and departments met and made recommendations about the possibility of disallowing college-level courses for students who needed to improve reading and writing skills. The recommendations were considered by the Ad Hoc Committee on TASP, which decided to continue allowing counselors and faculty members to use professional judgment in helping students select appropriate college-level courses.

As another result of Dr. Matthews' visit, the director of counseling and new student relations suggested Kilgore College as a TASP Test Center. The college was approved as a center and received registration bulletins and other TASP information for distribution to faculty, staff, and students. Thus the TASP became known to all on campus.

Kilgore College Students Help Develop the TASP Test

At 6 A.M. a rainy October 18, 1988, I bussed twenty-one freshmen twenty-five miles west to the campus of athletic arch rival Tyler Junior College to take the TASP field test. The students were chosen with the help of a table of random numbers found in a psychological statistics textbook. The students were given two orientation sessions to help them understand the importance of their participation and to help them take the matter seriously. The students originally asked "Why me?" But soon they realized their "luck" and dubbed themselves "the lucky triple seven."

Educating the College Service Area

Anyone who had at least three semester credit hours of college-level work before fall 1989, was exempt from the TASP requirements (the "grandfather clause"). Getting grandfathered from TASP seemed almost as important to high school seniors in the Kilgore College service area as getting admitted to a college with a scholarship. The Ad Hoc Committee on TASP attempted to "grandfather" as many students as possible. The response was high, with 161 high school seniors from twenty-three area high schools enrolling in fifty-two different courses at Kilgore College during the spring semester of 1989. During the two summer semesters, 322 high school seniors-to-be from twenty-four area high schools enrolled in thirty-seven different courses. The Ad Hoc Committee on TASP attributed this significant response to several things they had done to educate as many students as possible about the mandates of the TASP. These steps were as follows:

1. An on-campus TASP briefing for more than forty superintendents and assistant superintendents was conducted in December 1988. They gave these school officials a nineteen-point fact sheet on TASP.

2. They developed and distributed 6,680 copies of a TASP brochure to all juniors and seniors in thirty area high schools in December 1988, and met individually with the school principals and counselors.

3. High school assemblies for hundreds of seniors were conducted from October 1988 to March 1989.

4. There were scores of programs on TASP to area service and civic clubs during the spring of 1989.

5. A TASP statement was published including information on how to get "grandfathered," in the *Kilgore College Catalog, 1989-90*.[1] The catalog was mailed to area high school seniors in the spring of 1989.

6. TASP information was included in college class schedules during the spring and summer of 1989.

7. During the spring of 1989 regional meetings were conducted with area high school teachers, who were provided information about TASP requirements in reading and writing skills.

8. A workshop on TASP was held in February 1989 for area high school and college counselors.

9. There were several radio, television, and newspaper interviews about TASP during the 1988-1989 academic year.

10. The college developed and printed a TASP information brochure that was included in all college mailouts from the Admissions Office to prospective students.[2]

The Committee Makes Waves

The Ad Hoc Committee on TASP was extensively involved in educating the college community and service area about the various aspects of TASP. During the 1988-1989 academic year, it also developed several recommendations that significantly changed developmental education at Kilgore College. Four of its recommendations were made in an effort to ensure that all Kilgore College students were prepared to pass the reading and writing sections of the TASP Test. Some proved to be controversial and difficult to implement, notably recommendations to:

1. Develop a third developmental reading course for students who read between 10.0 and 12.9 reading grade levels.

2. Raise the ACT English subtest cutoff score from 12 to 14 for placement in college-level English.

3. Develop a third developmental English course immediately below the first college-level English course for students affected by the above recommendation.

4. Require students enrolled in the first college-level English course to pass an exit examination--the writing section of the Pre-TASP Test.

These recommendations were suggested by the reading and English faculty at the urging of an English instructor who had served as an essay grader for the writing section of the TASP Test. She was impressed with the requirement that students must be able to write a multiparagraph essay on a whole message to a specific audience for a particular purpose. She educated her colleagues and the committee members about the reading and writing performance standards of the test.

Even though the recommendations were unanimously passed for implementation, resistance by students and others in the college community began to develop during the fall semester of 1989. They were especially concerned about the requirement that students pass an exit writing examination.

Because of the diverse nature of the Kilgore College student body, it was nearly impossible to find a single time period when all students could reasonably take the examination and write about one topic. Eventually, the requirement was abandoned when forty-eight students failed the test. Of those, forty-four would otherwise have passed the course based on their performance in the other course requirements. Obviously, some of these students made their situation known to almost anyone who would listen. Thus, the college would have to determine if students could master the writing objectives established for the course through various means. Also, we would have to determine if students could write an effective multiparagraph essay without basing course grades solely on one example of writing. The other three recommendations fared better and are still standing.

New recommendations, to take effect during the 1989-1990 academic year, were also approved. The college would:

1. begin teaching human development courses in study skills and thinking and reasoning skills;

2. staff the mathematics laboratory with a full-time mathematics paraprofessional;

3. staff the mathematics laboratory with tutors, which require adding $5,000 to the mathematics budget to pay for qualified tutors; and,

4. purchase computers and software for the mathematics laboratory.

The human development courses were recommended for students who needed two or more developmental courses, such as reading and English. We recommended that the mathematics paraprofessional assist the instructors of self-paced developmental mathematics courses and the students who were expected to "drop in" the laboratory for help. An eight-week, one-credit-hour developmental mathematics course and individualized assignments for specific students were developed for both these students and those with near borderline, failing scores. Three-credit-hour developmental courses in prealgebra and beginning algebra and an eight-week, one-credit-hour developmental English course were also developed.

In the summer of 1990, the reading and writing laboratory, then housed in the library, was moved into a larger and better-organized space at a new facility.

Others Help Implement the TASP

In fall 1989, a new committee of administrators was appointed to make recommendations for improving admissions and registration. This committee recommended that the college establish an Office of Testing and Developmental Counseling and that the computer be used to monitor and track students on TASP as well as developmental course requirements. A coordinator of testing was named, effective June 1, 1990, and testing facilities were prepared to open that summer.

The committee also recommended that the TASP Test and

the Pre-TASP Test be included with the ACT and SAT as acceptable diagnostic tests for admission and course placement. Several members of the Ad Hoc Committee on TASP developed correlations among the four tests so students could submit TASP scores as well as ACT or SAT scores for admission and placement. Low-scoring students or those who do not submit scores from one of these three tests must take the Pre-TASP Test for placement.

The committee also recommended that all testing and placement occur prior to registration and the beginning of classes. Effective in the summer of 1990, this new policy ended possible schedule changes and various disruptions for most students. Consequently, the Nelson-Denny Reading Test, the Descriptive Test of Mathematical Skills of the College Board, and the Kilgore College English Diagnostic Test are no longer used at the college for course placement except as challenge examinations for the ACT, SAT, TASP Test, or Pre-TASP Test.

Preliminary Results of the TASP

The TASP Test was administered five times during 1989. Performance for the students enrolled in Texas community colleges and technical institutions revealed that 56.1 percent of the students passed every section of the test they attempted. According to the Texas Higher Education Coordinating Board, 333 of the 1,436 students who entered Kilgore College for the first time in 1989 took the test. Of these students, 85.6 percent passed the reading section, 73.6 percent passed the mathematics section, and 73.3 percent passed the writing section.[3] It is important to note that the 333 students represent only 23.2 percent of the 1,436 first-time enrolling students. Nevertheless, these passing percentages are significant when compared to the statewide average passing percentage.

In 1989, Kilgore College joined the North Texas Community/Junior College Consortium. The fifteen-college group was established in cooperation with the University of North Texas as an interinstitutional, two-year-college consortium devoted to improving undergraduate education through a variety of research and staff development projects.

The consortium's first research project is to determine the effectiveness of the developmental education programs at consortium member colleges by studying retention and successful performance in courses where developmental skills are required. Very preliminary findings of the research project reveal that Kilgore College does relatively well in relation to member colleges of the consortium.

Kilgore College has changed considerably since it became involved in developmental education as a result of the TASP. We believe these changes will benefit all concerned in the years ahead.

NOTES

1. *Kilgore College Catalog, 1989-1990*, Kilgore, TX, 1990.

2. Texas Academic Skills Program, Kilgore College. *You, TASP, and College.* Kilgore, TX, 1989.

3. Texas Higher Education Coordinating Board. *Texas Academic Skills Program Summary Test Results, 1989*, Austin, TX, 1989.

11
Implementation in Universities
Richard C. Meyer, Robert D. Gratz, and
H. Paul Kelley

Three types of universities were chosen to illustrate the different ways that policy and practice were put into place. The University of Texas at Austin is a highly selective research institution with a strong set of doctoral programs. Southwest Texas State University is moderately selective, at one time graduating more teacher education candidates than any other university or college in the nation. Texas A&I University is located in a rural county and has a high Hispanic student population. Problems regarding the Texas Academic Skills Program and priorities for these institutions required customized solutions for each setting.

Implementation of the Texas Academic Skills Program (TASP) at four-year schools presented a plethora of problems. Although there were many common problems that faced all universities in implementing TASP, each institution had its own unique problems as well. School size was one of the key variables that greatly influenced implementation at different institutions. This chapter will give readers a glimpse at TASP implementation at three universities.

The specific schools span the gamut of institutional size from the largest, most selective public institution in the state to a midsized, rapidly growing school, and to a small school serving predominantly minority students. Each institution was faced with implementing the same state-mandated program, but it is interesting to note how each school emphasized different aspects of the program and went about the business of implementation in very different ways.

This information could be useful to those who must put a

large mandated program into practice and for those who are contemplating or involved in planning for similar programs. A simple examination of the things that must be considered in the planning stages and learning how different institutions organized or reorganized for the program are eye openers in themselves. Here the three representative schools speak for themselves about the effort they made to put a one-page statute into practice.

RICHARD C. MEYER: TEXAS A&I UNIVERSITY

Texas A&I University is one of seven senior-level institutions on the mainland United States with a Hispanic student enrollment of 50 percent or more. It is the only such institution in the country offering degrees in both engineering and agriculture. In addition, the university offers a doctoral-level program in education and advanced-level programs through its College of Arts and Sciences and its College of Business Administration. These programs and others complete the picture of a comprehensive university responsive to the educational needs of the South Texas region and continuously evolving to respond effectively to emerging needs.

Coupled with its mission as a comprehensive regional university is a mandate from the Texas A&M University System to focus on minority education, particularly in the areas of science, mathematics, and engineering.

Texas A&I University's enrollment reflects the South Texas population. Hispanic students make up about 57 percent of the student body, blacks are 4 percent, and Anglos and others constitute 39 percent. Students from all fifty states and twenty-two countries attend Texas A&I University, but 75 percent of the enrollment is from South Texas. The university is located in Kingsville, thirty-five miles southwest of Corpus Christi.

The university enrolls approximately 5,800 students and has a full-time-equivalent faculty of 230. It is organized into seven colleges: Arts and Sciences, Agriculture and Home Economics, Education, Business Administration, Engineering, College I, and

Graduate Studies. It has the usual array of student services and support units. The faculty are participants in the administration of the university through a well-defined and functioning faculty senate. The faculty is generally tenured in the upper professional ranks and enjoys close personal relationships with its students. Academic programs are varied and diverse and offer traditional as well as nontraditional academic programs.

Approximately 1,200 freshmen enter the university each year. Many transfer students are admitted from area community colleges. Nontraditional-age students also are present on the campus. The average student age is twenty-five years old.

The advent of the TASP coincided with major strategic planning efforts at the university. Part of the strategic plan called for the university to develop strategies to improve its retention efforts, create a more proactive enrollment management program, and reorganize other student services into more effective units. As the requirements of the legislation creating TASP became clearer, it became evident that the university had an opportunity to do something significant--something it knew it should have been doing all along given the nature and preparedness of its student body.

In many ways TASP encouraged the university to design a program that would truly address the needs of students and provide the kinds of services it had never funded previously. Priority for funding advisement and remediation was always low in annual budget considerations. Opportunity seemed to be knocking as administrators and faculty contemplated ways of implementing plans for the TASP.

With the recommendations of its strategic plan and TASP legislative requirements, the university thought it wise to address all the issues within a single plan. From related discussions and planning sessions came the College I concept, which brings together activities for the TASP, counseling, advisement, remediation, and the learning lab.

In addition, a TASP task force had been previously appointed to study TASP issues and make recommendations. This task force contained faculty, high school principals, townspeople, and administrators. They did much of their work prior to beginning discussions of College I. They helped communicate to secondary schools and the general public the issues contained in TASP legislation.

College I was developed as the seventh academic college and the first new college to be created since 1947 at Texas A&I University. The major goals of the *1988 Strategic Planning Report* called for new efforts and commitments to improve student achievement, retention, depth and quality of instruction, and services. College I is an outcome of this renewed commitment to a long-standing tradition of attracting, retaining, and graduating well-prepared students from Texas A&I University.

College I provides a home for all new freshmen students and will incorporate the major educational activities of the critical first year of enrollment. College I is student-centered and organized to improve academic achievement and performance of first-year students. Its mission is to provide high-quality programs and academic services to assist students in being successful at the university. College I attempts to do what is necessary to improve academic performance and success. It models a philosophy of providing excellent service to students and academic departments in the six degree-granting colleges.

To carry out its mission, the following divisions are included in College I:

Marketing-Recruiting-Admissions concentrates on the recruitment and admission of qualified new students. A direct link with the overall university marketing effort provides an added impetus to the recruiting effort. The recruitment and admission of students builds on the first-year experience program within College I.

Testing and Orientation administers a wide variety of state and national tests, including the TASP Test. Orientation is organized to build on current strengths and to link with academic advisement, course planning and placement, academic departments, and student services.

Academic Advisement provides an extensive advisement

process for all first-year students. Academic advisors utilize TASP Test results to assist with course planning decisions. The advisement process includes planning and review meetings with students throughout the freshman year. This division provides the basis for the university-wide advisement program.

Developmental Studies and Learning Skills provides workshops and precollegiate instruction in reading, writing, mathematics, and algebra. The Developmental Studies Program is designed to prepare students for successful entry into their regular college-level academic classes. The Learning Skills Center provides a comprehensive academic skills lab with computer-assisted instruction, supplementary instruction, tutoring, and mentoring. Assistance is provided in many areas, with particular emphasis placed on the TASP competency areas of reading, writing, mathematics, and algebra.

Counseling provides services and programs related to career, personal, and life development with an emphasis on career counseling. Workshops are offered on topics and directly related issues relevant to the career, personal, and professional development of students. This division also plays a major role in developing and teaching a student-success course required of all first-year students.

Cooperative Education and Placement focuses its efforts on career planning, placement, and cooperative education. A commitment to cooperative education and applied work experience is administered in this department with strong links to the academic departments.

Student Data Management is administered to provide for the tracking, evaluating, and reporting requirements of the TASP. In addition, Student Data Management provides leadership to College I by evaluating and validating student outcomes and program results and by conducting institutional research relevant to retention and academic achievement.

In addition, continuing university efforts with General Studies and Pre-Professional Studies are coordinated in this college. International Programs are also administered in College I and provide an added impetus to foreign study and international offerings at the university. This office provides the services and expertise to work with international students, as well as assistance in developing student-faculty exchange and semesters-abroad programs.

As word of this new proposed college spread rapidly across the campus, the usual uproar followed. Departments feared budget cuts and losing control of advising, curricula, and the hiring of faculty. Reassurances went out daily, frequent small and large meetings were held, but rumors and misinformation flowed. "We do not need any of those slimy developmental types around here," one English professor was alleged to have commented about needed faculty for College I. Fortunately, it was not a typical reaction. Faculty who had previously participated in national conferences on advising freshmen and who had years of experience in counseling became strong supporters of the College I concept and helped as the faculty were brought into detailed planning for each of College I's components. Nevertheless, there was great evidence of a need to proceed slowly and carefully with planning. Campus politics sometimes helped in the distribution of facts and correct information. At other times it seemed as though too much time had to be spent on the planning process instead of on the plan itself.

Six committees, involving more than seventy-five faculty and staff, spent several months developing plans, curriculum, and staffing needs for College I. Without their dedicated work, the university would not have been able to implement its new college. Faculty on the committees became stronger advocates for the college and have become faculty in the college since it began in the fall of 1989.

As College I began, a former TASP task force was converted to an advisory committee for it. The committee's role in representing its various constituencies remains important. For instance, many Hispanic community members of the task force at first thought that TASP was an organized way to keep Hispanic students out of college. As they worked with the task force and learned about statewide efforts to remove all bias from the test and to ensure that scores would not be a part of any admissions decision, they began to concentrate on other things. Soon they wanted to ensure that developmental courses, advising, counseling, and learning labs were indeed planned and operated for those needing help. They continue to be interested in the numbers of minorities and Anglos needing help and to study statewide passing scores for all groups of students. This remains a political issue for the TASP on this campus, but openness of records and involvement in planning and evaluating have quieted many fears.

The former Board of Directors of the University System of South Texas, of which Texas A&I University was part, contained a majority membership of Hispanics. The university assured the board that minorities would be employed within College I for administrative, teaching, and staff positions. We are proud that Hispanic, black, and female role models for freshmen students teach or otherwise work within College I.

Several faculty and staff had served on Coordinating Board statewide advisory committees for the TASP. Their experiences were extremely helpful in planning for the campus. Throughout the statewide and campus planning efforts, communication became the key to success. The very detailed and careful planning for the TASP at the state level involved many of Texas A&I's faculty and staff. Their involvement gave greater credibility to what was being planned on the campus. The campus TASP liaison took great care to keep informed on each and every issue happening at the state level.

Coinciding with campus planning efforts were the necessary Board of Regents and state Coordinating Board approval for College I. The university assured its Board of Directors of its intentions concerning the employment of Hispanics. Coordinating Board staff indicated that Texas A&I had proposed a very comprehensive plan for implementing TASP requirements. Even legislators heard of the plans and sent letters of praise and encouragement. Newspapers were most interested in

TASP, and several, by feature articles and editorials, helped readers better understand TASP within the College I context. We, too, saw the whole TASP issue as an opportunity and not as a punitive or negative law we had to tolerate. This positive attitude was important for us during planning, and it remains a basic philosophy of College I today. As a result, the institution was viewed as addressing freshman concerns, remediation, advising, and counseling in positive ways.

Faculty committees recommended that the university require all freshmen to take a success course, in addition to developmental courses (less than college-level) in reading, writing, mathematics, and algebra. This course is where the university advisement system starts. Teachers use the text *Becoming a Master Student* and meet with each of their students three times a semester for personal and academic advising away from the classroom. They also assist the students as they register for future enrollment periods.

Space needs arose but were quickly addressed when an unused dormitory in the center of the campus was designated for College I needs. The building had minimum renovation. A separate building also gives the college a visual presence. Students now talk about "going over to College I."

Equipment was borrowed and loaned, and the university committed funds for the purchase of other equipment for the Learning Center. It became apparent that students learn independently with appropriate technology and that learning centers improve the skills of students. The Learning Center is open to any student--not only freshmen--on the campus. Having sophomores, juniors and seniors roll in and out of the Learning Center lab, the counseling offices, and the Cooperative Education and Career Placement office assures freshmen they are a part of a larger, diverse group. Many of these same upperclassmen and women enjoy taking on peer-tutoring or counseling roles.

Staffing College I turned out to be a politically sensitive issue. The head of the Counseling Center was named acting dean. Other existing directors (placement, testing, admissions) were realigned or reorganized into the College I structure. A search was begun for a director of developmental studies. A recent faculty hire in English happened to have had extensive experience in establishing and directing developmental or remedial programs on other campuses. He did a superb job for College I until he left. It is alleged that his former English faculty colleagues became concerned about his move to College I and some distrust set in. That concern may have motivated the person's decision to leave the university, because he needed complete cooperation from his former teaching colleagues to plan and implement the developmental courses for College I. Previously, six College I English faculty taught a remedial writing course and the mathematics faculty taught one remedial math course. In the planning efforts for College I, it became apparent that these two faculties would not be teaching the courses directly or have administrative control over College I. Fortunately, some of the faculty teach some of the developmental courses establishing an essential link.

The English and mathematics professors in the College of Arts and Sciences developed the curriculum for the developmental courses and recommended teachers to the dean of College I. The academic departments are assured they have a voice in the curriculum and in selecting faculty to teach "their" courses in College I. Many graduate students are instructors for developmental courses which allowed the departments to recruit and offer them teaching assistantships.

College I is under close scrutiny. Some have concerns about its costs, but others asked how we could do without it when retention figures began to flow. Without the TASP legislation there would not have been a College I, and without College I the university would not be able to provide better-prepared sophomores to our faculty. Only time and more data will tell how this relates to longitudinal retention efforts and success rates for our students.

ROBERT D. GRATZ: SOUTHWEST TEXAS STATE UNIVERSITY

Southwest Texas State University (SWT) is the largest of the four schools that comprise the Texas State University System. Southwest Texas State University's fall 1989 enrollment of 20,770 included 18,168 undergraduates, 3,071 of whom were beginning freshmen. The ethnic distribution of the student body was 80 percent anglo, 13.5 percent Hispanic, 4.5 percent black, less than 1 percent oriental, less than 1 percent native American and 1 percent international. The undergraduate population makeup included 48 percent men and 52 percent women.

Southwest Texas State University is organized into seven undergraduate schools, a graduate school, and a College of General Studies. The College of General Studies serves as an academic home for students who have not selected an academic major, a category that includes more than 30 percent of entering freshmen. It also coordinates SWT's General Studies Curriculum. The university offers more than 130 undergraduate programs and more than forty master's programs in a wide variety of disciplines. In the fall of 1989, the average SAT verbal plus mathematical score was 863 for first-time freshmen. A total of 34 percent of the first-time freshmen ranked in the top quarter of their class, and an additional 43 percent were in the second quarter. Admission requirements have increased several times in the last few years. The latest increase affected freshmen entering in fall 1990, and another will affect fall 1992 freshmen. In 1992, a specified high school curriculum will also be *required* rather than merely *suggested*. A summary of these admission standards appears in Table 11.1.

Table 11.1
Admission Requirements at SWT: Fall 1989 to Fall 1992

High School Quartile	Fall 1989		Fall 1990		Fall 1991	
	SAT	ACT	SAT	ACT	SAT	ACT
Top 10%	no minimum		no minimum		no minimum	
1st	no minimum		no minimum		800	20
2nd	750	17	800	20	900	22

Table 11.1 Cont'd

Admission Requirements at SWT: Fall 1989 to Fall 1992

			Fall 1989		Fall 1990		Fall 1991
High School Quartile	SAT	ACT	SAT	ACT	SAT	ACT
3rd	800	19	900	22	1,000	24
4th	900	21	1,100	26	1,100	26

Early Involvement of SWT with TASP

Southwest Texas State University's involvement with the TASP began well before the state legislation that created it. The blue-ribbon committee that studied the need for a state-mandated testing program was chaired by Robert L. Hardesty, then president of SWT, and several staff members at SWT provided support to the committee in its work. The work of the committee was the subject of frequent discussions on campus during its deliberations. The role of basic skills testing in undergraduate preparation had also been widely discussed at SWT during an earlier major review of the core curriculum.

Following a comprehensive curriculum review, SWT's new general studies core curriculum was implemented in 1986. This 52-54 credit hour core curriculum includes twelve hours of course work in essential skill areas, 36-38 hours of coursework in selected disciplinary perspectives, and four hours of integrative courses. Nine hours of coursework in English are a part of the core. The curriculum also requires eighteen additional hours in writing-intensive courses and demonstration of competency in basic skills areas through earning a passing score on the rising junior General Studies Examination in Writing and the General Studies Examination in Mathematics. Both examinations are based on college-level skills. With them, the SWT campus had accepted testing as an appropriate means of demonstrating competence in basic skill areas as TASP implementation began.

One of the earliest local questions about TASP implementation was deciding if SWT should conduct its own remediation activities or contract with an outside agency, such as an area community college, for this job. This question was considered by the Council of Academic Deans and the Executive Council (president's cabinet). In early October 1987, the Executive Council concluded that remediation was an institutional responsibility that would be met internally.

One week later, the Vice Presidents' Council endorsed a recommendation from the vice president for academic affairs to appoint a HB 2182 steering committee. This ad hoc committee monitored the progress of the same committees developing the TASP Test and other program elements and began preparations for implementing TASP at SWT. The committee included representatives from the English, Mathematics, Curriculum and Instruction (reading program) departments, the Student Learning Assistance Center (SLAC), the College of General Studies, a Special Services grant program, Computing Services, the Testing Center, the Office of Institutional Research and Planning, and Continuing Education. In February 1988, Dr. Joan Matthews of the Texas Higher Education Coordinating Board visited the SWT campus to discuss TASP developments with the committee. The committee followed this visit with a survey of SWT's existing academic support services.

Preparing for TASP Implementation

During the next few months several faculty members and administrators took part in TASP Test development and implementation processes, participating in the Academic Skills Development Committee, the Content Advisory Committee, the Tests and Measurements Committee, the Bias Review Committee, the Special Committee of Academic Officers, and other groups. I was asked to join the Special Committee of Academic Officers several times before the end of 1988 to participate in discussions of emerging TASP policy issues and initiated discussions of those issues on the SWT campus. Inquiries about

TASP were answered, and information was shared with individuals whose activities would be directly affected by TASP. Texas Academic Skills Program survey forms were distributed to faculty members and students. Formal reports about TASP were made to the Executive Council, the Council of Academic Deans, and the Instructional Council (department chairs). Campus representatives attended statewide conferences, and many comments and suggestions were submitted in response to Coordinating Board requests.

In late July 1988, the vice president for academic affairs distributed a list of questions from an Austin TASP conference to the Executive Council, the Council of Academic Deans, and the Instructional Council. As a member of the Special Committee of Academic Officers, I had participated in the panel at that conference. In August, the vice president for academic affairs asked chairs of the departments that would offer remedial instruction to revise earlier estimates of the number of fall 1989 remedial sections needed. He also asked deans to discuss emerging TASP issues with chairs in their school councils. The potential impact of remedial courses on financial aid eligibility was reviewed. In early October, a team from SWT participated in the TASP Administrators' Conference in San Antonio.

When SWT was requested to be a TASP Test Center, the director of SWT's Testing Center reviewed internal capabilities and developed a recommendation. Test administration requirements limited the number of spaces that could be provided. The university could offer only 600 of the 989 requested spaces. Even this number required a financial outlay for SWT because sound-baffling materials to reduce noise had to be installed in two gyms and portable chairs had to be purchased to make suitable testing facilities.

APPOINTMENT OF AN ACTING DIRECTOR OF REMEDIATION SERVICES

Following discussions at the Council of Academic Deans in August of 1988, the vice president for academic affairs recommended to the Vice Presidents' Council and the Executive Council the creation of a director of remediation services position. The deans recommended a position that would report to the dean of general studies, but others supported a more visible position within the office of the vice president for academic affairs. The vice president recommended that the new director report to him through the dean of the university.

The estimated annual cost for a half-time director plus operating expenses, including secretarial support, was nearly $70,000. This recommendation was approved by the Executive Council for implementation in January 1989, even though state appropriations to support the office did not begin until Fall 1989.

The search committee included representatives of departments that would offer remedial courses (English, Mathematics, and Curriculum and Instruction's reading program), the Admissions Office, the University Testing Center, and the Office of Student Financial Aid. After October's search for a good candidate within the university, the vice president named a member of the mathematics faculty and a former acting chair of the Mathematics Department to be acting director of remediation services. The director's office was established as a unit in the Office of the Vice President for Academic Affairs.

Clarification of Major TASP Issues

At a March 2, 1989, meeting, the dean of the university and the director of remediation services reviewed questions on TASP implementation to clarify pending major issues that needed resolution and to identify the appropriate individuals or groups responsible for each issue. That same day several faculty members and administrators met with Representative Eddie Cavazos of Corpus Christi. Representative Cavazos had previously asked how SWT was addressing the new TASP requirements, and he had been invited to visit the campus. He was given an analysis of institutional issues under current review as a result of TASP requirements. The analysis identified four curriculum and instructional program issues, four support services issues, and one budgetary issue as follows:

I. Ramifications of Changes Related to the TASP Test on Remediation at SWT

   A. Curriculum and Instructional Program
      1. Introduction and development of placement practices for two new remedial courses.

      2. Possible modification of placement practices for two current remedial courses.

      3. Identification of new staffing needs in English, mathematics, and reading.

      4. Identification of the role SWT's new master's degree in developmental education can play in remediation efforts.

   B. Support Services

      1. Establishment of a structure for coordination of remedial programs.

      2. Review of current special laboratories and tutoring services.

      3. Review of SWT's academic advising programs.

      4. Creation of computer programs and reports required by the TASP.

   C. Budget

      1. Provision of necessary support in the fiscal year 1990 budget to meet TASP requirements.

Creation of the TASP Advisory Council

Before the end of January 1988, the director of remediation services recommended to the dean of the university that an advisory council be established to review emerging TASP issues and to develop related policies. During the next few weeks the role of this council was clarified and potential membership was discussed. The TASP Advisory Council was appointed by the vice president for academic affairs on March 22, 1989, to provide a forum for discussion of issues related to TASP implementation, to provide a formal link for the departments and programs most directly involved in delivery of services related to TASP, and to provide advice to the director of remediation services. Council members included the director of minority student affairs, the assistant dean of general studies, the director of the student learning assistance center, one representative each from the departments of English, Mathematics, Curriculum and Instruction (reading program), Developmental Education, administrative data processing, the faculty senate, and associated student government. The council was chaired by the director of remediation services.

Over the next several months, the TASP Advisory Council met at least monthly to discuss policies and procedures related to TASP implementation. This was a very active time for the council. Many issues had to be resolved before freshman orientation began in early July. Others had to be completed before the fall semester began. The director of remediation services surveyed departments, asking them to identify courses that should be unavailable to students until part or all of the TASP Test was passed. The council reviewed this information but took no formal action. To facilitate academic advising, the council recommended the inclusion of TASP information on internal advising transcripts.

In early June, the TASP Advisory Council approved an advising plan. That plan proposed that TASP Test results (if available) and local placement methods should be used to determine whether students should pursue remediation. Data gathered over several years suggested that higher standards than those required for passing the TASP Test were necessary for student success in the first collegiate-level courses in mathematics and English at SWT. Therefore, performance on the TASP Test was regarded as only one of the relevant criteria to be considered for entry into these college-level courses.

Under this procedure, some students who pass the English or mathematics sections of the TASP Test must still begin their work in a remedial course. In addition to passing the TASP Test or having no recorded TASP Test score, a student must have an ACT English score of fifteen or higher or an SAT verbal score of 376 or higher to enroll in the first collegiate-level English course. In addition to passing the TASP Test or having no recorded TASP Test score, to enroll in the first collegiate-level mathematics course a student must have an ACT mathematics score of twenty-one or higher, an SAT mathematics score of 435 or higher, a local Mathematics Placement Test score of twenty-six or higher, or previously earned credit in Mathematics 1311 (the second-level remedial course). In cases where a student failed more than one part of the TASP Test, this plan call for required remediation in one area with recommended remediation in all areas each semester. This plan also recommended that SWT apply the nine-hour rule limit for its entering freshmen, thereby requiring that a TASP score be on file after no more than nine hours of college-level work has been completed. These proposals were subsequently approved and implemented.

In late July, the director of SWT's Student Learning Assistance Center (SLAC) sent a proposal for TASP noncourse remediation to members of the TASP Advisory Council. This proposal complemented an earlier recommendation from the council, which said that the primary mode of remediation at SWT should be course-based. The proposal also suggested that in special cases where a student fails the TASP Test, but has exceptionally high scores on the ACT, SAT, or the local mathematics placement test, noncourse remediation would be available through an individual contract with SLAC. These contracts would require two to three hours of work per week per semester.

This alternative was deemed appropriate for only a very small number of students per semester. It was to be based on individual referral by the director of remediation services, the chair of one of the departments offering remedial courses, or the dean of general studies. The center also agreed to perform additional diagnostic testing and appropriate tracking for these students. It began the development of a microcomputer-based tracking system for students in noncourse remediation.

During its first few months of operation, the council also discussed the impact of noncourse remediation on financial aid recipients and on student athletes. Other issues that were considered included institution-wide, computer-based tracking systems for TASP and a variety of academic advising issues. Many issues related to remedial courses were also under review.

Development of Remedial Courses

Even before the TASP requirements, SWT offered a sizeable remedial program in two courses. Many students were seriously underprepared in mathematics, and a lesser number were underprepared in English. In the 1988 fall semester, 1,915 students enrolled in the remedial mathematics course and 480 enrolled in the remedial English course. Many faculty had been concerned about the relatively low success rate of students in the mathematics course, and evidence suggested that the mathematical deficiencies of many students were far too great to be overcome in a single course.

When the Texas Higher Education Coordinating Board authorized an additional remedial course in mathematics and a new remedial course in reading, SWT moved quickly to obtain necessary approvals for these courses. The dean of the School of Education submitted a plan for remedial reading work to the vice president for academic affairs in late spring 1988. A new remedial course in reading was approved by the Texas State University System Board of Regents in February 1989. It was followed with approval of remedial course in mathematics in May. The mathematics curriculum development process included a review of the existing course and the creation of a new course using a modular approach. Department faculty also developed a program that included audio and video material, electronic tutoring, and electronic testing to supplement both courses. The revised program, with all four remedial courses, was offered for the first time in the fall semester of 1989. All the courses showed a decrease in enrollment from the fall 1989 to the spring 1990 semester, except for the reading course which increased by almost 10 percent. The four courses and their corresponding enrollment figures are shown in Table 11.2.

Table 11.2
1989-1990 Remedial Course Enrollments

	Fall 1989	Spring 1990
English 1300	533	160
Mathematics 1300	262	243
Mathematics 1311	1,705	961
Reading 1300	9	40

When the number of remedial courses was increased from two to four, their impact on calculations of grade point averages was reviewed. Previously, the two remedial courses were graded on the same A-B-C-D-F scale used in other courses. They had been included in grade-point-average calculations. During the summer of 1989, the Council of Academic Deans debated the impact of more remedial grades on academic standing. The council recommended continuing the grading of remedial courses in the same way as other courses, but it also recommended dropping these grades from future grade-point-average computations. But since this request would have required significant new programming during a computer migration period, an alternative plan was devised. All four remedial courses are now graded on a three-grade scale:

F (Failure) --- for students who have made little or no

progress typically with a numerical average of about fifty or below (a punitive grade that is included in GPA calculations) in the course.

P (Progress) ---   for students who have made progress (a nonpunitive grade that is excluded from GPA calculations).

Cr (Credit) ---   for students who have completed course-based remediation and are ready to move on to the next course (a nonpunitive grade that is excluded from GPA calculations).

Initial TASP Funding

The Coordinating Board's request to the legislature for TASP funding would have provided nearly $700,000 to SWT for fiscal year 1990. During the spring and summer of 1989, many of those involved in TASP planning expressed their concern about projected costs of the new program. These costs were very difficult to estimate, since many of the details about the level of performance that the test itself would require were still ambiguous. This was particularly true for reading, where little information was available. One internal estimate in spring 1989 suggested that program costs could exceed state funding by nearly a million dollars per year. In this context, most discussions, even those intended to focus on qualitative programmatic issues, included some comments about likely program costs and the probable difficulty of delivering a program of the desired quality within the available budget. During this period additional faculty had to be recruited for remedial courses, including faculty for an entirely new remedial program in reading, despite uncertain funding for the program.

In the summer of 1989, I served on the Coordinating Board Ad Hoc Committee on the Allocation of Remedial Funds. That committee developed recommendations for first-year TASP funding. The legislature had already appropriated $50,000 for each university. This committee was to recommend a system for allocating additional funds that had been appropriated to the Coordinating Board for distribution to junior and senior colleges. The system developed by the committee provided up to $200,000 to senior colleges according to a formula based on anticipated student need. The university submitted the proper information to qualify for the maximum allotment of $200,000. The internal budget for fiscal year 1990 was approved by the president in late August. The budget included support for the director of remediation services' office operations as well as for additional faculty in mathematics, English, and reading. Additionally, a director of the remedial reading unit was hired with other university funds. Therefore, this initial funding was immediately allocated by the university.

First-Year Implementation

Many specific steps were taken during the first year of TASP implementation to tell entering freshmen as much as possible about TASP requirements through these steps:

1. During the six summer freshman orientation sessions, the Office of Remedial Services' desk was placed just before a "final check" station that all students had to pass. As each student passed this table, he or she received a written notice that summarized the TASP Test requirement and provided the fall semester test dates and application deadlines. TASP Test registration bulletins were also distributed. Students were asked to sign up for the September test administration. The same general procedure was used during fall registration for students who did not attend summer freshman orientation.

2. On September 25, 1989, the director of remediation services wrote to 2,400 students required to take the TASP Test and encouraged them to take the September test if they had signed up for it or to register for the November test if they had not.

3. On October 16, 1989, flyers providing general information about the TASP Test requirement and about how to get additional information were posted around the campus.

4. On November 1, 1989, the director of remediation services sent 2,100 letters with information about late-registration procedures via telephone for the November test administration. The consequences for failing to take the test at the appropriate time were also provided.

During the fall semester, other TASP activities were also moving forward. In September, the director of remediation services gave a progress report to the Council of Academic Deans. That same month, the vice president for academic affairs distributed the final report of the TASP Council's Academic Advising and Placement Committee to the Council of Academic Deans. The Council of Academic Deans also had several very lively discussions about the potential cost of providing adequate remediation and about the propriety of including remedial education as a part of the university's mission. These discussions made it very clear that several of the deans remained concerned about growing demands for remediation in a university setting.

According to statistics provided from SWT's database in November of 1989 (prior to the receipt of results of the November test administration), 209 students had failed the TASP Test and were, therefore, required to take remedial work. These students fell into three subgroups: Ninety-six were enrolled in one remedial course, forty-one were enrolled in two remedial courses, and seventy-three students were not enrolled in any remedial courses.

The records of these seventy-three students were reviewed by the director of remediation services. Many had just taken the test during the September administration. However, a few had not been identified at the proper time. These cases were reviewed in detail in an effort to develop screening procedures that would prevent similar problems from recurring. The same report indicated that an additional 1,072 students were subject to TASP requirements but had no TASP Test score on file. Of these 1,072 students, 336 were taking one remedial course, sixty-three were taking two remedial courses, and three were taking three remedial courses.

On November 10, 1989, the commissioner of higher education sent letters to university presidents telling them to allow a one-semester waiver of the enrollment restrictions on students who had failed to take the TASP Test during the fall semester. This suggestion was approved by the director of remediation services and implemented. Before the spring semester began, the Council of Academic Deans expressed concern about a lack of consistent performance levels required for each of the three grades among the three departments teaching remedial courses. The vice president for academic affairs asked for more compatible definitions, and refinement was made by the TASP Advisory Council in consultation with the departments.

The university could not have complied with TASP requirements without significant computer support. This was a particularly difficult effort because SWT was in the midst of a three-year migration of mainframe hardware and software when the TASP requirements became effective. On February 1, 1990, the vice president for academic affairs reported to the director of computing services that no students were in violation of TASP requirements for the spring semester of 1990. He credited this achievement to exceptional computer support. By the end of the spring semester 1990, the director of remediation services reported that SWT had automated support that could

1. provide information about TASP status to academic advisors on an advisement transcript;

2. allow beginning freshmen to register with no TASP prohibition;

3. identify students with one to eight hours of college credit to permit consultation prior to registration;

4. identify students who had failed any portion of the TASP

Test and require that they participate in an appropriate remedial program; and,

5. identify students with nine or more collegiate hours who have not taken the TASP Test, thereby allowing consultation with them prior to registration.

In February 1990, the director of remediation services requested that faculty review TASP implications for student advising during advanced registration. Shortly thereafter the TASP Advisory Council responded to a new state interpretation that students who fail a portion of the TASP Test during a semester need to begin remediation immediately. Departmental representatives presented plans for dealing with students who had failed the February test. The Mathematics Department provided remediation through special work prescribed through the math lab. The Reading Department used individual student contracts to specify goals, provided individual learning packets, and prescribed work in the reading lab. The English Department provided individual counseling and remedial work for writing through the English lab. During the spring semester, the council, the director of remedial services, and the director of admission developed plans for dealing with summer transient students. The council also discussed ways to emphasize the substance of academic advising, suggesting possible training workshops for advisors and other alternatives.

Looking Ahead

We now know that in the first year we greatly overestimated the extent of remedial work that would be needed in reading. With no accurate basis for prediction, we assumed that the best predictor of our student's reading ability would be the deficiencies previously demonstrated in English. We estimated that the need for remedial work in reading might approximate remedial needs in English. However, for the 1,587 entering freshmen from SWT who took the TASP Test during the five 1989 administrations, passing rates on the three sub-sections were as follows: reading, 95.3 percent; mathematics, 90.0 percent; and writing, 88.3 percent. Nearly 80 percent of the students passed all three sections of the test.

The coming year will call for enhancing many elements of SWT's TASP program. The state allocation of funds to support remedial efforts is $521,791. This allocation is based on projected remediation needs for 615 students, the second highest number in the state. These funds will be used to provide additional sections of remedial courses and to expand noncourse remedial activities. During the year we expect to pursue the following specific TASP-related activities:

1. Operating the program under full-load conditions. Roughly twice as many freshmen will be subject to TASP requirements this year as last, and we will closely monitor the effectiveness of our systems under a full load.

2. Devoting further attention to academic advising issues. Existing academic advising systems will be reviewed and alternatives will be evaluated. Special attention will be directed toward changes required by an expected transition to telephone registration in the near future.

3. Promoting the effective use of data presently being gathered for internal and external reforms. We have scheduled a four-day visit by Dr. Charles Pine. His association with the Algebra Project in New Jersey should provide us with ideas about making the most effective curricular improvement and instructional development use of the data we are gathering.

We have begun a major remedial program, and we have invested a great deal of time and money in the effort. Continued funding remains a concern, and the Texas Academic Skills Program provides a very visible target for internal and external critics.

H. PAUL KELLEY: THE UNIVERSITY OF TEXAS AT AUSTIN

The University of Texas at Austin (U.T. Austin) is the largest of the University of Texas System's fourteen component institutions. In fall 1989, it had 50,245 students. Of the 38,118 undergraduates, 6,361 were first-time freshmen. The student body was 73 percent white, 10 percent Hispanic, 6 percent Asian American, 4 percent black, less than 1 percent native American and 7 percent international. The university consists of fourteen individual colleges and schools with more than 270 degree programs and approximately 6,500 courses. It has selective admission requirements and attracts large numbers of academically talented students. In fall 1989, the average SAT verbal plus mathematical score was 1,098, while 86 percent of the first-time freshmen ranked in the top quarter of their high school class. More than half--52 percent--ranked in the top 10 percent of their high school class.

Enactment in late spring 1987 of legislation authorizing TASP and providing limited funds to get the program started produced mixed reactions among U.T. Austin administrators and faculty members. While there was widespread agreement that academic assistance should be made available to all students who are admitted to the institution, many persons also believed that a formal program of remedial instruction should not be a part of this institution's role and scope.

First Stage of Implementation: October 1987-July 1988

The initial implementation stage, which began in October 1987, was characterized by careful compliance with the law and a very cautious, deliberate approach to planning. The first step taken was my appointment to serve as the U.T. Austin TASP liaison representative. I had served on the Committee on Testing that had recommended TASP and was serving at that time on the Texas Academic Skills Council and as chair of its Tests and Measurements Committee. Within U.T. Austin,

Dr. Kelley was serving as director of the Measurement and Evaluation Center (MEC), which is responsible for local TASP administration, and as the elected secretary of the general faculty.

Next, faculty and staff members were nominated to take part in the test development and implementation processes for TASP. Inquiries about TASP were answered, and information was transmitted to persons whose activities would be directly affected by TASP. Survey forms about TASP were distributed to faculty members and students. Formal reports about TASP were made to the University Council (the general faculty's governing body), the Academic Deans Council, department chairs in the College of Natural Sciences, and the Academic Counselors Association. Campus representatives attended two statewide TASP conferences, and everyone concerned submitted comments and suggestions in response to Coordinating Board requests.

As director of the MEC, I negotiated arrangements for U.T. Austin to be a TASP Test Center. Because of the many candidates that were expected, far more classrooms and auditoriums were needed for administering the TASP Test than had ever been needed for even the largest of the national testing programs. By July 1988, there was a growing awareness among U.T. Austin administrators that the TASP planning process had to be accelerated.

Second Stage of Implementation: July 1988-May 1989

Continuation of Earlier Activities. In late July 1988, implementation efforts shifted into second gear. Activities began in the first stage were continued, and new activities were initiated, while TASP publications were distributed to all faculty members. Proposals being considered by various Texas Academic Skills Council committees were circulated on campus for reactions and suggestions. The U.T. Austin Learning Skills Center (LSC) began to consider how its established noncredit reading, mathematics, and writing skills development programs might be adapted to the needs of students preparing for the TASP Test. For the first time, inquiries about TASP were received from officers of the student government organization. Formal reports were made to the Faculty Senate (a subgroup of the University Council) and to the Academic Sub-Deans Council. The Admissions Office began sending information about TASP to high school counselors. In addition, TASP information was published in the 1988-1989 "General Information" part of the U.T. Austin catalog.

Ad Hoc Working Group on TASP. In late July, each institution received from the Coordinating Board a suggested catalog statement about TASP, and in August each one received a worksheet on institutional policy considerations resulting from the implementation of TASP. These documents stimulated discussions among the provost, the vice president for student affairs, and members of their staffs.

In September, the presidents of The University of Texas at Austin and Austin Community College (ACC) agreed that a joint working meeting on TASP would be helpful. The provost appointed the U.T. Austin Ad Hoc Working Group on TASP, consisting of a vice provost (convener), an associate dean of the College of Liberal Arts, an associate dean of the College of Natural Sciences, the director of the MEC (TASP liaison), an Admissions Office senior administrative associate, the director of the Office of Institutional Studies, and the assistant director of the LSC.

In October, the U.T. Austin group began meeting separately and jointly with a corresponding working group from ACC. The first joint meeting concerned possible contractual arrangements between the two institutions for the delivery of remedial services. Both working groups established subgroups to work together on various issues, and those joint subgroups met several times. The discussions bogged down, however, because no one could make an adequate estimate of the number of U.T. Austin students who would need remediation each semester.

Contact at the vice provost level was also established with Texas A&M University, and a meeting of representatives from the two institutions was held to share information about TASP implementation plans.

The U.T. Austin Working Group continued drafting an implementation proposal and discussed a series of drafts of various options, including remedial courses that would be offered (at least initially) by U.T. Austin. In May, the U.T. Austin and ACC presidents and provosts discussed contractual options based on the expectation that U.T. Austin would initially offer its own remedial courses under the auspices of the provost's office. The U.T. Austin Working Group prepared drafts of course descriptions and discussed the possibility of hiring a TASP coordinator early in the summer.

During this period, the U.T. Austin LSC devoted an extensive amount of staff time to adapting its existing diagnostic and instructional resources and to developing new resources related to the three sets of skills measured by the TASP Test. It was generally assumed that, whatever remedial courses evolved at U.T. Austin, the LSC would provide optional noncredit TASP Test preparation just as it does for many other standardized tests taken by U.T. Austin students.

The second stage of implementation extended through the middle of May 1989. By that time, the 71st Texas Legislature had appropriated special funds for colleges and universities to use in 1989-1990 and in 1990-1991 to help defray start-up costs for the new student services required by TASP regulations. In May, the Coordinating Board announced the amount of money each institution would receive for 1989-1990. It is probably not coincidental that the pace of implementation efforts increased very soon thereafter.

Third Stage of Implementation: May 1989-May 1990

Creation of the TASP Office. In mid-May 1989, implementation efforts moved into third gear. A rough draft of the implementation proposal prepared by the Ad Hoc Working Group was in hand. Independently, the LSC staff submitted to the vice president for student affairs a proposed model for

TASP advising and remediation.

Discussion of the LSC proposal with the vice president for student affairs led to the preparation by the director of the LSC, in rough-draft form, of a revised proposal. Under that draft proposal, a TASP office would be established that would report to the provost through the director of the MEC, and the LSC would provide TASP remediation.

After discussions with the provost and the president, the possibility of placing the proposed TASP office under the vice president for student affairs and of appointing an advisory TASP Academic Council was explored. By early August, however, a decision was made to recommend that the TASP office be established as a part of academic affairs rather than student affairs, and the directors of the MEC and the LSC were asked to develop comprehensive recommendations, with budgets, for TASP implementation in 1989-1990. The proposal was submitted on August 10, 1989. As subsequently modified and approved, the essential elements included the following:

1. Responsibility for TASP implementation will be shared by the executive vice president and provost (academic affairs) and the vice president for student affairs, through the directors of the MEC and the LSC, respectively.

2. The MEC director will hire a TASP coordinator and develop and supervise the TASP office, which will be separate from the MEC.

3. The LSC director will develop, within the LSC, additional services to provide developmental/remedial services for students who have failed one or more TASP subtests.

4. The TASP office will disseminate information, coordinate activities of other U.T. Austin agencies involved in TASP, monitor compliance with TASP regulations, evaluate the effectiveness of TASP activities, and prepare program recommendations and budget estimates.

5. Student advising will occur at three levels. Colleges or departments will be responsible for academic course and degree advising. The LSC will be responsible for diagnostic evaluation and advising of students needing developmental/remedial services. The TASP office will be responsible for advising students about their compliance with TASP regulations.

6. Two groups will be appointed to advise the provost and the vice president for student affairs with regard to the development and implementation of the TASP--the TASP Academic Council and the TASP Administrative Council. (The composition and functions of those groups will be described later.)

The proposal also included additional space and budget requirements for the TASP activities of both the TASP office and the LSC in 1989-1990. With only minor modifications of procedures, the proposal was approved on August 16th, and the TASP coordinator was hired immediately.

It was decided that for 1989-1990 the needs of the small number of students who had already taken and not passed the TASP Test could be adequately met by the LSC's noncredit remedial services.

Activities of the TASP Office

The TASP coordinator first developed and coordinated procedures with other agencies to get fall semester TASP students properly identified, advised, and enrolled. Then information-disseminating meetings were held with the Academic Deans Council, the Academic Sub-Deans Council, the Academic Counselors Association, the local chapter of the Texas Association of College Teachers, Office of the Registrar staff members, Men's and Women's Intercollegiate Athletics staff members, and the Institutional Research Council. Written information was sent to students and to campus groups, and news releases were issued. Information was exchanged directly with TASP counterparts at ACC, Texas A&M University, and other institutions.

Appointment of the TASP Administrative Council

As recommended in the TASP office proposal, the vice president for student affairs appointed a TASP Administrative Council to review the plans for, and the effectiveness of, U.T. Austin's administrative procedures used in connection with TASP students, to assist the TASP coordinator and others on campus in implementing those procedures, and to advise the provost, the vice president for student affairs, and the TASP coordinator on suggestedimprovements in those procedures.

The council consists of representatives from the administrative offices most directly involved in providing TASP services: senior administrative associate, Office of Admissions (chair); associate director, MEC; director, LSC; assistant dean of students for orientation; assistant dean of students for minority affairs; database coordinator, Office of the Registrar; director, Office of Institutional Studies; assistant athletic director, men's intercollegiate athletics; and academic advisor, women's intercollegiate athletics. The TASP coordinator serves as the council's administrative advisor.

The council met twice during the first operational year of the TASP; but since the initial problems to be considered involved academic issues and policies, it chose to wait until the most urgent of those decisions have been made before meeting again.

Appointment of the TASP Academic Council

Also, as recommended, the provost appointed a TASP Academic Council to review plans for, and the effectiveness of, U.T. Austin's academic skills development programs for TASP students. The council was also set up to advise the executive vice president and provost, the vice president for student affairs, the TASP coordinator, and the staff of the LSC on the types of academic skills development programs needed and the ways in which those programs should be implemented.

The initially-appointed members of the council were assistant dean and director of student teaching, College of Education, who is a specialist in the teaching of reading (chair); associate dean, College of Liberal Arts; associate dean, College of Natural Sciences; director, MEC (TASP liaison); and director, LSC. On the council's recommendation, its membership has been expanded by adding an English Department faculty member, who is a specialist in teaching writing, and a Mathematics Department faculty member, who is a specialist in teaching math. Both the TASP coordinator and the chair of the TASP Administrative Council serve as the council's administrative advisors.

Since its first meeting in October 1989, the Academic Council has been very active, dealing with academic issues of both procedures and policies. The procedural issues probably are unique to U.T. Austin, so little will be said about them.

Change from Fifteen-Hour Rule to Nine-Hour Rule

The law mandating the TASP specified that students must take the test prior to the accumulation of nine or more semester credit hours. The Community College Presidents' Association's concern about the nine-hour rule resulted in allowing institutions the option of allowing students up to fifteen semester credit hours if a diagnostic placement test were used and remediation provided. When TASP implementation began, administrators believed that the tests used at U.T. Austin for academic placement in English and mathematics met the TASP definition of "an appropriate diagnostic instrument." Thus the first TASP students, who entered in the fall and spring semesters of 1989-1990, were informed that they were under the TASP fifteen-hour rule. However, as program implementation continued, it became clear that the TASP nine-hour rule would be more appropriate for U.T. Austin students. Therefore, upon recommendation by the TASP Academic Council, the policy was changed so that, beginning with the 1990 summer session, all students entered U.T. Austin under the nine-hour rule.

Administrative Location, Designation, and Grading of TASP Courses

At an early meeting the Academic Council discussed with the provost where the TASP remedial courses should be located administratively and how those courses should be designated in catalogs and course schedules. The council recommendation, subsequently approved, was that the courses, whether they be noncredit or for (precollegiate) credit, should be administered as part of the Office of the Executive Vice President and Provost.

It was further decided that TASP remedial courses would be called Development Studies (DEV). Students who satisfy the TASP remediation requirements by participating in noncredit activities, such as those provided through the LSC, will be registered for DEV 000 with a letter (R, M, W) after the 000 to indicate whether the basic skills being developed are in reading, mathematics, or writing. Development Studies courses carrying semester-hour credit will be designated DEV 100, 200, or 300 (depending on the amount of credit to be awarded) with one of four letters (R, reading; G, geometry; M, basic mathematics and algebra; W, writing) indicating the basic skills being developed.

The performance of a student in a DEV course will be graded as S (Satisfactory) or U (Unsatisfactory), where S means that the student's participation satisfies the TASP requirement. In addition, instructors will be permitted to use the system of student evaluation they decide is most useful for instructional purposes. More will be said about credit-bearing DEV courses later. Grades in DEV courses will not affect a student's grade point average.

Prerequisite and/or Concurrent Remediation

Some members of the Academic Council believed that remedial services are most effective when they are provided concurrently with students' enrollment in related college-level courses; for example, remedial mathematics should be taken concurrently with the college algebra course. Other members believed that some first-time freshmen are so ill-prepared that their academic skills should be strengthened before they undertake any college-level coursework. Finally, some members of the council strongly felt all students should be exposed to some college-level coursework every semester; that is, a student should not be allowed to spend a full semester taking only precollegiate coursework. As a result, TASP students who are entering freshmen are required to take at least three semester hours of college-level coursework, and TASP students may take their required DEV courses either prior to or concurrently with the corresponding entry-level college courses.

Creation of Credit-Bearing Courses in Developmental Studies

Because it seemed certain that U.T. Austin would need to supplement its noncredit TASP courses with credit-bearing developmental studies courses, upon recommendation from the Academic Council, U.T. Austin requested and received Coordinating Board approval to add to its course inventory four new variable-credit courses (the first digit of the course number designates the credit value):

DEV 100R, 200R, 300R: Basic Reading Skills

DEV 100G, 200G, 300G: Basic Geometry Skills

DEV 100M, 200M, 300M: Basic Math and Algebra Skills

DEV 100W, 200W, 300W: Basic Writing Skills

The initial intent was to phase in one new credit course each year. However, as TASP Test scores were received, it became apparent that credit courses in all three areas would be needed by fall 1990. By late spring, it was clear that DEV credit courses would have to begin in the 1990 summer session.

As a result, DEV 300R, DEV 300M, and DEV 300W were offered in the 1990 summer session, and those three courses plus DEV 300G were offered in the fall 1990 Semester. Development Studies course instructors are required to have the equivalent of a master's degree and are appointed as specialists in developmental skills, a nontenure-track academic appointment. The specialists develop their own course curricula while subject-matter experts on the TASP Academic Council and at the LSC serve as their consultants and advisers. The Academic Council approves the DEV course curricula.

Credit for DEV courses counts as *hours undertaken* for certifying full-time enrollment and other purposes, but it will not count as *hours completed* for grade-point-average computations. Development Studies courses and semester hours of credit will be placed on a student's permanent record each semester and summer session and will appear on official grade reports and transcripts.

TASP Assessment System

By spring 1990, it was also clear that the credit-bearing TASP courses should be made available not only to students who had already taken and not passed the TASP Test but also to high-risk students who had not yet taken the TASP Test.

In brief, there are three routes (see Figure 11.1) students may follow to comply with TASP regulations. Students who have taken the test but have not passed all three parts are divided into two groups: high-risk students who are permitted to choose between the organized-courses route and the self-paced route, and low-risk students who must take the latter.

Students who have not yet taken the TASP Test are divided into two groups: high-risk students who are permitted to choose between the organized-courses route and the optional-help route, and low-risk students who must take the latter. Students who choose the organized-courses route must make important academic and time commitments. These students must take at least one Developmental Studies course. Students must use the Learning Skills Center services to prepare for the TASP Test in the optional help route. Risk assessment and advising are essential elements of both routes.

Figure 11.1
U.T. Austin TASP Assessment System (Preliminary Plan)

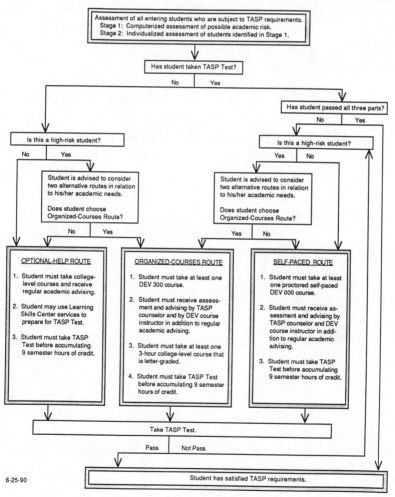

Next Stages of Implementation

Beginning in June 1990, TASP implementation at The University of Texas at Austin shifted into fourth gear. For the first time both noncredit and credit-based remedial services were available to TASP students. Policies and procedures were fine tuned, and course curricula were refined. Both formative and summative evaluations of the U.T. Austin TASP system began as did the reporting of evaluation results to the Coordinating Board.

The shift into fifth gear will take place when every aspect of U.T. Austin's TASP system has been fully elaborated, when many of its currently manually performed operations have been automated, and when all procedures have been reduced to smoothly functioning institutional routines.

REFERENCE

Ellis, David B., (1990). *Becoming A Master Student*. Rapid City, SD: College Survival, Inc.

12
Evaluating the Effectiveness of TASP

Gary R. Hanson and Richard M. Kerker

Few people want their programs evaluated, but everyone wants to know what works. That is the dilemma facing those responsible for any educational evaluation program. Evaluation of the Texas Academic Skills Program was mandated by law and required annual reports of the effectiveness of advisement and remediation at all public colleges and universities in the state. Of course, requiring evaluation and actually making it happen are two very different things. How much and what kind of data are necessary to do the job and still be tolerated by those required to submit reports? How soon can the public and legislators expect to be shown meaningful information about what works and what doesn't?

BACKGROUND

To this point, this book has focused on the issues, policies, and implementation strategies related to the Texas Academic Skills Program. This chapter will introduce another critical element of the TASP: the evaluation of the program's effectiveness.

The legislation mandating the TASP states, " Each institution shall report annually to the Board...the effectiveness of the institution's remedial program and advising program." This provision was responsible for considerable fear, anguish, debate, and resistance. Most institutional representatives had some apprehension about reporting data to the state that would be used to evaluate their programs. Their concerns were mostly with what the state would do with such information and who at the state level had the expertise to evaluate and report the data appropriately. A secondary, yet pervasive concern was whether or not institutions would be ranked or rated against one another on the basis of their evaluation reports. Most informed members of the higher education community realized the Texas legislature was concerned with accountability of higher education institutions and realized the necessity of the reporting component. They did not have to like this provision, however, and few did.

A second reporting provision that the higher education faculty and administration did like was the mandate to report TASP Test scores to the high schools. Most felt that the high schools were the source of the underpreparation problem and were delighted to see that data supporting this position were going to be collected and made available to the public. Many secondary school administrators were concerned that these data could be misinterpreted and would not fully represent the quality of secondary instruction. Thus, both secondary and postsecondary personnel were equally displeased with the evaluation component of the legislation. They did, however, realize that evaluations are a component of education and committed themselves to ensuring that these evaluations would be appropriately conducted.

The task of the staffs at the Coordinating Board and the Texas Education Agency was to develop reporting methods that would fulfill the legislative mandates while presenting the evaluation data in an appropriate, fair, and equitable manner. So they developed a process to arrive at the evaluation component of the TASP and bring it into existence. Emphasis on the process is important because it was the steps taken during the development process that ultimately reduced much of the anxiety over the evaluation component of this program.

In our continuing effort to include representatives from the colleges and universities in the development of the TASP, the Coordinating Board staff brought together research and evaluation experts from the institutions to serve on an advisory committee for the TASP evaluation. The membership of this committee included institutional researchers from both community colleges and senior universities. They were a group that collectively represented decades of experience in conducting and reporting evaluations of the effectiveness of institutional programs. It was natural to include such professionals in the evaluation of the TASP, both at the institution level and statewide.

The initial charge to the Evaluation Committee was to recommend the data elements used to evaluate the effectiveness of advisement and remedial programs, a method to track students longitudinally through the higher education system, formats for reporting the results of evaluations, and a method for evaluating the overall effectiveness of the TASP statewide.

The process of meeting the charge to the committee was quite interesting, to say the least. Many of the members of the committee were using new software that had been developed to provide institutions, particularly those with limited resources, a stand-alone institutional research tool. This software permitted institutions to track cohorts of students through various programs and generate aggregate reports on their academic performance. The members using this system (LONESTAR) felt that it should be the model for the state required reporting of effectiveness data. The initial recommendation coming from this group was that the colleges and universities should submit summary reports of the effectiveness of their remediation program to the Coordinating Board staff, who would then collate and publish the reports. The members supporting this recommendation felt that this method would be the most efficient way to collect and report data because of the system already in use on many campuses.

However, problems with this recommendation did exist. Not all institutions were using the same software for the purposes of conducting internal program evaluations. In fact, most of the senior institutions, especially those who could afford a substantial institutional research office, were not interested in using this research tool. These institutions did not want to purchase and use a software package designed to do what they had already been doing for quite some time. Further, many of the institutional researchers from the senior institutions resented even the possibility of the state mandating how they were to collect their data. They wanted only to be told what data elements were required, and they would supply the information in a manner of their own choosing.

The state also had reservations about allowing the institutions to provide summary reports. The Coordinating Board staff felt that the legislative intent was for the state to conduct the evaluation of the effectiveness of remediation programs, rather than merely publishing data results provided by the institutions. The State Attorney General's Office concurred with the state's opinion and added that they "did not want the fox guarding the chicken coop." They felt that the perception would exist that some institutions were manipulating their data to yield the most positive results. Although no staff member from either agency questioned the integrity of the colleges and universities, there was concern about the perception of impropriety. Finally, the Coordinating Board staff believed that the state could do a much better job of evaluation the effectiveness of the entire TASP if student unit record data were supplied by the institutions. Data collected on individual students would allow the state to investigate the impact of TASP from a variety of perspectives.

The pros and cons of unit record data versus aggregate summary reports were discussed in great detail by members of the Evaluation Committee, the TEA and Coordinating Board staffs, the State Attorney General's Office, and numerous institutional researchers not serving on any advisory committee. The results of these discussions were taken to the commissioner of higher education. After hearing all sides of the issue, he agreed that the state could best fulfill the legislative mandate of evaluating and reporting if unit record data were sent to the Coordinating Board. He was concerned, however, with minimizing the reporting burden of the institutions, and so he instructed the staff to design a reporting system that would take advantage of existing data and would call for adding as few new data elements as possible.

Once the Evaluation Committee had been redirected to recommend an evaluation system that utilized student unit record data, they began addressing the issues, underlying assumptions, and procedures of reporting system.

EVALUATION OF REMEDIATION ISSUES

Evaluating the effectiveness of remedial education efforts in the State of Texas hinges on this question: How will we know that our remedial program efforts make a difference in the academic performance of students who fail the TASP Test? To answer the question, we must examine a number of implicit assumptions about remedial and developmental education and raise important questions about how, when, and under what conditions we can expect remedial program efforts to work. These questions will guide the development of the criteria and standards used to judge the effectiveness of the remedial program efforts. In addition, several critical issues shaped the evaluation system designed for the TASP.

UNDERLYING ASSUMPTIONS

Four important principles or underlying assumptions guided the design of a statewide evaluation plan to evaluate the effectiveness of remedial program efforts. First, to evaluate the remedial efforts effectively, *student academic progress must be monitored longitudinally over time.* Improving the academic skills of students is not a process that will happen overnight, and sufficient time must be allowed for the application, synthesis, and integration of learning to take place. One important implication of this assumption is that indicators of the academic progress of students must be collected across several points in time during the students' educational careers. That students often pursue their educational objectives in sporadic intervals and across multiple institutions creates special data collection problems.

Second, *multiple indicators of student progress and performance are required* to judge the effectiveness of remedial programs. Because state law requires that all students who fail the TASP Test must participate in remedial programs, controlled experimental studies to isolate the program effects cannot be conducted. To compensate for this lack of control, multiple indicators are necessary to assess the effectiveness of the remedial programs. Any one indicator taken alone (for example cumulative grade point average) is subject to many different influences over and beyond the effects of the remedial program. Whereas no one single indicator can determine to what extent a particular program has been effective, patterns among multiple indicators will lead to informed judgments about the effectiveness of a given program.

The third principle or underlying assumption is that *the effectiveness of remedial programs* for students who fail one or more parts of the TASP Test *must be judged relative to the performance and progress of students who do not require remediation*. The ultimate test of whether a remediation program has been effective is that the remediated students are indistinguishable from students who did not require remediation. Hence, an effective remediation program should enable students to obtain similar grades in college level coursework and to progress toward the attainment of their college goals to the same degree as students who did not need the remediation services.

Finally, the fourth underlying assumption in the design of a statewide evaluation system was that *the cost and burden of collecting evaluation data at the local institutional level should be minimized*. Monitoring student progress over time with multiple indicators of academic performance could place a heavy burden on the local institutions. In addition, the volume of data generated from this kind of evaluation reporting system could be dysfunctional to the aims and goals of the evaluation process. This principle was especially important when deciding which criteria were most important, what data elements could be used as indicators of academic performance and progress, and when and how the data should be collected.

EVALUATION SYSTEM DESIGN QUESTIONS

Before the criteria to evaluate the effectiveness of these

remedial programs could be determined, a series of questions that influenced the design of the evaluation system were debated. These questions are fundamental to sound evaluation design and are highlighted here for those readers faced with designing an evaluation system for similar purposes. For some of these questions the legislation provided clear direction; other issues were debated and negotiated. What are these issues?

Who Needs Remediation?

A central issue in the design of an evaluation system is raised by this question: How do you determine who needs the remediation program? This is a critical question because the answer defines the cohort or sample of students who will be monitored as they participate in the remediation program. For the TASP, this issue was partially resolved by the legislation that required any student who failed a section of the TASP Test to take remediation covering the failed content area. Consequently, if students failed the mathematics portion of the exam, they would be required to participate in a remediation program in mathematics. If they failed the writing portion, they would be required to participate in remedial program dealing with writing. Students who failed more than one part of the exam were required to participate in remedial programs in each failed area, though students were not required to participate in remediation in all areas the same semester.

Who Receives Remediation?

A second design issue centered on the question: Did the students who needed remediation receive it? Since the legislation mandated that institutions must provide some form of remedial support but did not mandate how the remediation effort should be delivered, the individual institutions in the State of Texas were allowed complete freedom and autonomy to structure their remediation efforts at the local institutional

level.   Students were required by law to participate if they
failed one or more sections of the TASP examination.   For
institutions that elected to provide remediation using conventional instructional programs, the monitoring of student
participation was relatively easy.   For students who elected to
take a credit-based course, the institution entered the participation on the transcript as a grade upon completion of the course.
However, institutions who provided remedial programs through
non-course-based programs such as a learning and study skills
center tutorial program could not use the conventional instructional grade transcript as a record of the student's participation.
Other methods of tracking and monitoring the students'
participation were required.   The development of a computerized database for tracking student participation in remedial
activities over several semesters became a critical issue.

When Is Remediation Completed?

A third important issue was knowing when remediation was
complete or finished.   On this particular issue the legislation
was quite clear: The student would continue in remedial
activities until the TASP Test sections previously failed were
ultimately passed.   The student could not be allowed to register
beyond the sixtieth credit hour if any section of the TASP Test
was failed.   Even though the legislation provided clear guidelines for determining when students were finished with remediation, a problem of definition was evident.   A student may
participate in an institution's remediation program, pass the
TASP Test, but be unable to perform college-level work
successfully at that particular institution.   Has that student
successfully completed remediation?   According to the strict
guidelines of the law, the answer is yes.   In a broader sense,
however, the institution has not helped the student prepare for
a successful college experience.   One might logically argue that
remediation was not complete.

What Is Effective Remediation?

Defining effectiveness and the criteria used to satisfy the definition were central issues in the design of the statewide evaluation system. How do you know when a remedial program has been effective? This question is at the very core of the evaluation system. One way to define effectiveness is to consider whether or not the goals of the remediation programs were accomplished. Gardiner (1989) uses this definition: "Effectiveness refers to success in achieving the organization's purpose--doing the right thing."

GOALS OF REMEDIAL PROGRAM EFFORTS

While the decision to use multiple indicators to assess effectiveness was made very early in the design process, the decision of which indicators to use required considerable discussion and debate. For purposes of evaluating the remedial education efforts for the TASP the following goals were identified as important outcomes of the remediation process.

First, the legislation required that students pass the TASP examination before completing their sixtieth credit hour. The effectiveness of the remedial programs will be judged on the degree to which students who participate ultimately pass the TASP. If students cannot pass the TASP by the end of the remediation program effort, that will be one indicator that the program was not accomplishing an important goal.

A second goal mandated by the law was that students would be continuously enrolled in remedial education programs until all sections of the TASP Test were passed. The intent of this goal was to ensure consistent and adequate remediation efforts on the part of the student and the institution. Students were not required to participate in remediation in all areas every semester. Hence, students who failed one or more parts of the exam could participate in a remedial program to improve their skills in mathematics one semester and work on their skills in reading during a later semester.

A third goal was that the remediation program should help students successfully complete college-level coursework. One clear measure of that success is grade performance in college-level coursework. English and mathematics courses were chosen because they were most closely related to the basic skills assessed in the reading, mathematics, and writing portions of the TASP Test. Academic performance in college-level courses or more specifically, the grades achieved in the student's first college-level English composition and mathematics courses are adequate indicators of the success in meeting this goal.

The remedial education efforts should also lead to overall success in college-level work. In addition to improving specific skills in the basic areas of reading, writing and mathematics, students should begin to perform well in all the courses they take across the curricular domain. One reflection of how well students have generalized the skills they learned in the remedial education program is the cumulative grade point average. If the remedial education programs are working well, a high proportion of the students who participate should meet or exceed the college's minimum expectations for academic success.

Another goal of the remedial education programs is to ensure that the retention rate of students in the remedial education programs is at least as high or higher than the rate for students who do not need remediation. Although it is true that students leave college for many reasons, one of the primary factors in attrition is poor academic preparation. If the remedial education programs are improving students' academic skills, fewer students should leave for reasons of academic failure. Students may continue to leave the institution for all the other reasons, but if the remediation program is having a desirable effect, the retention rate for those students needing remediation should be at least as high as for those students who do not need remediation.

Finally, if the remedial education programs are working well, the graduation rates of students who participate should be as high as students who do not need the remediation. Like the retention rate, many factors influence whether or not students obtain degrees from their institution. If students lack the necessary skills to do college-level work, they most certainly will not graduate. However, if the remedial programs are effective, the net result should be at least comparable graduation rates for those students who need remediation and those who do not.

The effectiveness of remedial education programs must be judged on how well these multiple goals are met. Taken alone, achieving any one of the goals constitutes insufficient evidence to conclude that the remediation effort was working well. When multiple goals are achieved, additional evidence will accumulate and greater confidence can be placed in making judgments about how well the remedial education programs are working.

REPORTING THE RESULTS: ISSUES AND PROBLEMS

In developing a statewide evaluation reporting system, three critical issues were evident. The first general issue was the definition and development of indicators of the effectiveness of the remediation programs. The second issue was the development of reporting systems to summarize and communicate at a state level the results of the evaluation data. The third issue focused on the utilization of the evaluation data.

Indicators of Program Effectiveness

To determine whether or not the remediation programs provided by an institution were meeting the goals of the TASP, useful indicators of each goal were needed. Taken together and analyzed over time, these indicators should provide evidence about the extent to which the remediation was helping students become successful in doing college level work.

The indicators are a catalyst for future evaluative aspects for the program. All parties involved were obviously concerned with and inquisitive about the concepts and aspects of the program which would be the ultimate determinants of their individual program effectiveness and the subsequent impact the results of their evaluation would be. Table 12.1 shows the remedial program goals and the corresponding indicators used to assess the degree to which each goal is being met.

Table 12.1
Remedial Program Goals

	INDICATOR
1. Pass all sections of TASP Test prior to completing sixtieth credit hour	The percentage of students who pass the TASP Test by the end of each reporting period
2. Be continuously enrolled in remedial education activities until all sections of the TASP Test are passed	The number of students required to participate in remediation who do in fact participate
3. Successfully complete college courses with a cumulative grade point average of 2.0 (using a four point scale)	The percentage of students who obtained a C average or higher at the end of each reporting period
4. Achieve a retention rate as high or higher than students who do not need remediation	The percentage of students who persist from the date of entry to the end of each reporting period
5. Achieve a graduation rate as high or higher than students who did not need remediation	The percentage of students who obtain a degree by the end of each reporting period

Development of Evaluation Report Formats

The first evaluation report will be generated and distributed in the summer of 1991. The following is a discussion of the general issues and features of the evaluation reports.

One of the greatest concerns voiced by the colleges, particularly those with open or lesser admission requirements, was the erroneous comparisons that might be made among institutions. There is a fear that all colleges and universities will be ranked in terms of the number of semesters of remediation required for their students. If these numbers were interpreted as indicating the effectiveness of remedial interventions without regard to the level of erosion of entering students, institutions servicing students who are most underprepared would appear to be doing a poorer job than the highly selective institutions.

One approach that we have taken to ensure that interpretation of the data will be made in the appropriate context is to allow each institution to submit a narrative description as a prelude to the numeric report. This brief description includes a statement of the role and mission of the institution, the unique characteristics of its students, and a description of the academic erosion of the students who enter the institution. An open-admission institution may wish to describe the typical academic goals of its students (e.g., earn credit for transfer to a four-year university, obtain a one-year technical certificate, etc.), their level of erosion (e.g., non-college-bound high school diploma), and the types of programs that draw the greatest enrollment (e.g., vocational-technical). We believe that allowing the institutions, in their own words, to describe their students will ease some of the fear of misrepresentation and misinterpretation of the data.

The data for the evaluation reports come to us from a number of sources. Public higher education in Texas is funded on a formula system that reimburses colleges and universities for the semester credit hours of instruction offered. Each institution submits to the Coordinating Board a report identifying each enrolled student by social security number and the number of semester credit hours he or she is taking. These reports, which include demographic information about each become the source of the demographic information we use during the evaluation of remedial effectiveness.

A second source of data is the student test performance data we receive from our test contractor, National Evaluation Systems, Inc. (NES). The Coordinating Board staff receives a computer tape containing students' test performance after each test administration. Students are identified by social security number as well as by name and date of birth.

The final source of data is a report required annually identifying students by social security number. It includes data elements such as the need for remedial work, the type of remedial intervention, the number of semesters in remediation, and the grade point average in college classes (for a complete list of data elements on this report, please see "Student TASP Report-CBM 002" in Appendix 3). These data are reported on every student enrolled beginning with the fall 1989 semester. Since students' dates of entry into the institutions are included, we are able to look at an entire cohort of students who enter during a particular semester or academic year.

Once the data are received from all sources, they are entered into a student database. The database identifies students by social security numbers and includes the institution where the student is enrolled, as well as all demographic, academic, and test performance data we receive. This system allows us to track an individual from the time he or she enters public higher education until exit, via graduation or for other reasons. Since we can follow students from one institution to another, we can track transfers from a community college to a senior university and vice versa. The flexibility of this database should afford us some tremendous evaluation opportunities of the TASP and serves as a vehicle to conduct other academic research. At this time we have not yet fully utilized the potential of these data. Several staff members at the Coordinating Board do have research planned for the near future.

Summary data for each institution and for the state as a whole are presented in annual reports produced by the Coordinating Board staff. A separate report is produced for each cohort of students, consisting of a group of students who enter college for the first time during a given academic year. Appendix 3 presents information concerning the procedure to implement and to update the report. Therefore, the first evaluation report will contain first-year information about those students who entered college during the 1989-1990 academic year. The second annual report will include information about the second year of the 1989-1990 cohort and the first-year data from the 1990-1991 cohort. Each cohort will be tracked and reported until all students have either graduated or left the higher education system.

Remember, the evaluation reports will focus on comparisons of key indicators between those students who need remediation and those who do not. In addition, data will be reported by ethnicity, age, sex, and type of institution.

Evaluation Data Utilization

The TASP evaluation data and reports should serve several important functions. Three primary uses of the data are mentioned below.

The Texas Legislature and the Coordinating Board will view the TASP evaluation reports from a rather traditional perspective. Emphasis will be on determining the overall impact of the program on public higher education. It is critical to examine a program with the scope and expense of TASP to ascertain if the early identification of academic deficiencies and subsequent remedial efforts are having a positive effect on students. We would like to see that those students who need remediation are able to complete their education successfully at a rate similar to those who do not need basic skills development. This would be an indicator of overall program success and extremely helpful in determining the extent of underpreparation statewide. Focus would also be directed toward the success of different types of remedial interventions. Patterns may emerge to indicate that one type of remedial program tends to be more effective for a particular subgroup of students. This type of information could have direct bearing on funding for institutions that service particular types or groups of students.

Institutional personnel will use these data slightly differently.

They will be looking at their own institutions in an attempt to determine what is working best at their particular institution. They should also have the opportunity to examine data from other institutions similar to their own. This could lead to information sharing about successful programs. Quite frankly, we would be delighted to see institutions sharing ideas about what interventions tend to work best for different types of students. Although the statewide summary data will contain some of this information, individual institutions will be able to focus their attention on the successes of peer institutions. This should bring insight that the statewide reports will tend to wash out.

Finally, the TASP evaluation data will serve an important role for curricular evaluation and reform in Texas secondary schools. Both the TASP legislation and a separate piece of legislation called for the reporting of college students' academic performance to the graduating high schools. The TEA will report our data, by individual student and in summary form, to the Texas public high schools. The schools, school districts, and local communities should be able to use these results to evaluate the effectiveness of the high school programs in preparing students to go to college. Reports of remedial needs and overall academic performance could have a dramatic impact on high school counseling and programming. If, for example, a high school determines that its students tend to be underprepared in mathematics, greater emphasis on mathematics instruction could be implemented. On the other hand, if a high school determines that those students who took the college-preparatory courses are doing well but a surprising number of non-college-track students are in fact going to college, the advisors might be encouraged to guide more students into the college-preparatory programs.

Parents and community leaders should be able to take advantage of these reports. They might use the performance of students from a particular school to seek reforms in their children's secondary educations. As consumers of public education, parents should be informed of the level of erosion their sons or daughters will have upon graduation. This information could be used in determining what type of high school program is appropriate for their children. It is our hope that parents will use this type of information to get more involved in the education of their children. We believe they will find this information useful in ensuring that their children are getting what they deserve from the secondary schools.

EVALUATING ADVISING PROGRAMS

To this point the discussion has focused on the issues, process, and utilization of data from the evaluation of remedial programs. This final section will briefly discuss the evaluation of academic advising.

Evaluating the quality of academic advising is a tricky proposition. Typically, student retention data and graduation rates have served as the principle "hard" data available for this purpose. However, both of these data carry some problems. Good academic advising is necessary in retaining students. Unfortunately, students leave colleges and universities for a variety of reasons, many completely unrelated to advising. Most colleges and universities are unable to determine reliably why students have left, leaving unanswered the question of whether the institution could have prevented the departure. The same arguments pertain to why students fail to graduate. Given the lack of available information on the reasons behind leaving school and failure to reach graduation, these data are somewhat suspect for evaluating advising programs.

We have taken a somewhat different approach to the challenge of evaluating academic advising in Texas colleges and universities. Although we will have retention and graduation data, the focus of our evaluation will be "soft" indicators of advising effectiveness.

For the TASP first-year evaluation we have asked the institutions to supply some general information about their advising systems. This information will be used to get a baseline look at what is going on in the academic advising arena in Texas. The following guidelines for this narrative were sent to the institutions.

ACADEMIC ADVISING NARRATIVE

1. Describe any unique characteristics of your institution or the student body that might affect the advising process (that is, majority part-time enrollment, commuter institution, nontraditional population).

2. Describe your academic advisors. Please include the percentage of advisors who are faculty, professional staff, peer, or other.

3. Describe your academic advising system. Please include a description of the types of services available, the advising model (centralized, departmental, etc.), and which students are required to see advisors (freshmen only, all students, etc.).

4. Describe your system for training advisors.

5. Describe when and how advising occurs (e.g., during registration, at designated period before registration, on an individual basis, in groups).

6. Describe your process for evaluating advisors and/or the advising system. Please include how often evaluation is conducted, whether or not student input is included in the evaluation, when the last evaluation was conducted, and the results of the last evaluation.

7. Indicate what you believe to be the major strengths of your advising system.

8. Indicate what you believe to be the major problems or weaknesses with your advising system.

9. Describe what steps have been taken or are planned to

address the weaknesses or problems stated in item 8.

During the second year of the program, and every other year thereafter, we will ask each institution to draw a stratified sample of students and give them a questionnaire regarding their personal advising experience. We will specify which types of students (e.g., ethnicity, class, age, sex) are to be selected for this study. The results from this type of data should reveal the satisfaction and perception of effectiveness of advising from the perspective of the consumer. Evaluation of the advising programs at the colleges and universities is an important component of the TASP and is essential to the success of the entire process. Although school administrators might find the process bothersome, they acknowledge its necessity.

SUMMARY

At this time it is too early to tell how the program is working. We have heard of positive findings from preliminary studies conducted by a few colleges, but we need to have reliable data on students for three to five years before we can adequately address the questions of effectiveness. We are, however, hopeful that the first- and second-year reports reveal some encouraging trends in retention and academic success. One of the continuing responsibilities of the staff and the Evaluation Committee will be to convince the legislature and college officials that 1991 is too early to determine the effectiveness of the program. We will strive to assure them that, given adequate time, the data will exist to address the effectiveness question. Until that time, education administrators and lawmakers need to be patient and have faith in the educational reforms brought about by the TASP.

We hope that this chapter has given the reader a taste for the effort, agony, anger, delight, frustration, fear, loathing, and satisfaction that has gone into the design of the TASP evaluation system. Hundreds of educators, college administrators, and agency staff have been involved in the process. In spite of some contention, we have finally arrived at a point where most persons affected by this evaluation are satisfied that it is being done in a fair, equitable, and appropriate manner.

REFERENCE

Gardiner, L., *Planning for Assessment: Mission Statements, Goals, and Objectives.* Trenton, NJ. Office of Learning Assessment, New Jersey State Department of Higher Education, 1989.

13
Some Politics on the Way to Policy
William H. Sanford and Joan M. Matthews

With any major educational change as massive as this reform, institutional and state level politics figure heavily. We still trade war stories about some of the initiatives we had to deal with and shudder to think about all the ones that we haven't heard. The planning landscape was replete with covert and overt power plays. We remember more innocent and considerably less interesting days when politics were tales told from afar.

With tongue partly in cheek, we have come to believe that doctoral candidates in psychometrics who develop expertise in all kinds of testing and measurement may still be unprepared to deal on the front lines with a large testing program unless they also have an understanding of public speaking, a thorough knowledge of Byzantine politics, good diplomacy and negotiation skills, and, preferably, perfect knowledge of organizational dynamics skills. At all times we found the process of developing and implementing the Texas Academic Skills Program (TASP) to be challenging, invigorating, and complicated. This chapter concerns those complications that arose from the politics we faced. As an agency, the Coordinating Board didn't have to concern itself much with the politics that took place in the legislature. We were observers rather than actors. Politics began to play a part after the program was handed over to our agency and the Texas Education Agency. While some of the stories cannot be told, many of them can, and we hope they will be elucidating.

Since there were many forays against positions we took, or

against positions others feared we might take, our task became one of turning a power play back into a stated concern and attempting to address it in a forthright and legitimate fashion. That statement represents an ideal to which we aspired but did not always achieve. We, too, had our emotions engaged in the process in which we were involved, and we were not always able to be dispassionate about what was taking place. However, on both sides of any issue, many people are usually involved, and since they don't all react the same way at the same time, a natural human system of checks and balances results that helped us all stay on track.

To begin, it is important to start with the law we were charged with implementing. It is an axiom of government that broad-ranging legislation is more a statement of intent than a prescription for action. Such legislation requires extensive interpretation and elaboration to be made realistic and useful in guiding future actions and decisions. In the criminal justice system that interpretation and elaboration is a function of the courts. In higher education, it involves the state or federal agencies, institutions, and other affected and interested parties.

Legislation creating the TASP was enacted on the basis of simplified models of both the higher education system and the cohort of students who would be affected. The language of the statute did not account for essential distinctions among the philosophies, responsibilities, or cultures of the wide array of large and small universities, health-related institutions, community/junior colleges, and upper-level institutions across the state. It did not clearly delineate the special needs of citizens seeking training in highly focused vocational-technical programs, those receiving credit for courses offered out-of-state or overseas, college-going citizens incarcerated in state and local prisons, adult part-time students, the handicapped and learning disabled, or transfer students from other states. Developing the practical and realistic rules and guidelines necessary to address elaborations, complications associated with these, and other issues were assigned--as they must be in such cases--to the higher education community, the Higher Education Coordinating Board, the Texas Education Agency, the test development contractor, and the State Attorney General's Office. Trying to solve such multidimensional and sometimes amorphous issues in an environment of differing perspectives and self-interests is inevitably complex and sometimes contentious.

One of the first issues encountered was related to the impracticality and unintentional effects of the nine-hour limit on the longstanding and desirable practices of community colleges of the state. In Texas, these institutions are, by law, open admissions. They admit and strive to help, among others, students who are not fully prepared for college and who, without special attention and assistance, would never be able to succeed in such a challenging environment. In fact, community colleges historically have had the mandate to do almost all of the remedial instruction needed at the college level in Texas.

The legislation mandated that entering freshmen students must take the TASP exam during the semester in which they complete their first nine semester credit hours of college-level courses. If they fail to do so, they may not re-enroll in college-level courses in any public institution of higher education until they have taken the test.

The community colleges began to engage in a great deal of dialogue about the nine-hour limit. They had a number of concerns. From the extensive local testing, counseling, and remediation efforts already in place, they knew that a significant proportion of their students would not be ready to pass the test after only nine hours of college-level courses (remedial courses are not considered college-level in Texas). They feared it would be discouraging for students to pay $24 for a test that school officials could safely predict many would fail. They feared the colleges would not be well-perceived in the eyes of the public and possibly the legislature. Most of all, they were afraid their students might drop out of school.

Since the community colleges had existing services that permitted them to work with underprepared students over a period of several semesters so they could enter college-level instruction at a less demanding pace, the community college presidents' group asked that the nine-hour requirement be extended to permit colleges to continue to serve the special needs of their students.

This request raised several issues, both theoretical and legal. In the first case, if the intent of the legislature was that students demonstrate their current skill level in reading, writing, and mathematics immediately upon entrance to college, then how long can the initial taking of the test be delayed? If students have not taken the exam, how can they be counseled into the appropriate level of coursework? If students take a locally administered exam and prove to be weak in mathematics but adequate in reading and writing, should they be permitted to enroll in college-level courses that have no mathematics content or prerequisites? If not, the students are held hostage to a single type of unpreparedness; and what other courses could they take along with remedial mathematics to be eligible for student loan and scholarship programs? But if they are permitted to take some college-level courses not dependent on mathematics, how many such courses, and for how many semesters, may they be permitted to continue in college before achieving the minimum skill level in mathematics?

If the above students are successful in college for, say, two years, have they made a legally bona fide case that the TASP skills are not in fact needed for college success?

Do some skills actually deteriorate if delayed too long? For example, if students were permitted to wait a year or two to take all three sections of the test and in the meantime were taking remedial work in writing, is it possible that their mathematics skills, closely associated with the high school curriculum, could be jeopardized?

A different type of critical question was, how can a state agency, in this instance the Coordinating Board, change--or violate--the law, which specifically restricted students to a nine credit hour maximum before making a first attempt to pass the exam?

The initial reaction of the Coordinating Board was that no one except the legislature itself has authority to modify the restrictions stated in the statutes and that the community colleges would have to abide by them until the legislature made the desired changes. On the continued insistence of the community colleges, however, Coordinating Board staff approached the legislative sponsors of the bill and asked their counsel and advice. In this instance, the legislative leaders indicated uniformly that they would have no objection to the Coordinating Board extending the nine-hour rule to fifteen hours for some students if various conditions were imposed to protect the intent of the original statute. They said, in effect, that if the Coordinating Board did not make an appropriate modification through its rule-making authority, they would seek to change the legislation at the first opportunity. This would be possible either in a special legislation session or during the next regular session, which would be more than a year in the future.

On the basis of these assurances, the Coordinating Board enacted rules to permit institutions to choose between a nine-hour or fifteen-hour policy. If an institution chose the fifteen-hour plan, it could continue to use its locally developed and locally scored tests for placement of students in remedial activities and could extend the students' eligibility for enrolling in college level courses through the semester in which they completed fifteen credit hours. Institutions were asked to choose only one of the plans. Our attorney advised us that they could use both plans only if they could prove definitely that the groups of students affected were different and, thus, could be treated differently.

PRESIDENTIAL WATCHDOGS

What became known as the nine-to-fifteen-hour rule was one of the first instances when the community college presidents exerted their influence on the TASP policy-making process. One president told us in private that some of his peers tried to figure out if the TASP process could be derailed. Joan Matthews was present at a meeting of the group when a president stood up and said, "This train is out of the station and it's gathering speed!" With wide eyes and special emphasis he concluded, "and we don't know who's driving the engine!" Another president, speaking informally about the group, commented that the organization doesn't usually like to operate as a unified action group. But in the case of TASP policy and rule development, they did. The results were highly constructive with significant and important influence on the state. As time progressed, the leadership within the group assured members that TASP was going to happen, the law enacted and the funding found, and urged them to provide the input and take the opportunity to make the program to their liking. They met with the commissioner of higher education who confirmed simply and clearly that TASP *was* coming; and for some, the meeting defused a lot of concerns.

The group set up a "watchdog committee" to attend the Coordinating Board's many committee meetings systematically; they surveyed their members' concerns, got issues out for discussion, and were kept updated. This procedure turned them into a highly influential action group on the TASP process. The nine-to-fifteen-hour rule is a prime example, since the Coordinating Board's understandable tendency otherwise might have been a quick dismissal of the notion that we attempt to circumvent a highly specific element of the law.

Other related issues arose as discussions were going on regarding the nine- and fifteen-hour limitation. One of the most critical related to control of test security and residual testing. The community colleges regularly give a variety of local and nationally recognized tests when needed, maintain security for them, and score them. They wanted to have the same prerogatives regarding the TASP Test. Most of all, they wanted to have the ability to test students on demand and have immediate access to the results. At times, passions were high; presidents and other administrators took the position that if they could maintain security for the residual tests already in place, they could certainly maintain security for TASP. They believed that a failure to be able to test on demand might result in poorer service to students.

The Coordinating Board refused to permit this flexibility, maintaining that its obligations under the statute included guaranteeing the integrity and security of the testing program, and that this could be assured only through limited statewide test dates, uniform administration procedures and conditions, and centralized scoring. A compromise was worked out, however, which included the creation by the test development company of an unofficial version of the TASP exam that could be purchased at low cost by institutions and used for initial placement of individual students within the limits of their local nine-hour or fifteen-hour policies. The Pre-TASP Test (PTT), two-thirds the length of the official test, was developed. We also placed an important compromise into our official rules and regulations, allowing the PTT or any diagnostic basic skills measure to be used for the initial testing of entering students. We required remedial services for students who showed deficiencies, but we allowed them up to fifteen semester credit hours of college-level courses before they had to take the official TASP Test.

TASP legislation required that all students pass the exam before being enrolled in upper-level undergraduate coursework. And it also suggested that the intent of the legislature was that students in Texas should not be permitted to receive a college degree until they had shown proficiency in reading, writing, and mathematics. But what about associate-level degrees and certificate programs? Could students enter into and complete these programs and not be subject to TASP regulations? If so, could they use this as a method of avoiding the testing require-ment by completing two years of college and then declaring an intention to seek a baccalaureate degree?

Fortunately, in this instance, none of the educational leaders in the state, including the community college presidents, wanted such students to be excluded from the program. So, again, although the legislation did not specifically address these students, the Coordinating Board was encouraged to elaborate upon legislative intent and develop specific rules and proce-dures that included associate-level programs.

Even this solution, however, raised additional issues. For example, should technical-vocational programs with no or very limited college-level coursework be included under TASP regulations? Was it the intent of the state that students taking short-term job-training programs, equivalent to those available through proprietary schools or offered by community colleges, be required to demonstrate college-level basic skills? And if students started in such a program and then wanted to transfer to regular college-level programs, at what point should they come under TASP regulations?

The final answers to these questions did not receive unanimous agreement around the state, but it was decided that all public community college certificate programs containing nine or more credit hours of general education courses as defined by requirements of the Southern Association of Colleges and Schools would be included under TASP requirements. Programs with fewer than nine such credit hours were excluded. A student becomes responsible for satisfying TASP testing requirements when he or she enters into or transfers to a program with the nine-credit-hour requirement. This decision, too, was driven by the community college presidents.

As a result, it is possible for citizens to be trained in certain certificate programs without being subject to TASP. But no student may receive a certificate from an applicable program, an associate-level degree, or a baccalaureate degree without fulfilling the testing requirements.

Another important implementation issue for the TASP was that of settling on a fee structure for the examination. The advisory committee that had originally proposed developing a placement test for the state--the Committee on Testing--had firmly argued that the program should be established only if the state were willing to pay for all the costs of testing and remediation. This position was also adopted by the Coordinating Board and was a part of its formal recommendation to the legislature. But the legislature subsequently ignored this advice and mandated that students must pay for the exam. This produced another issue that had to be dealt with during the implementation process.

National Evaluations Systems, Inc. (NES), who won the contract to develop the TASP Test, originally proposed an examinee registration fee of $21.86 per student based on the services proposed in its contract specifications. The advisory committees of university and community college representatives involved in the test development process, however, recommended that additional services be contracted. Therefore, it was necessary to have further consultation with the contractor regarding fees.

The Coordinating Board was presented with a recommended set of additions that would have made the initial registration fee $29.00 per student. In addition to the base test administration fee, these services included the following:

- An increase from five to seven annual test administrations at up to 119 sites.

- Special test administration activities such as providing large test centers in metropolitan areas where colleges cannot accommodate all students.

- Paid chief test administrators for each site, paid assistant chief test administrators for large sites, and paid proctors for every thirty examinees.

- Individual examinees, institutional, and state test results reports.

The community college presidents and members of the Coordinating Board, however, expressed serious concern because they felt this would be too high a price for many of the students in the state. Deliberations by the Coordinating Board led to a deletion of these additional cost items and an agreement on a $24.00 test fee, with five test dates per year. A small amount in the fee went into a pool to fund necessary additional services as they arose.

BETWEEN A ROCK AND A HARD PLACE

The ten upper-level state institutions--those authorized to offer only junior, senior, and graduate courses/programs--were caught in an interesting dilemma. The legislation prohibited using passage of the TASP Test as a screening device, to prohibit any students from being admitted to a college or university. It also mandated that no students could be admitted to upper-level courses beyond 60 semester credit hours until they had passed the test. Taken literally this meant that upper-level institutions must admit students but then prohibit them from taking any courses. To add to the complexity of the issue, upper-level institutions are prohibited by law from offering remedial courses. Inadvertently, new laws and old ones had caught the upper-level institutions in a classic Catch 22. They had to admit deficient students without regard to TASP scores but then couldn't enroll them in upper-division courses. The law also said they had to remediate those students, but a different law prohibited them from doing so. Needless to say, the upper-level representatives with whom we met were highly frustrated. Once again, it seemed that significant legislation affecting them had been written considering the community colleges and four-year senior universities only. Once again, they felt like higher education's unconsidered stepchild.

Several meetings were held and a multitude of potential solutions were discussed. Some people wanted to find ways to ascertain that everything would be taken care of before any student was admitted. Others wanted to deal with the program just as the two- and four-year campuses were dealing with it. Practically nobody wanted to get upper-level schools in the remediation business. Ultimately, Coordinating Board staff made another visit to the leadership of the legislature to lay out the dilemma. The involved legislators were clear that they, too, did not want the upper-level schools doing remediation. With the consent of the sponsors of the bill, the Coordinating Board adopted rules allowing upper-level institutions to use passage of the test as an admission criterion. Even this policy causes some difficulty in relation to out-of-state and foreign transfer students, who may have to come to Texas to take the official test and learn their results. When remediation is needed, if non-course-based interventions are not available on an upper-level campus, the affected student will have to enroll concurrently at a community college to take remedial classes.

EVALUATION WARS

Perhaps one of the most problematic aspects of the TASP had to do with the evaluation reports required by law. Two laws called for extensive data collection for annual assessments of the effectiveness of remediation, advising, and reporting back to each high school the test results and first-year college performance of recent graduates. In planning for the evaluation reports, we divided the task, giving the design of the annual TASP reporting requirements to our Evaluation Committee and the high school reports to a subcommittee of a larger blue-ribbon group working on the quality of undergraduate education. The composition of the two committees was quite different. The Evaluation Committee was primarily composed of institutional researchers whereas the subcommittee was a group of college presidents and other administrators.

The Evaluation Committee members studied the problem extensively. Some of them accompanied staff to New Jersey and Tennessee to investigate reporting systems already in place. We became convinced that student unit records were the way to proceed--a departure from previous Coordinating Board methodology. But we wanted to be able to track our students across institutions and do the kind of retention studies that had not previously been possible. The Evaluation Committee made several suggestions to staff and ultimately developed what was jokingly referred to as the Cadillac of assessment plans, involving the creation of a new Coordinating Board report with forty-four data elements.

In the meantime, as their discussions progressed the subcommittee became increasingly concerned about the larger evaluation question--the charge that had been given to the other Evaluation Committee. Subcommittee members knew that staff wanted student unit records instead of aggregate data. As one president told us privately, that prospect raised a specter that few welcomed. The Coordinating Board, and thus the legislature, would have more information about the schools than ever before, making some officials extremely uncomfortable. The colleges and universities were unsatisfied with certain past Coordinating Board reports. The fact that we had hired an expert researcher for TASP reporting didn't serve to allay many fears. There was a strong push for aggregate reporting. Some committee members wanted their institutions to be able to turn in completed reports; on the other hand, we wanted data from which we would write the reports. Some of the presidents on the subcommittee were told that the way the staff wanted to conduct the evaluation process would require hundreds of thousands of dollars in computer upgrades and staff additions.

The Undergraduate Quality Committee decided to hold a public hearing related to its work with TASP evaluation one of the topics addressed. At the hearing, concerned testimony about the proposed evaluation requirements was heard from the president of a flagship university as well as from several other influential people, and they caught the ear of the commissioner of higher education.

Commissioner Ashworth decided that the cost and burden to the institutions might be alleviated if the number of data elements was reduced. He met with the TASP staff and planned out a reduction of data collection to fifteen items. Some additional information was available on other existing reports, and it would be up to the staff to merge them to minimize the reporting burden on the schools. One of our colleagues on the Evaluation Committee referred to the revised plan as the Pinto Evaluation Plan.

The commissioner, always amenable to a reasonable argument, told the staff to revise the number of data elements upward again after he heard from the State Attorney General's office. Dr. Ashworth was told by one of the attorneys who had been most active in litigation involving the two education agencies that more information would be needed in order to defend the program effectively. So a compromise was reached. We currently collect twenty-three data elements in a new report that is merged with other information to give us what is needed. We have not been told of any significant multimillion-dollar computer upgrades at the institutions based on new TASP requirements. We have arrived, we believe, at a "midsized car" evaluation plan. The subcommittee treated its original charge relating to reporting TASP scores to the public schools with some dispatch, and the Evaluation Committee returned to the charge that had been subverted by the other group and worked out the details of the new plan.

In reconsidering all the politics of the TASP, several conclusions occur to us. This is a particularly high stakes program. Stakes are high for students because the program has the potential to delay progress in college-level instruction but also to improve their chances for success. The program offers the legislature a way to assess institutions of higher education that was not previously available. It also means that the numbers and types of students served may shift and the quality of the curriculum will come under scrutiny. Given these assumptions, most college personnel took the TASP very seriously, and an outsider might be shocked to learn how frequently one party would "blow the whistle" on another. If a person on campus learned that plans were afoot to lessen the impact of TASP rules and regulations, we frequently got a confidential telephone call or letter. There were innumerable rumors for us to deal with or defuse. In several cases, a perfectly reasonable proposal would be put forth by an institution with no knowledge whatsoever that several other parties had already informed us of a potential self-serving aspect underlying the proposal. It soon became important for us to take all suggestions at face value with our mandate in mind--to set policy that clarified and extended the law and best served Texas students. If institutions also benefited from the results, so be it. It was always essential for us to try to keep our eyes on the horizon, for if we focused elsewhere our own hopes and fears began to interact and tangle nonproductively with the hopes and fears of our institutional constituents. We were not always successful, but we tried and were aided by an advisory process with many experienced institutional faculty and administrators acting as filters.

In the 1970s, one of us became acquainted with a small group of builders who named themselves the Ono Construction Company. When asked why, they said it was because of the many occasions they had to say "Oh *no!*" We often had reason to remember that anecdote as we moved through the early stages of this reform effort. The Ono Construction Company was responsible for well-constructed buildings in spite of its name. We believe that for all the interplay between forces for and against the TASP, all of us have combined to construct a good, solid reform, and even program detractors and nay-sayers have assisted us in finding constructive solutions. Even better, when a powerful group such as the community college presidents combined to share their concerns and led us to useful conclusions, we found ways to help each other. What may have begun as a relationship with an adversarial tinge became a productive alliance to solve problems effectively.

14
After Implementation:
The Role of the State
Joan M. Matthews and Elena de la Garza

What should the state's role be after the reform has been put in place and implementation of the program rests with the colleges and universities? We faced ongoing test and program administration combined with implementation efforts. In deciding how to be helpful without getting in the way of the institutions, we cast some long-range plans to formulate program development.

As the Texas Academic Skills Program (TASP) has moved from politics to policy and from planning to implementation, the focus of the program has changed from developing the test and its supporting policies to implementation. We have learned from states such as New Jersey, where a basic skills assessment program has been in existence more than ten years, that the full impact of a developmental education program of this magnitude will not be felt for years to come. But we can, based on our experiences and those of other states, predict those outcomes.

This transition in our role has been an interesting one, especially in light of the intense and unremitting activity of the first few years when everyone on staff worked overtime to design the total program. The Texas Education Agency (TEA) and the Texas Higher Education Coordinating Board were the lead players. Activities were limited by the law and by the sheer necessity of developing a product within eighteen months. The work seemed endless. Even after the test was developed in time to meet the TEA mandate for administration of the first test in March 1989, the time spent on policy development to support the program and communication with the schools intensified. And yet 1989-1990 was clearly a year of change for us. Early on, we engaged in staff discussions about our evolving role. It was clear to us that our part in ongoing test development and administration would quickly become more routine and that we would complete policy development. The schools, then, would assume their primary role on which the strength and potential of the program rested totally: the implementation of advising, placement, and academic skills development. What would be our role? How could we legitimately facilitate the important work of the schools without getting in their way? In this final chapter, we will discuss our solutions and how we have tried to stay involved in a meaningful, practical manner without interfering in the vital role the schools had assumed for implementation.

Our first job was to assess the ongoing tasks. The everyday administration of the program requires a number of simultaneous activities. Necessary for ongoing test development, a review for bias, content, and possible adjustment of standards requires annual meetings. In tandem with continuing development of new items, we must routinely deal with the interpretation of test results from across the state. As the program has evolved, we have experienced the emergence of unexpected and increasingly complex policy issues, as well as the need to revise and refine existing policies.

TEST DEVELOPMENT

Because we anticipate the possibility of litigation, activities in test development have become very important. Once a year, the content committees meet to consider items for the following year's test bank. The Bias Review Panel also meets to review questions and problems in each of the subject areas of reading, mathematics, and writing. Discussion at these meetings is often lively and sometimes confrontational because the members must determine if the items are equitably screened for college-level preparedness. Members must be constantly cognizant of the complexity of the test items and whether they are appropriate for the standards set by the Coordinating Board and the TEA.

Standards and test results are heavily scrutinized by the schools and other interested parties, such as legislators. Because the admissions standards are so varied in Texas' nearly 100 public institutions of higher education, test results and test standards always provide a lively topic of discussion wherever we meet with educators. For example, there is a small community college where most of the students fail the Pre-TASP Test, and there are other selective institutions where only a handful of students fail. Senior university faculty continue to bemoan the fact that students who pass the test believe they are ready for college-level mathematics such as calculus (they aren't), while some community college faculty complain about the "high" level of mathematics skills tested. In other words, some educators will probably always think that the test is too easy, whereas others complain that it is too difficult. The debate will continue, we believe, until the program settles, a more representative sample of students is routinely tested, and the academic support programs in the colleges and universities are running to their full satisfaction.

POLICY ISSUES

Although most of the policies supporting the program and its implementation have been set, we anticipate continual refinements. During the 1989-1990 academic year, we worked constantly on the Coordinating Board rules relating to the TASP. In such a massive educational reform, we realized that the mere thought that a group of bureaucrats from Austin (us) would independently set policy for the entire program was anathema to the schools. Even though almost all the Coordinating Board staff in the Universities and Health Affairs Division have backgrounds as college or university faculty or in administrative positions, we tend to be regarded with some distrust by our constituents. After all, we did defect to the state, some of them have told us, and thus we have lost credibility in dealing with current campus affairs. Although we chuckle at times about that attitude, both our constituents' perception and their beliefs have some validity and must be honored. As a result, we designed a policy-making process whereby input was sought and received both formally and informally from faculty and staff throughout the state.

Staff members then developed a list of policy questions and dilemmas that needed to be answered. All of them were filtered first through our Committee of Chief Academic Officers, a dedicated and, for a while, severely overworked group of vice presidents and deans of instruction. With their day-to-day experience and invaluable perspective of institutional administration, they guided us toward what we believe is a practical and usable set of policies. As their value to our process grew, we asked for and received special permission from the commissioner to allow this committee to communicate directly with their peers--an unusual departure from our normal procedures of receiving committee input as advice only to the staff, commissioner, or board members. But as part of our goal of facilitating program "ownership" by the institutions as quickly as possible, we wanted one group of chief academic officers communicating directly with others about the important issues under consideration.

Some "white papers" highlighting policy issues, problems, and suggested solutions were sent out, and the committee received some criticism for its efforts. For example, at a regular quarterly meeting of all university vice presidents of academic affairs, one vice president half-jokingly asked the chair of the committee who had died and made him king! Other committee members reported that they, too, sometimes had been questioned about why they, instead of the Coordinating Board, had sent out policy materials. In general, however, the materials were well received and stimulated the thought and dialogue that we had hoped would occur. Ultimately, policy questions were evaluated by our attorneys and staff before they went to the Texas Academic Skills Council, the final oversight group. After review by those groups, we would check the final decisions, forward them to the commissioner, and finally send them out to the schools. Our five policy papers were distributed during

1989-1990. Next, we will revise them into a single reference document so that the many complicated rules and policies can be accessed more easily.

EVALUATION

We are just beginning to deal with evaluation--one of the most important parts of the program. It is from this component that the impetus for further educational reform in Texas will emerge, especially with regard to accountability and curriculum reform. We anticipate that the required evaluation reports will occupy a considerable portion of staff time and will be carefully scrutinized both by the schools and by the legislature. We believe that although evaluation is perhaps the most feared element of the program, it will also be one of the most useful. For the first time, we will be able to provide institutional decision makers in public postsecondary education with information and feedback about some of their implementation efforts in remediation and advisement. We know that many colleges and universities are already engaging in the type of process evaluation studies that will enable them to have even more finite data to guide them in ongoing program refinements on individual campuses. Many more institutional studies will follow. The end result will be more efficient deployment of resources and better service to students. With its requirement for annual reports, the evaluation component of the TASP will provide the schools with program refinement and information to guide curriculum reform, the two agencies with standard information about program efficiency across the state, and the legislature with data against which to measure some future institutional requests.

COMMUNICATION

Communication with the schools and students about the TASP law, its requirements, resulting policies, and implications for the campuses remains a major initiative of both agencies. There are 1,184 high school districts in Texas, and each one of them must have information about the program. As a result of the TASP, colleges and universities have made massive changes in policy, curriculum, programs, student tracking, and reporting within the institutions and to the state.

Traditionally, new legislation and minutes from the Coordinating Board's quarterly meetings are the two major communication signals studied by college and university presidents and vice presidents. Minutes are regarded as official information about state laws, Coordinating Board rules, and policy decisions. Administrators summarize and forward them to faculty and staff as needed. We then follow up with letters and phone calls allowing us to count on the presidents and vice presidents to disseminate information to the appropriate personnel on campus.

Obviously, TASP was too large a program to rely on these traditional methods. In retrospect, we wish we had had the foresight to seek professional advice on developing and implementing a statewide communications plan as soon as the law was passed. In spite of our best efforts, several principles that must be almost instinctive to communications professionals slowly became obvious to us. Given a complicated new reform (which is usually intrinsically threatening) with massive implications for change, information must be provided frequently and repeatedly to people because they tend to retain little of what they have heard and remember only selective bits and pieces and distort the bits and pieces they do remember. These are natural and expectable reactions, but they are extremely frustrating to those trying to learn about the program and to those trying to impart accurate information.

In addition to the traditional means described previously, our communication efforts involved printed materials, speeches, and conferences. In the early stages of development, the TASP staff from both agencies concentrated on providing information about the law, the test, and the various components of the program in an effort to educate people and ease their fears about the consequences of implementation at their educational institutions.

We began with a number of concurrent activities. The first issue of the *TASP: FYI Newsletter* was published in May 1988. This newsletter is published once every semester, including summer. Like the other elements of the program, it has evolved from a medium for policy issues to a medium for overall program implementation. Articles by guest writers in recent editions discuss program development in mathematics, reading, writing, and critical thinking. We publish information on current projects and activities, meetings, testing issues, and test results as well as the whimsical *"Ask Dr. TASP,"* a regular column on policy issues. The change in content reflects an effort to give administrators, counselors, educators, parents, and students "ownership" of the newsletter and, thereby, provide a viable, friendly tool for communication. Sent to approximately 3,500 college counselors, advisors, developmental educators, and administrators in all high schools and colleges in the state, each issue is prominently marked "please circulate." Undoubtedly, the content of the newsletter will again change to reflect changes in the program and to address the expanding needs of its readership.

Other publications also helped spread the word. National Evaluation Systems prepared a widely disseminated series of well-designed brochures about the program. A pamphlet on the program was distributed by the TEA to high schools and admissions offices at public colleges and universities. In addition, the TEA sent a letter about the program to every high school junior and senior in the state.

From the beginning, we designed a series of conferences for institutional leaders and practitioners--those faculty and staff on campus who actually did the advising and remediation. We started with a conference for presidents and chancellors in January 1988. After providing extensive information about the law, we organized the participants into groups based on their school sizes and asked them to advise us on state policy questions. As with all our subsequent conferences, our goal was to provide information and sensitization about the role and scope of the TASP and to begin the important process of involving as many people as possible in the planning process.

In July 1988, we held a second conference--this one for vice presidents. Dr. Anthony De Giorgio, then the vice president of academic affairs at Trenton State College in New Jersey, told how a similar basic skills testing program in his state had helped provoke major, positive changes at his college. Dr. Di Giorgio's speech was followed by a panel discussion among our Committee of Chief Academic Officers. They had prepared a handout outlining the implications for institutional policy changes within a college or university's key instructional or service areas. Finally, we organized the vice presidents into groups based on institutional type and size and had them discuss where new or changed institutional policy was needed.

In Fall 1988, we held a series of three regional conferences in different parts of the state for deans and mid-level managers. We especially wanted to reach the people responsible for the most important parts of the program: advising, placing, instructing, evaluating, and tracking students. At these conferences, we again provided general information followed by extensive dialogue. Work done by the Faculty Development, Academic Skills Development, and Advising Committees then provided information about effective models, annotated bibliographies for each area, and on-the-spot expertise for informal consultations.

Although we had an excellent plan, the first administrators' conference was an unmitigated disaster. Our inexperienced staff made several glaring errors first in handling registration and then in sharing information. We had not adequately anticipated the hostility and lack of information about the program among many of our participants. We naively assumed that the information disseminated had reached them; obviously not much had, and they were angry and appalled that there was less than a year left to prepare for TASP. Our own errors, combined with their fears and anger, provided fuel for the fire. We thought we were experienced at dealing with upset constituents, but we experienced more concentrated hostility and concern at that meeting than ever before.

With two more conferences facing us over the next two

weeks, the staff was in crisis. A key secretary in charge of conference registration quit in distress, but others in the division quietly and competently arose to help us. By the time the director of TASP was informed that she had lost her secretary, another staff member had taken over the conference registration job voluntarily. Meanwhile, we used an organizational consultant to help us assess why things had gone wrong.

We scrutinized our errors and the conference evaluation forms (which still smolder in our files). To our dismay, we learned that even some of the metaphors used in remarks to the audience had probably fed the fire!

The second conference was only a few days away. We approached it with trepidation but were determined to turn things around, and we did. At the initial reception, we were prepared for and found the same levels of threat, fear, and anger present at the previous conference. We worked the room like a group of politicians, listened, acknowledged fears, and reinforced good institutional efforts already underway. We were able to convert our image from one of officials who "were doing something to them" to an image of fellow participants in a major reform still fraught with unknowns. In the end, some of the persons who were initially most hostile thanked us for our efforts. Since that time, some of them have generously contributed their talents to our committees. Even though the conference evaluations were good, we made more refinements for the third and last conference the following week. It was as much a success as the first conference was a failure, and the staff began to feel as if we were back on track. We learned our lesson, though and to prevent future fiascos, shortly thereafter we filled a part-time position with a professional public relations person who had extensive experience in conference planning.

In spring 1989, we held the first conference for practitioners. Directed at experienced developmental instructors, the conference provided programs about successful remediation. We added an exhibit show of numerous companies demonstrating educational products, many of which were TASP oriented. We stated the hope that some of the experienced instructors would become involved in training the new instructors who would be hired during the summer to deal with increased demand for remedial courses. Given the low standards for remedial instructors outlined by the Southern Association of Colleges and Schools criteria, we feared that poorly qualified persons would be hired for these important positions. The first practitioners conference, co-sponsored by the Texas Academic Skills Council, Houston Community College, and North Harris County College, was successful and judged by participants to be very useful. It led us to the second conference for practitioners, held during Fall 1989.

At this conference, we piggy-backed our meetings onto a well-established 24-hour annual conference known as the Conference of Academic Support Programs (CASP), sponsored by the Texas Association of Developmental Education and the College Reading and Learning Association. Participants could register for either or both meetings, and most chose both. We provided variable-length training opportunities with experienced developmental educators as faculty and trainers. It was an economical way for college administrators to send new faculty for timely and needed professional development. In the future, the CASP group will continue to provide this service.

The following conference, in Spring 1989, featured academic advising. We worked hard to combine faculty advisors and professional advisors--two groups who usually don't attend the same professional meetings. In the future, the Texas Academic Skills Council plans to study faculty development and sponsor conferences with that focus. Tentative plans involve regional conferences within a few years after the program is implemented. The council believed that the initial demand would be for remediation, which not all schools had been providing. Academic advising was thought to be the next need. Last, they thought the schools would look at the appropriate androgogy for developmental courses. Future conferences will be held on an as-needed basis. In the meantime, we and National Evaluation Systems, Inc. have held a series of conferences and meetings directed at the testing personnel and chief test administrators on campuses.

As with the newsletter, the conferences took an identity of their own as participants became more familiar with the details of the TASP and with the communal vision of the characteristics for an ideal program at their respective schools. Hosting this conference series involved the cooperation of literally hundreds of people and many institutions in higher education across the state serving as co-sponsors for conference organization committees, presenters, juries for programs, participants, and exhibitors. This cooperation created fertile ground for new ideas to grow.

That fertile ground for new ideas took the form of a state-wide TASP network. At the first TASP conference for practitioners held in April 1989, the idea of a TASP network was informally discussed among many participants. A meeting was held at the practitioners' conference in October of the same year. The results were encouraging. The meeting was well attended and the discussion was always animated, sometimes intense and vehement. Participants generally agreed that a forum for sharing ideas, problems, and solutions was needed to develop on Texas campuses effective programs related to the TASP. Further discussions were held at the advising conference in 1990, and a consensus for action resulted. A networking meeting was held in October 1990, to organize the TASP Network. More than 200 campus TASP liaisons and coordinators from schools across the state attended for a day of discussion about logistics, goals, and objectives for their local TASP implementation efforts. The network participants agreed to meet again on a regional basis.

Speeches soon became another primary method of communication. The demand for TASP staff members to speak to faculty, staff, and students was enormous, as were the requests from professional groups in the state. We quickly found that the division's travel budget, although large, was so strained by the demand that the requesting groups had to pay our travel expenses. It was not unusual for the TASP staff to make as many as ten speeches a month at the height of the demand. Frequently we spoke to the entire faculty and staff of a school. Public speaking had not been planned as a primary method of dissemination of TASP-related information, but the resulting dialogues were excellent. We typically allowed at least a half an hour to talk with the audience after our remarks. The question-and-answer sessions helped educators in the state realize that they could call or write or follow up quite informally later with their ideas and concerns. They could circumvent the traditional, formal channel of communications up the line within the school and then from the vice president to our division or from the president to the commissioner of higher education. Speeches on the TASP are still frequently scheduled on campuses and at professional meetings, but, as it should be, faculty and staff are listening to each other and sharing their experiences, which now are much more relevant than anything we can tell them.

Communication about TASP took on an organized, orchestrated effort with the organization of the TASP Communications Task Force in late 1988. With the assistance of the Community Colleges and Technical Institutes Division of the Coordinating Board, a group of public information officers from colleges and universities throughout the state were assembled to discuss ways to distribute information about the TASP. Over the next year, the task force enlisted the assistance of the communications department at the University of Texas at Austin to develop a slogan for the program and produce public service announcements. This slogan, *"Skills for Success"*, is used in all communications efforts. Texas personalities such as Henry Cisneros, former mayor of San Antonio, and Earl Campbell, former star football player for the Houston Oilers, were portrayed as role models in the public service announcements. Members of the task force also produced a TASP information brochure with space for each college and university to insert personalized information about its program.

In 1989, a toll-free TASP telephone hotline was provided to answer questions about the program. A bimonthly question-and-answer column, with frequently asked questions about TASP, was sent to newspapers in the state. The work of the TASP Communications Task Force continues as needed. Among the future projects planned are a TASP communication package that will be sent to every public institution of higher education in the state. A statewide TASP poster contest will offer donated college scholarship money as first prize.

The Texas Academic Skills Council also initiated an exciting new program called the TASP Information Clearinghouse, which is designed to provide practical information about TASP implementation efforts in the colleges and universities. The clearinghouse is co-sponsored by the Texas Higher Education Coordinating Board, Southwest Texas Junior College, and Texas A&M University. The clearinghouse provides information through a catalogue about useful, effective programs for faculty and staff working with students in the state. Complete copies of the programs are kept at the clearinghouse location at the Center for Teaching Excellence at Texas A&M University. They are available upon request for the cost of duplication of materials, handling, and postage. The *TASP Clearinghouse Catalogue* is scheduled for publication in the Spring of 1991 and will be updated every two years. It includes abstracts of programs in assessment, placement, developmental instruction, support services, and counseling and advising. Experts have contributed annotated bibliographies in critical thinking, developmental education, reading, faculty development and learning strategies. A low cost consultant bureau available to schools that are implementing TASP-related programs is advertised.

We believe that the most relevant role for the Coordinating Board's staff is to facilitate implementation by bringing together people to learn from each other. The schools have made it clear that aside from more money, their greatest need is to know what works in remediation, advising, faculty development, and the tracking of students. We are well situated to serve as a central point to collect and disseminate that information. In fact, we hope the clearinghouse will become a primary vehicle for information about effective programs. We can serve as the focal point for regional conferences, such as the faculty development conferences currently under consideration.

Being on the ground floor of a major educational reform certain to transform the face of higher education in a state as large as Texas was an experience that nobody associated with it will ever forget. It was not always an enjoyable experience, but we never doubted its worth. Now, from our perspective, comes the enjoyment, for it is our privilege to watch the institutions of higher education do what they do best: educate underprepared students using the new TASP mandate and resources and grapple effectively with a significant educational reform. At last all schools will be uniformly addressing the problems of underprepared students. They will have addressed raising their expectations to accommodate the already prepared and the newly prepared freshmen students in college-level courses. Faculty members have already told us that their expectations had so eroded over the years that it had been too easy to drop to the lowest academic common denominator. Since then, they have echoed their colleagues in other states we visited who told us that until faced with students who had successfully completed remediation, faculty had been unaware of how much their standards had slowly and subtly lowered over the years. Now we will have the privilege of witnessing refinements in curriculum and programs and teaching to accommodate better prepared students and track them to, we hope, increased rates of graduation.

Appendix 1
Vernon's Texas Codes (Annotated)

I.   <u>Section 51.306. Testing and Remedial Coursework</u>[1]

  A. In this section, <u>board</u> and <u>institution of higher educa-</u><u>tion</u> have the meanings assigned by Section 61.003 of this code.

  B. All students in the following categories who enter public institutions of higher education in the fall of 1989[2] and thereafter must be tested for reading, writing, and mathematics skills:

     1. all full-time and part-time freshmen enrolled in a certificate or degree program;

     2. any other student, prior to the accumulation of nine or more semester credit hours or the equivalent; and

     3. any transfer student with fewer than sixty semester credit hours or the equivalent who has not previously taken the test.

For that purpose, the institution shall use a test instrument prescribed by the Coordinating Board. The same instrument shall be used at all public institutions of higher education in the state.

C. The test instrument adopted by the board must be of a diagnostic nature and be designed to provide a comparison of the skill level of the individual student with the skill level necessary for a student to perform effectively in an undergraduate degree program. In developing the test, the board shall consider the recommendations of faculty from various institutions of higher education.

D. An institution may not use performance on the test as a condition of admission into the institution.

E. The board shall prescribe minimum performance standards for the test instrument. A student whose performance is below the standard for tested skill must participate in a remediation program. An institution may require higher performance standards.

F. If the test results indicate that remedial education is necessary in any area tested, the institution shall refer the student to remedial courses or other remedial programs made available by the institution. Each institution shall make available those courses and programs on the same campus at which the student would otherwise attend classes. The courses or programs may not be considered as credit toward completion of degree requirements.

G. A student may not enroll in any upper-division course completion of which would give the student sixty or more semester credit hours or the equivalent until the student's test results meet or exceed the minimum standards in all test scores. The board shall establish other assessment procedures to be used by institutions in exceptional cases to allow a student to enroll in upper-division courses in cases where student test results do not meet minimum standards.

H. The state shall continue to fund approved non-degree credit remedial courses. Additionally, the board shall develop formulas to augment institutional funding of other remedial academic programs. The additional funding required under such formulas shall be met by state appropriation for fiscal years 1990-1991 and thereafter.

I. Each institution shall establish an advising program to advise students at every level of courses and degree options that are appropriate for the individual student.

J. The unit costs of each test shall be borne by the student. Costs of administering the tests to students shown to be financially needy under criteria established by the board shall be borne by the state through appropriation to the board for that purpose or other sources of funds. Additionally, appropriation shall be made to the board to cover overall administrative costs of the testing program.

K. Each institution shall report annually to the board, on or before a day set by rule of the board, concerning the results of the students being tested and the effectiveness of the institution's remedial program and advising program. The report shall identify by name the high school from which each tested student graduated and a statement as to whether or not the student's performance was above or below the standard. For the purposes of this report, students shall not be identified by name.

II.   Section 51.403. Reports of Student Enrollment and
       Academic Performance[3]

   A. All higher education institutions of this state shall
       offer only such courses and teach such classes as are
       economically justified in the considered judgment of
       the appropriate governing board.

   B. After the end of each spring semester the chief
       executive officer of each institution shall provide its
       governing board a report for the preceding fall and
       spring semesters indicating for each instructor the
       number of students enrolled in each class, the number
       of semester-credit hours accrued to each course, the
       course number and title, the department in which the
       course is offered, and the identity and academic rank
       of the instructor.

   C. A report prepared under Subsection B of this section
       must compare student enrollments in each class on
       the last day of each semester with enrollments at the
       beginning of that semester.

   D. Each institution shall file with its governing board and
       the Coordinating Board a small class report, excluding
       individual instruction courses, indicating department,
       course number, title of course, and the name of the
       instructor. Small classes, for the purpose of this
       report, are undergraduate-level courses with less than
       ten registrations and graduate-level courses with less
       than five registrations. No small classes shall be
       offered in any institution except as authorized by the
       appropriate governing board, within the guidelines
       established by the Coordinating Board.

   E. Under guidelines established by the Coordinating
       Board, Texas College and University System, and
       State Board of Education, postsecondary institutions

shall report student performance during the first year enrolled after graduation from high school to the high school or junior college last attended. This report shall include, but not be limited to, appropriate student test scores, a description of developmental courses required, and the student's grade point average. Appropriate safeguards for student privacy shall be included in the rules for implementation of this subsection.[4]

NOTES

1. Section 51.306 was added by Acts 1987, 70th Legislature, chapter 807, Section 1, effective August 31, 1987.

2. Section 51.306, 1987 Legislation, Section 2 of the 1987 Act provides that "the test required by this Act shall be administered to students beginning with those students entering institutions of higher education for the first time no later than the fall semester of 1989."

3. Section 51.403 was amended in the heading, adding "and Academic Performance", by Acts 1987, 70th Legislature, chapter 665, Section 2, effective August 31, 1987.

4. Section 51.403 was amended by the 1987 legislation adding subsection E.

Appendix 2
TASP Skills

The Texas Academic Skills Program (TASP) is an instructional program designed to ensure that students attending public institutions of higher education in Texas have the academic skills to perform effectively in college-level coursework. The TASP includes a testing component designed to provide information about the reading, mathematics, and writing skills of students entering Texas public colleges and universities.

The purpose of this document is to provide general information about the academic skills that may be assessed by the test.

TEST

The TASP Test consists of three sections: reading, mathematics, and writing. Each section of the test is defined by a list of five to ten broadly stated academic skills. The academic skills defining each section of the test have been reviewed and judged by thousands of Texas college faculty, the Texas Higher Education Coordinating Board, and the State Board of Education. The skills represent the knowledge students entering college in Texas should have if they are to perform effectively in their courses.

The academic skills that are eligible to be assessed by the TASP Test are listed on the following pages. Each skill is accompanied by a description of aspects of the skill that may be assessed by the test.

Each section of the test will consist of approximately forty to fifty four-option, multiple-choice questions. Only one of the options will be the correct or best answer. The writing section will also include a writing sample.

TEST REGISTRATION BULLETIN

The *TASP Test Registration Bulletin* will help students register for the test. The bulletin will include general information about the TASP and its testing component, instructions for registering for the test and receiving test scores, and background information about the development of the test. The bulletin can be obtained, starting in November 1988, from the advising office of either a Texas public college or university or a Texas teacher education program.

STUDY GUIDE

The *Official TASP Test Study Guide* will help students prepare for the TASP Test. The guide will include a description of the TASP and its testing component, strategies for preparing for the test, a description of the skills eligible for the test, a chapter of study materials and exercises for each skill, and a practice test.

TASP READING SECTION

General Description

The reading section of the TASP Test consists of approximately ten to twelve reading selections of 300 to 750 words each. The selections were chosen from a variety of subject areas; they are similar to reading materials (e.g., textbooks, manuals) that students are likely to encounter during their first year of college. Students will be asked to answer several multiple-choice questions about each reading selection.

Skill Descriptions

The reading section of the TASP Test is based on the skills listed below. Each skill is accompanied by a description of the content that may be included on the test.

Skill. Determine the meaning of words and phrases. Includes using the context of a passage to determine the meaning of words with multiple meanings, unfamiliar and uncommon words and phrases, and figurative expressions.

Skill. Understand the main idea and supporting details in written material. Includes identifying explicit and implicit main ideas and recognizing ideas that support, illustrate, or elaborate the main idea of a passage.

Skill. Identify a writer's purpose, point of view, and intended meaning. Includes recognizing a writer's expressed or implied purpose for writing; evaluating the appropriateness of written material for various purposes or audiences; recognizing the likely effect on an audience of a writer's choice of words; and using the content, word choice, and phrasing of a passage to determine a writer's opinion or point of view.

Skill. Analyze the relationship among ideas in written material. Includes identifying the sequence of events or steps, identifying cause-effect relationships, analyzing relationships between ideas in opposition, identifying solutions to problems, and drawing conclusions inductively and deductively from information stated or implied in a passage.

Skill. Use critical reasoning skills to evaluate written material. Includes evaluating the stated or implied assumptions on which the validity of a writer's argument depends; judging the relevance or importance of facts, examples, or graphic data to a writer's argument; evaluating the logic of a writer's argument; evaluating the validity of analogies; distinguishing between fact and opinion; and assessing the credibility or objectivity of the writer or source of written material.

Skill. Apply study skills to reading assignments. Includes organizing and summarizing information for study purposes; following written instructions or directions; and interpreting information presented in charts, graphs, or tables.

TASP MATHEMATICS SECTION

General Description

The mathematics section of the TASP Test consists of multiple-choice questions covering three general areas: fundamental mathematics, algebra, and geometry. The test questions focus on a student's ability to perform mathematical operations and solve problems. Appropriate formulas will be provided to help students perform some of the calculations required by the test questions.

Skill Descriptions

The mathematics section of the TASP Test is based on the skills listed below. Each skill is accompanied by a description of the content that may be included on the test.

Fundamental Mathematics

Skill. Use number concepts and computation skills. Includes adding, subtracting, multiplying, and dividing fractions, decimals, and integers; using the order of operations to solve problems; solving percentage problems; performing calculations using exponents and scientific notation; estimating solutions to problems; and using the concepts of "less and greater than".

Skill. Solve word problems involving integers, fractions, or decimals (including percents, ratios, and proportions). Includes determining the appropriate operations to solve word problems and solving word problems involving integers, fractions, decimals, percents, ratios, and proportions.

Skill. Interpret information from a graph, table, or chart. Includes interpreting information in line graphs, bar graphs, pie graphs, pictographs, tables, charts, or graphs of functions.

Algebra

Skill. Graph numbers or number relationships. Includes identifying points from their coordinates, the coordinates of points, or graphs of sets or ordered pairs; identifying the graphs of equations or inequalities; finding the slopes and intercepts of lines; and recognizing direct and inverse variation presented graphically.

Skill. Solve one- and two-variable equations. Includes finding the value of the unknown in one-variable equations, expressing one variable in terms of a second variable in two-variable equations, and solving a system of two linear equations in two variables.

Skill. Solve word problems involving one and two variables. Includes solving word problems that can be translated into one-variable linear equations or systems of two-variable linear equations and identifying the equation or equations that correctly represent the mathematical relationship(s) in word problems.

Skill. Understand operations with algebraic expressions. Includes factoring quadratics and polynomials; adding, subtracting, and multiplying polynomial expressions; and performing basic operations on and simplifying rational expressions.

Skill. Solve problems involving quadratic equations. Includes graphing quadratic equations, solving word problems involving quadratics, identifying the algebraic equivalent of stated relationships, and solving quadratic equations.

Geometry

Skill. Solve problems involving geometric figures. Includes identifying the appropriate formula for solving geometric problems, solving problems involving two- and three-dimensional geometric figures, and solving problems involving right triangles using the Pythagorean theorem.

Skill.   Apply reasoning skills.   Includes drawing conclusions using the principles of similarity, congruence, parallelism, and perpendicularity; and using inductive and deductive reasoning.

TASP WRITING SECTION

General Description

The writing section of the TASP Test consists of two parts: a multiple-choice part and a writing sample part. The multiple-choice part will include questions assessing a student's ability to recognize various elements of effective writing. The writing sample part will require students to demonstrate their ability to communicate effectively in writing on a given topic.

Skill Descriptions: Multiple-Choice Part

The multiple-choice part of the writing section of the test is based on the skills listed below. Each skill is accompanied by a description of the content that may be included on the test.

Please note that the term *standard* as it appears below refers to language use that conforms to the conventions of edited American English.

Skill.   Recognize purpose and audience.   Includes recognizing the appropriate purpose, audience, or occasion for a piece of writing; and recognizing writing that is appropriate for various purposes, audiences, or occasions.

Skill.   Recognize unity, focus, and development in writing. Includes recognizing unnecessary shifts in point of view or distracting details that impair the development of the main idea in a piece of writing and recognizing revisions that improve the unity and focus of a piece of writing.

Skill.   Recognize effective organization in writing.   Includes recognizing methods of paragraph organization and the appropriate use of transitional words or phrases to convey text structure, and reorganizing sentences to improve cohesion and the effective sequence of ideas.

Skill. Recognize effective sentences. Includes recognizing ineffective repetition and inefficiency in sentence construction; identifying sentence fragments and run-on sentences; identifying standard subject-verb agreement; identifying standard placement of modifiers, parallel structure, and use of negatives in sentence formation; and recognizing imprecise and inappropriate word choice.

Skill. Recognize edited American English usage. Includes recognizing the standard use of verb forms and pronouns; recognizing the standard formation and use of adverbs, adjectives, comparatives, superlatives, and plural and possessive forms of nouns; and recognizing standard punctuation.

Description: Writing Sample Part

The writing sample part of the TASP Test consists of one writing assignment. Students are asked to prepare a writing sample of about 300 to 600 words on an assigned topic. Students' writing samples are scored on the basis of how effectively they communicate a whole message to a specified audience for a stated purpose. The following characteristics may be considered in scoring the writing samples:

- APPROPRIATENESS--the extent to which the student addresses the topic and uses language and style appropriate to the given audience, purpose, and occasion.

- UNITY AND FOCUS--the clarity with which the student states and maintains a main idea or point of view.

- DEVELOPMENT--the amount, depth, and specificity of supporting detail the student provides.

- ORGANIZATION--the clarity of the student's writing and the logical sequence of the student's ideas.

- SENTENCE STRUCTURE--the effectiveness of the student's sentence structure and the extent to which the student's writing is free of errors in sentence structure.

- USAGE--the extent to which the student's writing is free of errors in usage and shows care and precision in word choice.

- MECHANICAL CONVENTIONS--the student's ability to spell common words and use the conventions of capitalization and punctuation.

Appendix 3
Public Senior Colleges and
Universities; Student TASP
Report: CBM-002

This report will include all undergraduate students, including transfer students, who meet all of the following requirements:

1. are enrolled in the reporting institution during the reporting period;

2. have completed fewer than three semester credit hours of collegiate-level work prior to the fall semester of 1989;

3. are registered for one or more Coordinating Board approved semester-length courses for resident credit.

This report will not include students:

1. who withdraw prior to or on the official census date, or

2. who have a baccalaureate degree, or

3. who have three or more semester credit hours in collegiate-level work earned prior to the fall semester of 1989.

Each student described above will be reported on the CBM-002 every reporting period that the student is enrolled at your institution, whether he or she has or has not taken the TASP Test and whether he or she passed or failed the TASP Test.

Rather than requiring two separate reports, TASP and the student performance data required by SB 543 have been combined on this report. Therefore, students who meet the above criteria, even though they may be enrolled in a TASP-exempt program, will be reported.

After all CBM-002 reports for a fiscal year have been received and processed, the Coordinating Board will send the student performance data to the Texas Education Agency (TEA), who will distribute it to the respective high schools.

For the purpose of this report, course-based remediation occurs when the remedial courses being taught are on your Coordinating Board approved course inventory for funding purposes.

The following instructions are to be used to complete the report. If there are any questions, please contact the TASP office at the Coordinating Board.

INSTRUCTIONS:

Item 1   Record Code. Always enter '2'.

Item 2   Institution Code. Enter the FICE code of the institution.

Item 3   Student Identification Number. Enter the social security number of the student. The institution will assign unique (nine-digit) identification numbers to students without social security numbers.

Item 4   First Semester Enrolled. Enter the code indicating the semester the student was first enrolled. This data will remain constant throughout the student's collegiate career at the reporting institution.

            1. Fall   2. Spring   3. Summer I   4. Summer II

Item 5   Year First Enrolled. Enter the last two digits of the calendar year in which the semester in item 4 occurred.

Item 6   Educational Objective. Enter the code indicating the student's educational objective at the institution.

1. Nondegree
2. Certificate
3. Associate Degree
4. Baccalaureate Degree
5. Undetermined

NOTE: Institutions will update the student's file if the educational objective changes.

Item 7   Testing Status at Entry. Enter the code of the status of the student when the student first entered the institution.

1. TASP Test scores
2. Other placement test scores
3. Not tested
4. TASP not required

Item 8   Math Remediation Required. Enter the code indicating the student's status for required math remediation.

0. Not TASP tested
1. Yes---based on TASP score
2. Yes---based on other placement test/advisement
3. Not required

Item 9   Math Remediation Provided during Reporting Period. If math remediation has been provided during any part of the reporting period, enter a code of 1, 2, 3, or 4 based on the type provided. Enter a 6 if remediation is not required. Enter a 5 for remediation delayed only if codes 1-4 or 6 do not apply. Code 7 is to be reported if none of the other codes apply.

0. Not TASP tested
1. Yes---course-based program
2. Yes---non-course-based program
3. Yes---combination of 1 and 2
4. Yes---at correctional institution
5. Delayed
6. Not required
7. Completed in previous reporting period

Item 10   Number of Semesters in Math Remediation. Enter the code indicating the number of semesters in which the student has been in Math Remediation during the reporting period. Enter 0, 1, 2, 3, or 4. (On a semester report only codes 0 or 1 are appropriate.)

Item 11   Writing Remediation Required. Enter the code indicating the student's status for required writing remediation.

0. Not TASP tested
1. Yes---based on TASP score
2. Yes---based on other placement test/advisement
3. Not required

Item 12   Writing Remediation Provided during Reporting Period. If writing remediation has been provided during any part of the reporting period, enter a code of 1, 2, 3, or 4 based on the type provided. Enter a 6 if remediation is not required. Enter a 5 for remediation delayed only if codes 1-4 or 6 do not apply. Code 7 is to be reported if none of the other codes apply.

0. Not TASP tested
1. Yes---course-based program
2. Yes---non-course-based program
3. Yes---combination of 1 and 2
4. Yes---at correctional institution
5. Delayed
6. Not required
7. Completed in previous reporting period

Item 13   <u>Number of Semesters in Writing Remediation</u>. Enter the code indicating the number of semesters in which the student has been in Writing Remediation during the reporting period. Enter 0, 1, 2, 3, or 4. (On a semester report only codes 0 or 1 are appropriate.)

Item 14   <u>Reading Remediation Required</u>. Enter the code indicating the student's status for required reading remediation.

0. Not TASP tested
1. Yes---based on TASP score
2. Yes---based on other placement test/advisement
3. Not required

Item 15   <u>Reading Remediation Provided during Reporting Period</u>. If reading remediation has been provided during any part of the reporting period, enter a code of 1, 2, 3, or 4 based on the type provided. Enter a 6 if remediation is not required. Enter a 5 for remediation delayed only if codes 1 - 4 or 6 do not apply. Code 7 is to be reported if none of the other codes apply.

0. Not TASP tested

1. Yes---course-based program
2. Yes---non-course based program
3. Yes---combination of 1 and 2
4. Yes---at correctional institution
5. Delayed
6. Not required
7. Completed in previous reporting period

Item 16   Number of Semesters in Reading Remediation.
            Enter the code indicating the number of semesters
            in which the student has been in reading reme-
            diation during the reporting period. Enter 0, 1, 2,
            3, or 4. (On a semester report only codes 0 or 1
            are appropriate.)

Item 17   Grade in First College-Level Mathematics Course
            at Your Institution

            1. A 2. B 3. C 4. D 5. F 6. Credit
            7. No Credit 8. Incomplete 9. Withdrawn/Quit
            0. Not taken as of reporting date

Item 18   Grade in First College-Level English Course At
            Your Institution.

            1. A 2. B 3. C 4. D 5. F 6. Credit
            7. No Credit 8. Incomplete 9. Withdrawn/Quit
            0. Not taken as of reporting date

Item 19   Semester Credit Hours Attempted.   Enter the
            number of semester credit hours in nonremedial
            courses (for which a grade of A-F is given) at-
            tempted at this institution for the reporting period
            (right justified, zero filled). Do not include incom-
            pletes (unless they have been resolved prior to the
            reporting date), withdrawn, or credit/no credit
            hours attempted.

Item 20   Grade Points Earned. Based on a four point system, enter the number of grade points earned in nonremedial courses attempted at this institution for reporting period (right justified, zero filled).

Optional Items 21-23---Mismatched CBM-002 records. To be entered only for first-time reported CBM-002 records for which a corresponding CBM-001 record cannot be found. A mismatch report showing those CBM-002 students who cannot be matched to the CBM-001 will be provided.

Item 21   Sex. Enter the sex of the student.
           M = Male   F = Female

Item 22   Ethnic Origin. Enter the code indicating the ethnic origin of the student.

           1. White-non-Hispanic
           2. Black-non-Hispanic
           3. Hispanic
           4. Asian or Pacific Islander
           5. American Indian or Alaskan Native
           6. Non-resident Alien

Item 23   Date of Birth. Enter the month, day, and the last two digits of the year of the birth of the student.

Optional Item 24-Prior Student ID-Social Security Number Change. To be entered only for those CBM-002 students whose social security numbers have changed since the last reporting period. If the CBM-002 record submitted for the current semester/year does not match the master TASP file at the Texas Higher Education Coordinating Board (THECB), a CBM-002 mismatch report will be printed.

Optional Items 25-30. Mismatched TASP Scores. TASP scores are normally provided by National Evaluation Systems (NES). These fields should be entered only if the CBM-002 record cannot be matched to a NES record and the CBM-002 data (Item 7 = 1 or Items 8, 11, or 14 = 1 or 3) shows that the TASP Test has been taken. A report listing those records for which TASP scores should be provided by the institution will be supplied. If a section(s) of the TASP Test was taken more than once, enter the most recent TASP Test score in the respective items 25-27. If a student retook a section that was previously passed, report the highest score for that section.

Item 25   Most Recent TASP Reading Score. Enter the three-digit scaled score for reading provided by NES.

Item 26   Most Recent TASP Math Score. Enter the three-digit scaled score for math provided by NES.

Item 27   Most Recent TASP Writing Score. Enter the three-digit scaled score for writing provided by NES.

For the initial TASP Test scores, enter the score of the test taken just prior to remedial intervention at your institution. If the TASP Test was passed on the first attempt, report the scores in items 28-30.

Item 28   Initial TASP Reading Score. Enter the three-digit scaled score for reading provided by NES.

Item 29   Initial TASP Math Score. Enter the three-digit scaled score for math provided by NES.

Item 30   Initial TASP Writing Score. Enter the three-digit scaled score for writing provided by NES.

Item 31   Reporting Period. 1. Fall 2. Spring 3. Summer 4. Annual

Item 32   Year. Enter the last two digits of the calendar year of the reporting period. For those reporting annually, enter the last two digits of the fiscal year.

Item 33   <u>Update Code</u>. Enter the appropriate code.
A=Add   C=Change   D=Delete

Data Processing Record Layout
Student TASP Report - CBM002

		Beginning Position	Length
Item 1	Record Code-Always enter '2'	11	
Item 2	Institution Identifier-FICE Code-(N)	26	
Item 3	Student Identification Number	8	9
Item 4	First Semester Enrolled (N)	17	1
Item 5	Year First Enrolled (N)	18	2
Item 6	Educational Objective (N)	20	1
Item 7	Testing Status at Entry (N)	21	1
Item 8	Math Remediation Required (N)	22	1
Item 9	Math Remediation Provided (N)	23	1
Item 10	Semesters in Math Remediation (N)	24	1
Item 11	Writing Remediation Required (N)	25	1
Item 12	Writing Remediation Provided (N)	26	1
Item 13	Semesters in Writing Remediation (N)	27	1
Item 14	Reading Remediation Required (N)	28	1
Item 15	Reading Remediation Provided (N)	29	1
Item 16	Semesters in Reading Remediation (N)	30	1
Item 17	Grade in First Math Course (N)*	31	1
Item 18	Grade in First English Course (N)*	32	1
Item 19	Semester Credit Hours Attempted**	33	3
Item 20	Grade Points Earned**	36	3
Item 21	Sex (Alpha)	39	1
Item 22	Ethnic Origin (N)	40	1
Item 23	Date of Birth (N)	41	6
Item 24	Prior Student ID (N)	47	9
Item 25	Most Recent TASP Reading Score (N)	56	3
Item 26	Most Recent TASP Math Score (N)	59	3
Item 27	Most Recent TASP Writing Score (N)	62	3
Item 28	Initial TASP Reading Score (N)	65	3
Item 29	Initial TASP Math Score (N)	68	3
Item 30	Initial TASP Writing Score (N)	71	3
Item 31	Reporting Period (N)	74	1
Item 32	Year (N)	75	2
Item 33	Update Code	80	1

N=Numeric* = College-level**= right justified, zero filled

EXAMPLE

TEXAS   HIGHER   EDUCATION   COORDINATING
BOARD

SR-CBM002 SUMMARY OF INITIAL STUDENT TASP

DATA FROM   DATE: 11/11/89

LONE STAR UNIVERSITY   FALL 1989

FIRST SEMESTER ENROLLED
FALL	4,318
SPRING	529
SUMMER	582
TOTAL	5,429

EDUCATIONAL OBJECTIVE
NONDEGREE	53
CERTIFICATE	0
ASSOCIATE DEGREE	123
BACCALAUREATE DEGREE	5,036
UNDETERMINED	217
TOTAL	5,429

TESTING STATUS AT ENTRY
TASP	3,561
OTHER TEST	733
NOT TESTED	1,135
TASP NOT REQUIRED	0
TOTAL	5,429

MATH REMEDIATION REQUIRED
YES, TASP	1,221
YES, OTHER	98
NO	4,110
TOTAL	5,429

MATH REMEDIATION PROVIDED
YES, COURSE-BASED	121
YES, NONCOURSE-BASED	117
YES, BOTH	198
YES, CORRECTIONAL	0
DELAYED	305
NOT REQUIRED	4,110
COMPLETED	578
TOTAL	5,429

WRITING REMEDIATION REQUIRED
YES, TASP	812
YES, OTHER	80
NO	4,537
TOTAL	5,429

WRITING REMEDIATION PROVIDED
YES, COURSE-BASED	112
YES, NONCOURSE-BASED	107
YES, BOTH	45
YES, CORRECTIONAL	0
YES, DELAYED	215
NOT REQUIRED	4,537
COMPLETED	413
TOTAL	5,429

EXAMPLE

THE TEXAS HIGHER EDUCATION COORDINATING
BOARD　　　　　　　　　　　　　　　　　PART B

SR-CBM002 SUMMARY OF INITIAL STUDENT TASP
DATA FROM　　　　　　　　　　　　　　　11/11/89

LONE STAR UNIVERSITY　　　　　003304　　　　FALL 1989

READING REMEDIATION REQUIRED
YES, TASP	1,124
YES, OTHER	84
NO	4,221
TOTAL	5,429

READING REMEDIATION PROVIDED
YES, COURSE-BASED	117
YES, NONCOURSE-BASED	103
YES, BOTH	178
YES, CORRECTIONAL	0
DELAYED	286
NOT REQUIRED	4,221
COMPLETED	524
TOTAL	5,429

Appendix 3: Student TASP Report: CBM-002

EXAMPLE

CBM002 EDIT SUMMARY   PAGE 1 OF 3
LONE STAR UNIVERSITY   003304   FALL 1989

		NORMAL RANGE	QUESTIONABLE	ERROR VALUES
1	RECORD CODE	5,429	0	0
2	INST. CODE	5,429	0	0
3	STUDENT ID	5,429	0	0
4	1ST SEM. ENROLLED	5,429	0	0
5	YEAR 1ST ENROLLED	5,429	0	0
6	ED. OBJ.	5,429	0	0
7	ENTRY STATUS	5,429	0	0
8	MATH REQUIRED	5,429	0	0
9	MATH PROVIDED	5,429	0	0
10	SEM. REM. MATH	5,429	0	0

EXAMPLE

CBM002 EDIT SUMMARY   PAGE 2 OF 3
LONE STAR UNIVERSITY   003304   FALL 1989

	NORMAL RANGE	QUESTIONABLE	ERROR VALUES
11 WRITING REQUIRED	5,429	0	0
12 WRITING PROVIDED	5,429	0	0
13 SEM. REM. WRITING	5,429	0	0
14 READING REQ.	5,429	0	0
15 READING PROVIDED	5,429	0	0
16 SEM. REM. READING	5,429	0	0
17 1ST MATH GRADE	5,429	0	0
18 1ST ENG. GRADE	5,429	0	0
19 SCH ATTEMPTED	5,429	0	0
20 GRADE PTS EARNED	5,429	0	0

<u>EXAMPLE</u>

CBM002 EDIT SUMMARY   PAGE 3 OF 3
LONE STAR UNIVERSITY   003304   FALL 1989

	NORMAL <u>RANGE</u>	<u>QUESTIONABLE</u>	ERROR <u>VALUES</u>
28 REPORTING PERIOD	5,429	0	0
29 YEAR	5,429	0	0

TOTAL CBM002 RECORDS PROCESSED   5,429

CONTROL DATA   1

DISCREPANCY   0

ADDS   0

CHANGES   1

DELETES   0

REJECTS   0

CBM-002 "Questionable" and "Error" Values

The following values are used in the Coordinating Board's edit programs to determine Questionable and Error Values for each element.

ITEM NUMBER	QUESTIONABLE	ERROR VALUES
1. Record Code	N/A	Any value except '2'
2. Institution Code	N/A	Must match value on transmittal document and be on the list of valid FICE codes
3. Student ID Number	Not on CMB001	Blank, special Characters
4. First Sem. Enrolled	N/A	Any value except 1-4
5. Year First Enrolled	N/A	Any nonnumerical values
6. Educational Object.	N/A	Any value except 1-5
7. Testing Status	N/A	Any value except 1-4
REMEDIATION		
8., 11., 14. Required	N/A	Any value except 0-3
9., 12., 15. Provided	N/A	Any value except 0-7
10., 13., 16. No. Sem.	N/A	Any value except 0-4
17. First Math Grade	N/A	Any value except 0-9

ITEM NUMBER	QUESTIONABLE	ERROR VALUES
18. First English Grade	N/A	Any value except 0-9
19. SCH Attempted	Sem. value > 22 Annual value > 54	Any nonnumerical value
20. Grade Points Earned	Sem. value > 22	Any nonnumerical values
	Annual Value > 216	Value > 4 times SCH

OPTIONAL		IF PROVIDED
21. Sex	N/A	Any except M or F
22. Ethnic Origin	N/A	Any except 16
23. DOB	N/A	Month < 1 or > 12 Day < 1 or > 31YY
24. Prior SSN	N/A	Special Characters
25. R Reading Score	N/A	Number < 100 or > 300
26. R Math Score	N/A	Number < 100 or > 300
27. R Writing Score	N/A	Number < 100 or > 300
28. I Reading Score	N/A	Number < 100 or > 300
29. I Math Score	N/A	Number < 100 or > 300
30. I Writing Score	N/A	Number < 100 or > 300
31. Reporting Period	N/A	Must match value on transmittal document
32. Year	N/A	Must match value on transmittal document

CBM002 Student TASP Updating Procedure

The updating procedure for the CBM002 is different from the other CBM reports. Updating of the other CBM reports is confined to one semester. The CBM002 data will be input to a TASP Master file that will be continually updated. Consequently, each semester/reporting period is tied together by the student ID (social security number). The update code of A will be used when reporting any new information. A change code (C) will be used to modify an item that was erroneously reported. Each semester the data will be reported as adds whether they be the initial record for a first-time entered or first-time transferred student or only the Semester Credit Hour and Grade Points Earned data being submitted for reporting periods after the student entered school. If you are required to report any of the Optional Information (items 21-30) it too, will be reported as adds. All the CBM002 information will be transmitted to the Coordinating Board in the same format, whether on a form or on a magnetic medium.

Items 4, 5, 7, 8, 11, and 14 (First Semester and Year Enrolled, Testing Status at Entry, and the Remediation Required items) will not be updated with data from subsequent add records, except items 8, 11, or 14, which can be changed from a 2 (other placement test) or 3 (not required) to a 1 (TASP Test). If any of these fields was reported incorrectly, a change record with only the specific field(s) to be modified should be submitted. To change the data, enter item 1, 2, 3, 4, 5, 31, 32, and the item(s) to be changed, and enter C in item 33.

Items 17 and 18 (Grades in First College-Level Math and/or English Course) will only be changed with a subsequent add record if a code of zero (Not taken as of reporting date) is the current code in the TASP Master file. If either of these fields was reported incorrectly, a change record with only the specific field(s) to be modified should be submitted. To change data see instructions in paragraph 2.

Items 9, 12, and 15 (Remediation Provided) will be updated on the Master TASP file with subsequent add records if initially coded as a 5 (Delayed). When a student has been remediated in a non-course-based program (code 2) during one reporting period and in a course-based program (code 1) in a subsequent reporting period, or vice versa, an update coded as a combination (code 3) will be allowed. If remediation has been provided and completed during the reporting period, enter the appropriate code 1-4 (which indicates the type of remediation), instead of a code 7 (which indicates remediation has been completed). On the subsequent report show that the remediation provided was completed (code 7). A passing TASP Test score will also show that remediation has been completed. If any of these fields were reported incorrectly, a change record with only the specific field(s) to be modified should be submitted. To change the data see instructions in paragraph 2.

Items 10, 13, and 16 (Number of Semesters in Remediation) will be reported each reporting period on an add record until the remediation is completed for that section.

Items 19 and 20 (Semester Credit Hours Attempted and Grade Points Earned) will be reported every reporting period that the student has attended your institution or until a baccalaureate degree has been reported.

When a student ID has changed since the last reporting period, enter the new number in item 3 and the old number in item 24. This can be reported along with other information to be added to the TASP Master file. If a mismatch occurs due to the student ID changing and the old student ID is not in item 24, a printout showing the mismatch will be sent to the reporting official.

Appendix 4
Examinee Score Report

EXAMINEE SCORE REPORT

TEST DATE:

TASP™ TEXAS ACADEMIC SKILLS PROGRAM

READING

SKILL AREA PERFORMANCE

WORD MEANING:

MAIN IDEA AND DETAIL:

WRITER'S PURPOSE:

IDEA RELATIONSHIPS:

CRITICAL REASONING:

STUDY SKILLS:

For further information about these skills, consult your advisor or study chapters 4 – 9 in *The Official TASP® Test Study Guide*.

TEXAS INSTITUTIONS TO WHICH YOUR SCORES HAVE BEEN REPORTED

SEE THE BACK OF THIS REPORT FOR INFORMATION ON HOW TO INTERPRET YOUR SCORE

MATHEMATICS

SKILL AREA PERFORMANCE

FUNDAMENTAL MATH:

ALGEBRAIC GRAPHING AND EQUATIONS:

ALGEBRAIC OPERATIONS AND QUADRATICS:

GEOMETRY AND REASONING:

For further information about these skills, consult your advisor or study chapters 10 – 19 in *The Official TASP® Test Study Guide*.

YOUR NAME AND ADDRESS

Your Social Security No.:

TASP STATUS		
READING	MATHEMATICS	WRITING

WRITING

WRITING SAMPLE

WRITING SAMPLE SCORE:

YOUR WRITING SAMPLE SHOWS

WRITING MULTIPLE CHOICE
SKILL AREA PERFORMANCE

PURPOSE AND AUDIENCE:

UNITY, FOCUS, AND DEVELOPMENT:

ORGANIZATION:

EFFECTIVE SENTENCES:

USAGE: [1]

For further information about these skills, consult your advisor or study chapters 20 – 26 in *The Official TASP® Test Study Guide*.

References

AERA/APA/NCME Committee. (1985). *Standards for Educational and Psychological Testing*. Washington, DC: American Psychological Association.

Berk, R. A. (Ed.) (1982). *Handbook of Methods for Detecting Test Bias*. Baltimore, MD: John Hopkins University Press.

Board of Curators, University of Missouri v. Horowitz, 435 U.S. 78, 98 S.Ct. 948 55 L. Ed. 2d 124 (1978).

"Council Committees," Attached to April 8, 1988, TASP Council Minutes.

Debra P. v. Turlington, 644 F. 2d 397, 408 (5th Cir. 1981).

Debra P. v. Turlington, 730 F. 2d 1405 (11th Cir. 1984).

Demography and Higher Education in the Changing Southwest-Texas, Western Interstate Commission for Higher Education (WICHE), March 1988.

Eiland v. Wolf, 764 S.W. 2d 827 (Tex App.---Houston (1st Dist.) 1989, *writ den.*).

Ellis, David B. (1991). *Becoming a Master Student*. College

Survival, Inc., Rapid City, SD.

Gardiner, L., *Planning for Assessment: Mission Statements, Goals, and Objectives.* (1989) Trenton, NJ: Office of Learning Assessment, New Jersey State Department of Higher Education.

A Generation of Failure: The Case for Testing and Remediation in Texas Higher Education. (1986). Austin, TX: Coordinating Board, Texas College and University System.

Johns, V., and D. W. Viehland. (1986). "Migration Patterns of First-Time Freshmen in the United States." *Research in Higher Education*, 30, 5.

Kilgore College 1989/90 Catalog. (1989) Kilgore, TX.

Kulick, C. C. and J. H. Kulick and B. J. Shwalb. (1983)" College Programs for High-Risk and Disadvantaged Students: A Meta-Analysis of the Findings." *Review of Educational Research*, 53, 3, 397-414.

Marshall, R. F. and L. F. Bouvier. (1986). *Population Changes and the Future of Texas*, Population Reference Bureau, Washington, DC.

Murdock, S. H., R. B. Ham, K. P. Beckman and S. S. Hwang. (1988). *The Future Population of Texas: Alternative Scenarios of Growth and Their Implication for Public and Private Services*, College Station, TX: Texas Agricultural Experiment Station in cooperation with the Texas Department of Commerce.

New Jersey Basic Skills Council. (1984). *Effectiveness of Remedial Programs in New Jersey Public Colleges and Universities: Fall 1982-Spring 1984*. Newark, NJ: Department of Education.

"Pre-Professional Skills Test Longitudinal Data, March 1984 through November 1986," accompanying Albert H. Kauffman, staff attorney, Mexican-American Legal Defense and Education Fund, to Dear Friends, March 24, 1987.

Pollard, J. S. (1987). *A Case Study of the Mobilization of an Interorganizational Collaboration in Higher Education.* Doctoral Dissertation, Texas Tech University, Lubbock, TX.

PSAT/NMSQT Summary Report and Summary Report Worksheet, Admissions Testing Program of the College Board, 1988.

Regents of University of Michigan v. Ewing, 474 U.S. 214, 106 S. Ct. 507, 88 L. Ed. 2d 523 (1985).

70th Texas Legislature. (1987). *House Bill 2182.*

70th Texas Legislature. (1987). *Senate Bill 543.*

71st Texas Legislature. (1989). *Senate Bill 692.*

Southern Region Education Board. (1988). *SREB Book on Higher Education.* Atlanta, GA: SREB.

Texas Academic Skills Program, Kilgore College. (1989). *"You, TASP, and College."* Kilgore, TX.

Texas State Teachers Association v. Star, 711 S.W. 2d 421 (Tex. App.---Austin, 1986, *writ ref'd, State V. Project Principle, Inc.*, 724 S.W. 2d 387 (Tex, 1987).

Texas Higher Education Coordinating Board. (1987). Texas Administrative Code 5.311, Subchapter P.

Texas Higher Education Coordinating Board. (1989). *"Texas Academic Skills Program Summary Test Results,"* (1989), Austin, TX.

U.S. Dept. of Education. (1983). *A Nation at Risk.* National Commission on Education, Washington, D.C.

United States v. Texas, 28 F. Supp. 304 (E.D. Tex. 1985).

United States v. LULAC, 793 f. 2D 636 (5th Cir. 1986).

Index

About the Editors and Contributors

DAN ANGEL is the president of Austin Community College.

KENNETH H. ASHWORTH is the commissioner of higher education for the State of Texas.

MILTON R. BRYANT, formerly vice president for academic affairs at Prairie View A&M University, a historically Black institution, has returned to the business faculty. He served as co-chair of the Bias Review Committee and is an original member of the Texas Academic Skills Council.

ELENA DE LA GARZA is currently working at the Texas State Technical Institute in Harlingen, Texas. She was an associate program director in the TASP office at the Texas Higher Education Coordinating Board.

THE HONORABLE WILHELMINA R. DELCO is Speaker Pro Tempore of the Texas Legislature. She previously chaired the Higher Education Committee in the House of Representatives and is a national spokesperson on educational and testing issues.

CHARLES B. FLORIO is dean of academic instruction at Kilgore College.

ROBERT D. GRATZ is vice president of academic affairs at Southwest Texas State University in San Marcos, Texas. He also serves on the Committee of Chief Academic Officers, advising staff on all policy matters relating to the TASP.

GARY R. HANSON is the research coordinator, Office of Admissions, at The University of Texas at Austin. He has served on the Texas Academic Skills Council and as the co-chair of the TASP Evaluation Committee.

ROBERT L. HARDESTY, who now lives in Washington, D.C., has long been associated with higher education in Texas. He was president of Southwest Texas State University in San Marcos from 1981 to 1988.

JOSÉ ROBERTO JUÁREZ was the vice president for instruction at Laredo Junior College located on the Texas-Mexico border. He was also a member of the Texas Academic Skills Council and co-chair of the Bias Review Committee. He recently joined the history faculty at St. Edward's University in Austin.

ALBERT H. KAUFFMAN is a staff attorney for the Mexican-American Legal Defense and Educational Fund (MALDEF). He lives and works in San Antonio, Texas, and is actively involved in litigation related to public school finance, discrimination in higher education, and testing.

H. PAUL KELLEY has acted as an expert consultant on testing to the Coordinating Board staff and is a member of the Texas Academic Skills Council, chairing the Tests and Measurements Committee. He directs the Measurement and Evaluation Center at The University of Texas at Austin.

RICHARD M. KERKER is a program director in the TASP office of the Texas Higher Education Coordinating Board.

JOAN M. MATTHEWS has been associated with the Texas Higher Education Coordinating Board since 1984. As director of special projects, her overall responsibility includes the Texas Academic Skills Program.

RICHARD C. MEYER, vice president for academic affairs at Texas A&I University in Kingsville, Texas, is also a member of the Committee of Chief Academic Officers.

PAULA M. NASSIF is vice president for research and operations at National Evaluation Systems, Inc., in Amherst, Massachusetts.

KEVIN O'HANLON is now the general counsel for the Texas Education Agency. He formerly served the state as an assistant attorney general.

THE HONORABLE CARL A. PARKER, an attorney from Beaumont, Texas, chairs the Education Committee of the Texas State Senate. He also serves on Executive Committees of the Southern Regional Education Board and the Southern Legislative Conference.

ROBERTO REYES, a former member of the Texas Academic Skills Council and co-chair of the Academic Skills Development Committee, is dean of college and community educational development at El Paso Community College.

WILLIAM H. SANFORD is the assistant commissioner, Division of Universities and Health Affairs, at the Texas Higher Education Coordinating Board.

RONALD G. SWANSON is the associate director of the TASP for the Texas Higher Education Coordinating Board.

PAMELA TACKETT has experience in many different testing programs in her position as director of programs in the Division of Teacher Assessment at the Texas Education Agency.

LARRY E. TEMPLE is an Austin attorney. He is the former chair of the Texas Higher Education Coordinating Board and of the Select Committee on Higher Education.

MARVIN VESELKA is the interim associate commissioner for assessment at the Texas Education Agency.

NOLAN WOOD is the director of the Division of Teacher Assessment at the Texas Education Agency.